HISTORY AND POLITICS

SPAIN IN REVOLT
by Harry Gannes and Theodore Repard

THE MAGIC OF MONARCHY
by Kingsley Martin

THE TRAGIC FALLACY
A STUDY OF AMERICAN WAR POLICIES
by Mauritz A. Hallgren

TSUSHIMA
by A. Novikoff-Priboy

AN ATLAS OF CURRENT AFFAIRS
by J. F. Horrabin

MARIA THERESA
by Constance Lily Morris

These are Borzoi Books, published by
ALFRED A. KNOPF

THE SIEGE OF ALCAZAR

PLATE 1

Major GEOFFREY McNEILL-MOSS
[GEOFFREY MOSS]

THE
SIEGE
OF
ALCAZAR

A HISTORY OF THE SIEGE OF THE
TOLEDO ALCAZAR, 1936

NEW YORK · ALFRED · A · KNOPF

1937

Copyright 1937 by Geoffrey McNeill-Moss

Manufactured in the United States of America

FIRST AMERICAN EDITION

FOR

ESTHER ROSE

ACKNOWLEDGMENTS

The Author is grateful to—

Sir Fisher Dilke, Mr. Christopher Holme, Mr. Thomas Cadett, Don Paul Merry del Val, Mr. Maresco Pearce, who has given him the sketch plan of the Alcazar, and el Conde de la Sisla.

PREFACE

Here is the history of the defence of the Alcazar. I knew Toledo and the Alcazar before the siege. Since then I have been round it so often, alone, or with those who defended this or that special corner, that I have come to know what remains of it as well as a man knows his own garden.

I have been aided by the High Command of the Spanish Nationalist Army; by the military authorities in Toledo; by several officers, many of the men, and by one lady, all of whom endured the siege. I am intensely grateful to them.

I have had at my disposal a diary kept by an officer of the garrison. I have been helped, to some extent, by a series of letters which another officer in the Alcazar wrote for the lady to whom he was engaged; though, of course, he had no chance to dispatch them.

As for the other side, I have had practically nothing to go on. The forces which besieged the Alcazar were large but they have melted away. Very many of the besiegers must by now be dead; in a year's time there will be still fewer of them left alive. They were in revolt against tradition, they despised established methods, so it is doubtful whether they kept records. If they did, it is unlikely that any will have survived.

Perhaps in the future someone will write the tragic history of these men. They were poor, ill-educated. Most were sincere. Many must have seen themselves as prophets of a new age. The Government gave them arms, brought them to Toledo, and there before them was the Alcazar. They had heard of it. They saw it, huge and grey; once a royal palace, lately a military school and cradle of the military caste. To them it must have seemed like the ghost of things they hated and believed they

ix

had already swept away. They were brave: they squandered their lives in vain assaults: they failed. Good luck to him who writes a book for them!

Those who held the ancient building stood for things little related to our own problems and politics. So for us the defence of the Alcazar can be seen divorced from the causes of the moment and can remain, like Thermopylæ, a military episode.

CONTENTS

CONTENTS

CONTENTS

CONTENTS

APPENDIX I

APPENDIX II

ILLUSTRATIONS

THE ARCHITECTURAL DRAWINGS ARE BY MIRIAM PEARCE

THE SIEGE OF ALCAZAR

CASTILE

Spain, with Portugal, forms a great square tableland five hundred miles each way, and in the centre of it stands the city of Toledo.

The first impression of the landscape of Castile is its immensity and emptiness. The air is clear, for the whole tableland is of mountain height, and where in other lands the skyline may be seven miles away, here it is sixty.

Trees grow with difficulty; there are none except upon distant mountain-sides. The plain rolls on, billow after billow of prairie or interminable plough; no hedge, no boundary; nothing to break the thought of a world rolling on for ever.

The villages are leagues apart. There are no isolated farms. The plain rolls on; corn stubble; dry maize-fields; parched prairie; bare hillsides studded with dwarf bushes; dust. And very far away, against the sky, there runs a line of saw-edged sierras.

The colour scheme of this world is different from that of northern lands and the normal descriptive phrases lose their use. There are no contrasts, no rich greens and sombre browns, no misty blues and purple distances. Here all is a harmony, ranging but little and never far from the tint of human skin; though every slope may show a dozen subtly different shades; the warm yellow of amber, the yellow of parchment; the grey of hempseed; the warm tone of a walnut shell, of cork, of cedar-wood; the copper brown of dry beech leaves; the pale grey-green of an unshaven cheek, the deeper grey-green of lichen.

It is a landscape simplified; rolling away, subtle yet featureless, under the breath-taking vastness of its sky. And, miles apart, studding the plain, there stand the ancient castles which gave Castile its name.

TOLEDO

Across this upland plain of New Castile there flows the Tagus, held back by frequent weirs.

Above Toledo, and again below it, the river runs tranquilly between low banks. But as it comes upon the town it enters a gorge, cleft in the dusty rocks on which Toledo stands. It circles the town on three sides, leaving only one side undefended; and here the ridge falls steeply and the ramparts overlook low ground.

Seen from above, Toledo has nearly enough the outline of a pomegranate; the city forming the flattened circular shape of the fruit; and the single suburb of buildings of the Baroque and the Renaissance forming the stalk.

The town stands perched upon its hill. In the middle of it the cathedral raises a spire, ringed with a triple crown of thorns. At one side of it, overlooking the Tagus, there stood the Alcazar, square, immense, dwarfing all else.

THE HISTORY OF TOLEDO

Men must have lived upon this river-girt ridge long before there was history. For Nature had made here a perfect site for defence, while the narrowing of the river where it enters the gorge made bridging easy.

Under the Romans it was already a city. Indeed outside its walls exist the ruins of a forum and an amphitheatre. But so rich is Toledo in relics of other ages that these have never passed for much.

Roman power waned, and, as in the case of Gaul, Italy and the rest, barbarians from the North overran Spain. They conquered it and for nearly three centuries a line of Gothic kings reigned over all the Peninsula from their capital at Toledo.

Their power waned, too, and soon after A.D. 700 Moors from Africa conquered the Peninsula. Toledo became Moorish and remained so for some three-and-a-half centuries. This was a period of growth and the city rose to great importance. Indeed the influence of those days has never wholly disappeared and the general plan of the city dates from that epoch. Mosques have become churches, Arab market-places have become the little plazas of to-day. But the winding alleys and the trace of the ramparts are still those of the Moorish city.

Such of the Spanish Christians as had fled before the Moors, had taken refuge in the mountains in the north. Here they grew hardy, nurtured their grievance and in course of time began to fight their way southward again. The reconquest of their ancient territories was very slow. But in the eleventh century Alfonso the Brave, King of Castile, aided by that picturesque, much-sung and most treacherous ruffian, the Cid, captured Toledo. The city then became and remained the capital of Castile; though the kingdom of Castile was only one of the several Christian kingdoms which existed in Spain; and though the southern half of the peninsula was still in the hands of the Moors.

The town was far larger, richer and more civilized than any other in the Castilian kingdom. Nobles flocked to it and built palaces; some in the rugged and austere Gothic of Burgos and the north; some in the tender and sophisticated taste of the conquered Arabs who remained as craftsmen. Their contact with Toledo softened the dour Castilians and in this city there flowered an early Renaissance which at first had no link with that of Italy.

During four centuries Toledo remained the capital of the kingdom. Then towards the end of the fifteenth century the marriage of Isabella of Castile with Ferdinand of Aragon joined Castile with the only other remaining Christian state in Spain, and Toledo became the capital of them both. The conquest of Granada followed, the last of the Spanish Moors surrendered, the Catholic Kings became the rulers of all Spain, and the Archbishop of Toledo was the Primate of the whole land.

With Spain all his, Ferdinand set out upon an aggressive foreign policy. His veterans, trained in the long wars against the Moors, and hardened by the iron discipline of Gonsalvo de Cordoba, made Spain the first military Power in Europe— and for almost two centuries no soldiers could stand against hers.

Ferdinand gained a footing in southern Italy. He became the master of the western Mediterranean. His queen had financed the voyage of Columbus and the discovery of the New World, and the exploitation of its precious metals brought Spain an immense if fictitious wealth. And throughout this period of expansion, Toledo remained the Spanish capital.

The greatest period in the city's history was the next long reign, that of the Emperor Charles V, rival and conqueror of François Premier, and nephew of Henry VIII of England.

Charles inherited from his mother's father Spain, Sicily, the greater part of Italy, and the Spanish conquests in the New World; from his father's mother the Netherlands and counties bordering on them. Then as a young man he stood as candidate for the Imperial honours, was elected, and became Emperor of the Holy Roman Empire. Thenceforth all the German-speaking lands came nominally beneath his sway. His rule was acknowledged from Bruges to Vienna, and from Hamburg to Palermo. His fleets were supreme upon the ocean and the possession of those provinces (Lorraine, Alsace, Franche Comté, etc.) which now form the western and north-western departments of France, gave him a land bridge, from his Spanish Netherlands to his possessions in northern Italy.

By the mere extent of what he held, he dominated Europe, Europe at the height of the Renaissance. Toledo was the capital of his most-favoured country, and of the one which he made his home. The city took his shield, his crown, his eagle; she bears them still. Over the gates and the public buildings is Charles's double-headed eagle, with his Imperial crown. Hung around the eagle are the chain and pendant of the Golden Fleece. On either side is Charles's private crest, the Pillars of Hercules, joined by a ribbon with the motto . . . "Plus Ultra" . . . which made the boast that he ruled beyond those Gibraltar straits which had been the boundary of the Ancient World.

His son, Philip II, husband of Mary Tudor and rival of Elizabeth, abandoned Toledo. Inheriting the gloom and perhaps a little of the madness of his grandmother, Johanna the Crazy, he set about building a mausoleum for his family. This mausoleum grew even more gigantic.[1] He ruled half Europe, but the planning of this building absorbed much of his energies. Toledo proved inconveniently far from the site he had chosen, so when supervising the construction he stayed in a meagre market town called Madrid. He had half Europe to rule, and the Reformation to counter. He tried to do both, by diligence and an endless stream of letters from his inconvenient residence. His unwilling Court was forced to follow him.

Toledo had lost the King, and her rival, and this market town with nothing and no one to favour it, became the capital of Spain. Yet from one point of view Toledo has gained by being thus supplanted. Her days of expansion were over. There was no need to pull down her walls, her gates, her narrow medieval alleys; and the palaces abandoned by the great could house the lowly. Thus the appearance of the town has changed little since her greatest period. Though her importance, as seat of the Primate of all Spain, has given her baroque churches and convents, and wealth enough to save her from decay.

Nevertheless Toledo is a city of the past. The widest streets are narrow. In many the walls of houses have been grooved to

[1] The Escorial.

give room for axle-caps, and pedestrians draw back into doorways to allow even a single car to pass. Alleys, where a man can touch the walls on either side, wind up and down the many little hills on which the town is built. And as in the past, merchandise and even town refuse are largely carried in panniers slung across the backs of donkeys.

It is a city of churches and convents. Some date from Moorish days. Many have towers built by Arab craftsmen in a Christian-Moorish style. Some are of the high Renaissance. Some are of the Jesuit Baroque. It is, too, a city of abandoned palaces, of unexpected glimpses and odd corners. It is a town in which it is hard to find an ugly building. For Spain is the only country in the world where, for a reason which may be clear later, architecture has never died.

EVENTS IN SPAIN (1931–1936)

The average reader with no special interest in Spain has probably not followed very carefully the political troubles of that country between the years 1931 and 1936. It seems necessary, therefore, before beginning the story of the siege of the Alcazar, to give some account of the series of events which were of ever-increasing gravity, which appeared bound to lead to disaster, and which did actually culminate in the outbreak of civil war in the summer of 1936.

The provincial elections in 1931—which preceded the general elections by a few weeks—resulted in a landslide of the Monarchist Parties and in a spectacular success for the Republicans. The King, Alfonso XIII, without waiting for the seemingly certain triumph of the Republicans in the coming general elections, abdicated and left the country. A Government of the Left took office: Spain was declared a Republic: the crowns were removed from some of the public buildings and from official documents: in place of the ancient red-yellow-red national flag, another, of red-yellow-purple, was substituted. The most prominent supporters of the Monarchy, and some who did not interest themselves in politics but whose family names were illustrious, were imprisoned. They were kept in prison for periods ranging from six months to two years or more, without a charge being made and without a trial. Beyond these things little was done for the moment. In truth the end had come more quickly than the Republicans themselves had expected and it seems that they, somewhat taken aback, remained wondering exactly what should be done next.

Naturally enough the new regime failed to bring about immediately the miracles which its supporters had expected. For more than two centuries the power and prestige of Spain had been declining and, from being the greatest Empire in the world, she had sunk to being a stagnant second-rate Power. It seemed as though she had fallen asleep. And the departure of the last reigning Habsburg from the throne of a kingdom nearly fourteen centuries old, and to which his family had given so much fame, did nothing to bring back the glories of the past. The crown had been knocked off the decayed and crumbling national façade . . . that was all.

Parties of the Centre and of the Left were frankly disappointed. If these Moderate Republicans could do nothing more than this they must make way for others who could. A second Republican Government was tried; a third; a fourth; a fifth—and each successive Government was more to the Left.

The Monarchy was gone and yet the evils of which the Republicans had complained and had attributed to it, remained. Clearly the Church—the other great and ancient power in Spain—was the cause of this! The parties of the Left therefore began to organize themselves for an attack upon this other stronghold of tradition. Thus the struggle became one against the Church—and that in Spain, where there is no Protestantism, means only the Catholic Church.

The Church, however, had more means of defence than had the Monarchy. It had its pulpits, its schools, its influence in the hearts and homes of the people. This was less than it had been, but was still strong. The action of the Church, in defending itself when attacked, further angered its opponents. As often in revolutions, the Moderates had little to propose and the Extremists were able to force themselves to the front. They, too, failed. There came a reaction and for some two years they were replaced by Republicans more to the Right.

The pace had slowed and because of this the agitation of the Extremists of the Left increased. Now in opposition, they had no longer control of the Government machinery, so their attacks upon the Church took the form of violence and terrorism. It began with the burning of monasteries and convent schools, and continued with the murder of priests, monks and nuns.

The Moderates of the Republican parties rallied the forces of order. This led to a Communist revolution amongst the miners of the Oviedo district. It was suppressed with difficulty and only after Moorish troops had been called in.[1]

The forces of law and order had succeeded. But their success left extreme bitterness. Then, according to the Monarchists and the supporters of the Right, Moscow began to play a hand. Whether this is true cannot at present be decided. It is possible.

Meanwhile the difficulties of the Madrid Government increased. The Catalans, of somewhat different race from other Spaniards and joined to the rest of Spain only during the late fifteenth century, had long been claiming autonomy. The Basques, too, who have no racial affinities anywhere, demanded a federal government of their own. But these two provinces represented the richest districts in the country and, had they been given financial Home Rule, the monetary position of the Central Government would have become impossible.

---

[1] By his supporters, the action of General Franco in bringing Moorish troops into the Spanish Civil War is held to be but the continuation of a policy introduced by a Republican Government.

There were other troubles closing in. The faithful were demanding protection for their religious buildings and their religious education. Those who opposed the Church were weekly increasing the violence of their acts. The miners, whose revolt had been crushed, were clamouring for revenge; and, lest it might not be given to them, were making ready to take it. Throughout Spain disorder increased, till strikes and burning churches ceased to be "front-page" news.

The Government proved unable to protect the Church from its opponents. As early as the Spring of 1934 burnt-out convents gaped like broken teeth along the thoroughfares leading into the centre of Madrid. In other large towns such spectacles were proportionately common. It may well be that the great majority of the people were against such acts. But in times of danger and of stress it is always a determined minority, and not the majority, which rules. And all through this period in Spain the Extremists of the Left seem to have been more certain of what they wanted, and better organized to get it, than were their opponents on the Right.

The Monarchy was gone. The political power of the Church seemed at an end. The Extremists now prepared a programme for going farther. There seemed few things left for them to attack. They determined to attack them. Their next objective was the abolition of private property in most forms, of the family, of freedom of worship. For their attack on these the Extremists consolidated their forces and formed the Frente Popular. To oppose this the parties of the Right also formed a coalition, the National Counter-Revolutionary Front—for the issue now was whether Spain was to enter upon the revolutionary road at the end of which Moscow beckoned, or whether she were to hold to her traditions.

The general elections were held in February.

"The votes cast showed a fairly even division between Right and Left, with the Centre squeezed out. Of the total votes the

Right obtained 49 per cent., the Left 47 per cent., and the Centre a mere 4 per cent. But the electoral system gave the Left 256 seats in the Cortes, the Right 165 seats and the Centre 52, so that the Popular Front commanded an absolute majority."[1]

Supporters of the Right claim that the elections were held in circumstances of intimidation, violence and terrorism; that there was an actual tampering with the urns. They claim, too, that great sums of money were supplied by Bolshevik Russia to tip the scales in favour of the Communist Party. These claims may be true; they may not.

The Frente Popular had won and on its entry into power the Extremists in it at once began to call the tune.

"The first acts of the New Government were to grant an amnesty for the many political prisoners and to order the reinstatement of the dispossessed municipal councils.

"Another decree ordered the reinstatement of all employees dismissed in consequence of political strikes during the previous two years, and employers were required to restore pay-rolls to the level of October 4, 1934. The indiscriminate opening of the prison doors and the exuberance of extreme elements at their electoral triumph led to serious disorders, including the sacking of many churches and convents. Without waiting for legal authorization labourers began to seize the lands which they believed to have been promised by the Agrarian Law of 1932."[2]

Now, the evil of the absentee-landlord is a very old and a very real one in Spain. For it was true that the upper class, and even many of the well-to-do, lived in the large towns and drew their revenue from country estates which they may never

1 "Times Review of the Year, 1936."
2 "Times Review of the Year, 1936."

PLATE 2

THE VISAGRA GATE

The gate of Toledo which faces towards Madrid. On the upper storey is sculptured the Imperial eagle of the Emperor Charles V.

PLATE 4

THE ALCAZAR FROM THE NORTH-EAST

On the extreme left, rising above the slopes, is the "Quarters-of-the-Soldiers." The many win-
dowed building, low left of the Alcazar, is the "House-of-the-Military-Government." On the
right of it is the convent of la Concepcion.

even have visited. Some indeed hold this to have been the
chief cause of the poverty and lack of education to be found
everywhere in the countryside in Spain. But to confiscate
without compensation the estates of even the very rich was to
awaken the fears, not only of industry and commerce and
finance, but also of every little man who had his shop, his
trade, his savings.

At first insensibly, then rapidly, those who had anything to
lose drew back. The Right began to rally. The Church prepared for a final effort in the defence of all for which it stood.
Business men began to combine and consider what could be
done. Commerce commenced to organize itself. In the view
of the Extremists of the Left, Mammon was preparing to make
war upon the Workers.

The gap between the Left and the Right grew wider; it
yawned. Talk of revolution and counter-revolution was in the
air. It was rumoured that the Extremist supporters of the
Frente Popular, discontented at the slow progress of their
Government, were planning a Communist revolution for the
first of August. Many with no interest in Spain or Spanish
politics heard this rumour in London as early as the first weeks
of June. It is not yet possible to know whether it had good
foundation. It was generally believed by both sides in Spain.

A swift increase in the general violence made the situation
still more dangerous. The attacks upon churches developed
into attacks upon those attending Mass. Shots were fired, a
death or two would result. Retaliation followed. The funeral
of the victims of either side would produce more shots and
perhaps more deaths. The party spirit grew so bitter that routes
chosen for funeral processions became provocative. In the end
a state of affairs was reached like that in Belfast during its least
pleasant periods.

The politicians of the Right denounced the Government's
failure to protect life.

In July a crisis was reached. A lieutenant of the Assault

Guards (a Socialist-Communist Militia) was assassinated. Whether in revenge for this, or in accordance with plans already laid, the house of the three most important leaders of parties of the Right were visited. At two the visitors drew blank. At the third they were more successful.

"Before dawn the next morning a police van drew up outside the house of Señor Calvo Sotelo, the Monarchist leader, and uniformed men told him that he was under arrest. Suspicious and protesting, he entered their van, from which a few hours later his mutilated body was handed to the mortuary officials." [1]

Now Calvo Sotelo had the reputation amongst partisans of the Right of being the ablest statesman in Spain, and the country's hope. It was claimed that the names of his murderers were well known—they had been in Government uniforms and had taken him off in a Government prison van. All partisans of the Right clamoured for the punishment of these men. The Government took no action. Its opponents were convinced that this murder had been committed solely to clear the way for the much-talked-of Communist Revolution. They therefore determined to forestall it by making a revolution of their own; or, as they preferred to call it, a counter-revolution.

If pressed, supporters of the Right will offer the following justification:—that, though democracy has succeeded in Anglo-Saxon and certain Northern countries, it has failed utterly in Latin states; that this being so, the democratic principle has not for them the sanctity it has amongst Anglo-Saxons; that in Spain a corrupt democracy, subsidized by Russia, had come to mean the burning of churches and Church schools, the persecution of the religious, murder by terrorists, and the ruin of the nation and all that was for them sacred; that a coup d'état and the re-establishment thereby of a government of law and order was the only remedy then available. Their arguments

[1] "Times Review of the Year, 1936."

may have been specious, they may have been well-founded.

We have not as yet means of knowing how long this counter-revolution had been planned. To be successful, it had to have the support of the Army and of the Army chiefs, and especially of General Franco, the accepted leader of Army thought. It is said that until the murder of Calvo Sotelo he had loyally tried to fulfil his obligations to whatever government was in power. But at this point he threw in his lot with those who were planning a coup d'état, and his adherence was decisive.

To make the story of the defence of the Alcazar intelligible to those who have not followed these recent troubles in Spain, it has been necessary to give some account of these events. But here is a book written with no political purpose and it is hoped the reader will accept this.

THE CHANCES OF THE COUP D'ÉTAT

On what forces could those who planned this revolution count? To give the answer it is necessary to consider for a moment the organization of the Spanish armed forces.

The Army consists of three parts:—the Regulars, in the garrison towns of Spain itself; the Tercio [1] or Foreign Legion; the Moorish regiments stationed in Spanish Morocco.

But behind the Army proper there existed another entirely military force, the Guardia Civil. This was a very remarkable body of men. The attitude they took up would be important; it might be decisive.

The Regular Army was a conscript one. The officers and higher non-commissioned officers formed a permanent cadre, but the rank and file consisted of boys of seventeen or eighteen who were undergoing their one year of not too strenuous military service. It was on an average but a bare six months since

[1] For those it may interest, the "c" in Tercio is pronounced as a "th."

they had left their villages. Much of their time in the Army had been spent in the necessary fatigue duties, and, not infrequently, in learning to distinguish their right foot from their left. I hope to give no offence when I say that, while the officers had a higher standard of theoretical and military education than officers in corresponding British regiments, the short-service conscript army of Spain was not in the summer of 1936 a very efficient military force. The quality of its higher command and its general tone had lately, and deliberately, been weakened by the Government promoting to key positions only such officers as it believed held its own political views.

So much for the Regulars. The Moors and the Tercio were a very different matter.

The Moor is a born soldier, brave, prudent, a marksman; and by heredity and training a perfect skirmisher. He is hardy, stoical, obedient, patient, fatalistic.[1] He loves fighting for itself, almost as much as he does for the loot it brings him. In the Spanish-Moroccan army he serves for a long period and is highly trained. There is no race distinction in the Spanish forces. A Moor can rise to any rank and command Spaniards as well as Moors. He often does. But he seldom rises above the rank of captain, as to do so he must pass written examinations, for which perhaps he has not the mental development but which in any case he thinks tiresome.

The Tercio—the Legion—was in one way very different from the French Foreign Legion. For, though originally it had been intended to include volunteers of all nations in its ranks, actually ninety-five per cent. of the men were Spanish. They were long-service, highly paid soldiers. Their discipline, though elastic, was stern in the extreme. They lived always under almost active service conditions. They were keen, confident, self-reliant, alert.

---

[1] It is an astonishing sight to see these Moors flat on their stomachs and wriggling forward at high speed under machine-gun fire which would hold up any other infantry.

It had been intended that the Tercio should carry on the traditions of Alva's veterans; those pikemen and arquebusiers of the Spanish phalanx who tramped the Netherlands, defeating against impossible odds every foe they encountered, and who were probably the most redoubtable infantry the world has ever seen since the days of ancient Rome. To remind them of this the legionaries wore, embroidered upon the short-sleeved shirts which formed their normal uniforms, the arquebus, the cross-bow and the long straight trumpet of those days. They were young men but as soldiers they were mature. They were all men who for some reason or another preferred the rigours of Moroccan campaigning to the comparative ease of their homes. No doubt some had been black sheep, wild youths, square pegs which could not fit in round holes. Seen in war there was about them all a certain tough gaiety. Their officers formed the cream of the Spanish Army.

But, as has been said, behind the Regulars, the Moors, and the Tercio, there were the Guardia Civil. These were a police force, organized, armed and officered on an entirely military basis. They were distinct from the civil police and from the police of the towns. They were not concerned with the ordinary enforcement of trivial regulations and thus they were freed from the pettiness which an association with such matters is apt to produce. They had much less contact with the ordinary public than any normal police would have. They had their special rôle.

There are in Spain great stretches of wild country which often in the past have harboured outlaws and even armed guerilla bands. The Guardia Civil had duties in and about the towns and villages, but it was for the policing of these great wild places that their corps primarily existed.

They joined as young men of fine physique, of reasonable education and of proved good character. They served in the Guardia Civil until an age when their bodily activity might begin to decline. They were seasoned and responsible men and, on the average, in early middle age. Perhaps the nearest counterpart that could be found to them in any British force would be the non-commissioned officers of the Foot Guards. They were highly paid and well pensioned. But very much was expected of them. They were above all suspicion and there were no scandals in their corps such as sometimes come to light among, say, the London police.

It would have been as hard to bribe a soldier of the Guardia Civil as a British Secretary of State for Foreign Affairs; and harder to sway him by flattery. The officers of the Guardia Civil were like the men but came of a higher social class.

There remained two other branches of the armed forces of the State: the Navy, and an Air Force . . . which in Spain formed part of the Army.

The Navy was small, ill-equipped, antiquated. The Air Force had but few planes and these were mostly out of date.

The reason why more space has been devoted to the land forces than to those of the sea and air is that the land forces were far more numerous and appeared far more politically important.

Having considered the armed forces of the Spanish State it is now possible to judge better the chances of success that the coup d'état had in Spain during the summer of 1936.

What attitude would these various bodies adopt?

The Tercios and the Moors, both in Morocco and remote from the seat of government, and both dependent upon the authority of their own officers, were almost certain to follow the lead of the Army chiefs. But here the Navy, though small and decrepit, would be important. For, should it remain faithful to the Government, it would have seemed impossible for either the Tercio or Moors to cross the Straits of Gibraltar and take any part in the struggle in Spain itself. A knowledge of the naval history of any country should have made it easy to predict that the seamen of the Spanish warships would follow the Frente Popular Government in Madrid, whether this entailed mutiny against their own officers, or not.

As for the Regular Army, the position of the officers would be difficult in the extreme. Not only their own future but also that of their wives and families, would be at stake. They belonged to a service with a tradition of loyalty to the State; and their own loyalty, according to law and constitution, was to the Government in Madrid. But they were Catholics—which in Spain implies more, perhaps, than in any other land; they were probably at heart Monarchists; they had witnessed for months the Government's indifference or incapacity to prevent the burning of churches and massacre of religious orders; they, like everyone else, must have heard the rumours of a coming Communist revolution which, if successful, would sweep away everything in which they believed. It may well be understood that some, in all good faith and patriotism, made one choice, and that some, in equally good faith and patriotism, made the other.

As for the rank and file, this consisted chiefly of the rawest recruits. To what extent they would follow their officers, in whichever political direction they might choose, no one could tell.

The Spanish military Air Force was but a branch of the Army and it might have been expected that what applied to the whole would have applied to the part. But, while the decision of the Army proved to some extent divided, with the majority of the officers siding with the Right, the airmen of Spain, almost to a man, at once threw in their lot with the Frente Popular.

The Guardia Civil remain to be considered. The choice before all of that corps must have been similar to that before commissioned ranks of the Regular Army. Habitual loyalty to the Government and the future of their families had to be weighed against devotion to their Church, reverence for the past, and detestation of all that a Communist state would mean. The choice for them would be bitter and no one could foretell what their decision would be.

Taking a long view, in mid-July 1936, it would have seemed probable: that the Tercio and Moors would follow the Army chiefs but would be prevented by the Navy from crossing the Straits: that the choice of the Army would be divided and inconclusive: that the attitude of the Guardia Civil would decide the chances of a coup d'état.

Two things only seem to have been certain:—Firstly that none of the likely leaders of that coup d'état were personally ambitious or politically minded. Secondly that they were swayed, not by personal motives, but by a belief that only such a coup d'état could save their country.

Few perhaps can have foreseen that, while the failure of the coup d'état would mean the forfeit of their lives, an indecisive result would plunge the country into civil war.

Certain it is that those who revolt against an established government take upon themselves an awful responsibility. Yet neutral observers in Spain seem agreed that the situation had long been so serious, and was rapidly worsening, that in any case the outbreak of a civil war had become inevitable.

THE REVOLT IN MOROCCO

On Friday the 17th of July General Franco, speaking on behalf of the garrisons of Spanish Morocco, proclaimed them and himself unable any longer to take orders from the Government in Madrid.

Calvo Sotelo had been murdered on the 13th of the month, and during the four days which followed, those who had planned the "counter-revolution" must have acted quickly; especially as it is commonly accepted that General Franco had been against such a course and that it had been necessary to persuade him to take a part in it.

It is not yet possible to know whether a military rising had long been planned or whether the determination to make one dated only from the murder of July 13th. In either case the final steps must have been very rapid; necessarily so, as those responsible for it believed, or pretended to believe, that plans for a Communist revolution were almost complete. Yet by acting so quickly the organizers of the coup d'état ran the risk that previous knowledge of their own intended rising might not reach in time many on whose support they counted.

What exactly happened in Spanish Morocco is not yet clear to the world outside. All telephone and telegraph communication between Spain and the rest of Europe was cut off by the Government in Madrid. This automatically isolated Spanish Morocco. The pressmen of Paris and London then attempted to get into telephone communication with Portugal, in order to have news from there. But, as the wires pass through Spanish territory, this proved impossible. They then made telephone calls to various persons in French Morocco, editors of local papers or business men whose names were taken haphazard out of trade directories. All that they obtained from these sources was the rumour of a military rising in Spanish Morocco, and the fact that the frontier of it had been closed. On the next day, Saturday the 18th of July, the Spanish Government allowed pressmen in Madrid to make telephone calls to London and Paris; though these had to be made in the presence of a censor. In Madrid it was given out that the Moroccan rising was the work of a handful of officers and that it had already been practically suppressed. In such telephone messages as were sent to newspaper offices in other countries, accounts of the state of affairs in Spain, or in the capital itself, had to be much watered down.

Those who had organized the revolution in Morocco kept the frontier closed for some time. They had no intention of being spied upon or of having their action reported by newspaper men, until it was complete. One French journalist who without the necessary permission penetrated into Spanish Morocco, was rightly or wrongly accused of espionage and was dealt with summarily. This seems to have discouraged others.

For a while, therefore, all that the newspapers of the outer world could do was to collect the various rumours current in French Morocco, choose the most likely, and on them build up some idea of what had happened on the other side of the closed frontier. But within a few days civil war broke out in Spain itself and robbed Morocco "stories" of their news value. The interest of the world had passed on and it has been left to the historians to discover what really happened in Spanish Morocco at that time.

There were stories, of course; stories of small military detachments, returning under non-commissioned officers from field training to their barracks in Melilla, being booed by Socialists on the balcony of their political club; of the men breaking the ranks, forcing an entrance into the building and assaulting those in it; stories of a party sent by organizers of the coup d'état to occupy a telegraph and telephone building, in spite of the protests of its technical staff; of a company of soldiers who, as the officers with it were of junior rank and not in the secret of the movement, drove off the party which had seized the telephone building; of their occupying it themselves and defending it until officers of the High Command arrived and explained the situation.

But if in Morocco there was any resistance to the coup d'état, there was certainly not much. And within a matter of hours the revolt had been completely successful and Spanish Morocco was in the hands of those who had made it.

THE REVOLT IN SPAIN

It is as yet impossible to know how, or to what extent, the commanders of military garrisons in Spain itself had been informed beforehand of this Moroccan coup d'état It seems certain that neither telephone nor telegram nor post was generally employed—for obvious reasons. It seems likely that an officer was sent to convey the secret to each commander on whom the organizers of the coup d'état counted.

But, considering how desultory and disconnected the revolt by military garrisons in Spain was, it would seem that in many cases no previous information was received; or, if it were, was received too late.

In many garrison towns the revolt broke out. But in extremely few was it successful.

It may well be that the stories quoted in the last chapter were true and that the troops in Morocco began a revolt without any knowledge of one being planned. Indeed they may thus have forced the organizers of it to act, before the date for which they were preparing. In any case there seem to have been more signs of haste than of preparation.

But, whatever doubts there may be as to what happened in other parts of Spain, this book is concerned with what took place in Toledo. And in the case of Toledo it is possible to give exact information. A captain well acquainted with the town was despatched from Morocco. His instructions were, to inform the Military Governor of the Province as to what was being done, and then to return at once to Morocco and report himself to the officer who had sent him.[1]

[1] I had the story from the Captain himself.
On arrival in Southern Spain he found such disorganization that it took him much longer than he expected to reach Toledo. As a result he had no time to leave the town before the proclamation of a state of war made his departure impossible. He thus by chance became part of the garrison of the Alcazar and went through the siege.

TOLEDO IN JULY, 1936

In July, 1936, Toledo was a quiet and pensive old town, capital of the province which bears its name. It was the seat of the Primate of all Spain, and also of a provincial government—an elected body corresponding roughly to a county council in modern England.

It had its cathedral, with a large chapter of ecclesiastics. It had its school for priests and many monasteries and convents. It was one of the show cities of Spain. But, as it was but some forty-six miles from Madrid, not many of such tourists as visited the town, spent a night in it.

It was the terminus of a railway that ran from Madrid to itself. The highroad from Madrid was a good one, but after Toledo it led to nowhere in particular. Toledo was, in fact, a dead end. At the time of the last census the town had twenty-eight thousand inhabitants.

It was the centre of a moderately rich agricultural district. It had its market, its local trade, a theatre which was rarely open, and two small cinemas. Below the town, some two kilometres away and well hidden by trees, was the Arms Factory—a Government institution. But since the overthrow of the Monarchy the needs of the Army had been so neglected that chromium-plated bedsteads had become one of the main products of the Factory.

Toledo had one other small importance. Within the Alcazar there had long been established the Academy of Infantry. And in late years, as an economy, the Academy of Cavalry had been

---

Now it happened that the officer on whose instructions he had come to Toledo became commander of one of the columns that relieved the Alcazar. My captain, therefore, was able to present himself and state:—that he had carried out his instructions; that he had communicated to the Military Governor the message entrusted to him; that the military situation had prevented him from reporting himself before; that he did so now . . . and awaited further orders.

I am indebted to this captain for much besides this single story.

joined to this. Once, when the king had still been on the throne, there had been a thousand cadets, but by the summer of 1936 the great days of the Academy were over. For the Republican Government favoured promotion from the ranks, and so there were but a hundred and thirty cadets, in place of the thousand who had once filled the Alcazar. July in Spain is a holiday month. So the cadets, and the colonel commandant and most of the officer instructors were on leave.

There were no garrisons in the ordinary sense, either in Toledo or anywhere else in the province. Some two hundred soldiers, mostly young recruits, were attached to the Academy as grooms and batmen. But, as the cadets were away, a number of these, too, were on furlough.

Beside the Academy there was in Toledo a military Gymnastic School. But the number of instructors and those undergoing a course was never large, and at this season was particularly small.

No rich families lived in Toledo. If there were families of the aristocracy, they were few. There were business men, Army officers shopkeepers, some members of the learned professions, priests. The life of Toledo was a local life, with local interests. The great majority of the people who lived in the town had been born there; they would probably die there. That was the sort of place Toledo was.

The people of Toledo do not seem to have had much interest in politics. On the whole they were mildly Conservative. Indeed in the recent elections some eighty per cent. of the voters had polled for the parties of the Right. As in other places, there were some extremists of the Left; and these turned out to have been well organized, and also armed. There were no doubt extremists on the other side also, but they seem to have been unprepared.

This, then, was the town in which the captain from Morocco, mentioned in the last chapter, arrived on the 17th of July; and in which he gave certain information to a Colonel Moscardó, Military Governor of this not very militarily important province.[1]

THE EIGHTEENTH OF JULY

During the morning there were rumours everywhere in Toledo of a military revolt in Morocco. Radio-Madrid, the Government-controlled wireless station, minimized the story in its broadcast. But not many were reassured by this. Indeed it seems to have been realized by all classes that the situation, long so tense, had now reached a point where civil war was inevitable.

Before noon Colonel Moscardó ordered the acting-commandant of the Military Academy and the commanding officer of the "Gym" School to keep their men in barracks.

He followed this with another order of far greater importance. For he then instructed the officer commanding the Guardia Civil of the Province to concentrate them all upon Toledo. The messages were sent out by telephone and delivered in the late hours of that night or in the early hours of the next day.

Soon the Guardia Civil arrived from all the outlying stations, with their wives, families and movable belongings. They came in their waggonettes, patrol cars, or requisitioned private vehicles.[2]

The duties of the Military Governor of the Province in normal times seem to have been light—so light that no one was very certain what they were. But now, in view of develop-

[1] For those who may care, the name "Moscardó" is pronounced with the accent on the final "o".

[2] I have not been able to ascertain whether the bringing in of their families and belongings by the Guardia Civil was ordered; or whether it was a precaution taken by the men themselves in view of the unsettled condition of the countryside.

ments and of the concentration of the Guardia Civil, Colonel Moscardó found himself with a force of almost eight hundred armed men of various sorts at his disposal. He thereupon set up his headquarters in a building which had once, at some forgotten epoch, been the House-of-the-Military-Government; and which was still known by that name.

This building was a quiet, two-storeyed, eighteenth-century one, of stucco. It stood on the slopes below the Alcazar and just inside the grounds belonging to it.[1]

At midnight the Guardia Civil on duty in the Zocodover (the main plaza and general meeting-place of the town, and close to the Alcazar) were fired upon by extremists of the Left, three being wounded. In other parts of the town, too, Guardia Civil were fired upon. Throughout the early hours pistol shots were to be heard. By telephone enquiries the Military Governor learnt that a state of excitement existed throughout the province; while in some villages there had been ugly incidents and acts of violence committed by roughs and strangers coming in from a distance.

COLONEL MOSCARDÓ

At first, when studying amongst its ruins the siege of the Alcazar, one is amazed by the complexity of little isolated incidents; and there seems nothing to suggest that a single personality in any way directed and controlled them all. There had been, of course, a commander of the garrison. He had been there with the rest. Now he had gone away.

His name had been Moscardó. He had been a colonel, a man in late middle age, who had risen to the not very important post of military governor of a province. He was conscientious

[1] The House-of-the-Military-Government is seen on Plate 39. It is the long white building, low right from the Alcazar.

but not ambitious. He had lived a life of semi-retirement in Toledo for a long time. He was on the shelf. Then the events of July, and the convictions that he held, forced on him a certain course of action; and thus without intending it he found himself commander of the besieged Alcazar, in which, years before, he had been a military cadet.

For a few weeks the siege of the Alcazar remained first-column news, and his name was known. Then the relieving force arrived. His task was done. He asked for nothing more than some employment at the front. They gave him a column —which was more than he expected—and he slipped back into obscurity again.

He was a tall, reserved, gentle-mannered man; a little awkward, rather punctilious; happy enough with the few people he knew well, but shy in company. He had a strict sense of duty. He was religious. In a nation where most were slack, he was exact.

Here are two short impressions of him. The first is—that his glance seldom met anyone's; and that, being tall, he seemed always to look at something behind and above those with whom he talked. The second is—that if, when going round the posts of the defence, he found a barricade not to his liking, he would take stones and begin to make some alterations. Then, when the soldiers hastened to help him, he would let them have the stones; he would nod and pass on; having said nothing, and having left behind no sensation of reproof.

The siege once started, there is but one occasion on which anything that he said or did is recorded; and the occasion lasted only five minutes. Beyond that, he is not mentioned. Indeed at first I myself never thought of him.

Yet, as I followed the progress of those desperate weeks, I grew each day more conscious of this big, grave, shy man; hovering always just beyond the background of the tale. He was there, exact, honourable, conscientious.

I have no more to say of him. It may be that others, read-

PLATE 5

21ST OF
JULY

The young soldiers of the Academy marching down from the
Alcazar to the Plaza Zocodover for the reading of the Declaration of a State of War. The street is the Cuesta. The highest
line of openings in the wall on the left are the windows of the
"Simplon."

THE READING OF THE DECLARATION OF A
STATE OF WAR ON THE PLAZA ZOCODOVER

PLATE 6

THE GOLDEN DAYS OF THE ALCAZAR

Alfonso XIII reviewing the cadets.

ing this record of the siege, often in detail dusty and precise, and in which there is but one mention of him, will grow aware of him and, as I do, feel him ever there.

THE NINETEENTH OF JULY

All was calm next morning. By the normal hour idlers were lounging and strolling on the Zocodover. There was more to talk about than usual but there was then no newspaper published in Toledo. Those which presently arrived from Madrid made little of the troubles in Morocco, and of course did not mention the commotion in Toledo during the previous night. Slowly the shops opened. The sun grew hotter and the loungers on the Zocodover retired, as always, into the arcades which surrounded the little plaza on two of its three sides.

During the morning Colonel Moscardó in his new headquarters was called to the telephone by someone in Madrid. The speaker, who gave no name, stated that he was acting for the Secretary of State for War. He then said that the entire stock of munitions in the Arms Factory at Toledo was to be sent at once to the capital. For which purpose any or all motor vehicles in the district were to be requisitioned.

Actually during these twenty-four hours the War Ministry in Madrid changed hands three times. It is likely that Colonel Moscardó was not aware of this. But, if he had been, he would doubtless have found it confusing.

The Military Governor replied that as such a communication was extremely unusual and as the speaker was unknown to him, he must have telegraphic confirmation of these instructions in the approved cipher.[1]

---

[1] I have not been able to discover whether a cipher confirmation was ever received. The only person I met, who might have been in a position to know, told me that it was not.

The afternoon was breathlessly hot and no one in the town faced the glare of the sun for longer than was necessary. These hours therefore passed quietly.

As soon as it was cool a Socialist provincial deputy, of the name of Prat, called at the House-of-the-Military-Government, and asked to see Colonel Moscardó. This deputy, it must be explained, held no official position except that of being a member of the local Provincial Assembly. On being received he at once repeated, almost word for word, the demands which had been made in the telephone call from Madrid that morning. To it he added the demand that the Guardia Civil, the soldiers attached to the Academy and those belonging to the "Gym" School, should be disarmed and their weapons handed over to his own party's political militia, of which he stated himself to be one of the leaders.

Only a short while after this visit Colonel Moscardó was again called to the telephone by someone in Madrid. The speaker on this occasion gave his name as Sarata.[1] He also demanded that the munitions in the Factory should be loaded and despatched forthwith.

A little later still the Civil Governor of the town called at the Military Headquarters. He also, it appeared, had received a call from the deputy Prat, and the same demands had been put before him. Colonel Moscardó made it clear that compliance would be impossible.

THE TWENTIETH OF JULY

The night had passed quietly with the exception of a minor disturbance by unknown persons in some districts of the town. Owing to the narrowness and the tortuousness of the alleys,

[1] The name was unknown to the Military Governor and whether this was the same person as had telephoned that morning is not clear.

and to the lack of efficient lighting, it had been found impossible to apprehend those concerned.

During the morning it came to the knowledge of Colonel Moscardó that the demands of the previous day had been sent, also, directly to the officer in charge of the Arms Factory. It would seem strange that this officer had not informed the Military Governor but his subsequent conduct may offer an explanation. It was now agreed between them that no arms or munitions should be despatched for the present; and that for their better protection two hundred Guardia Civil should be posted at the Factory.

The afternoon passed without developments. But late that evening, however, the General-in-Chief of the Guardia Civil (of all Spain), speaking by telephone from Madrid, informed Colonel Moscardó that, unless the demands made on the previous day were at once complied with, he would be regarded as being in a state of mutiny. In which case a column of troops would be sent to Toledo and the town would be bombarded. If, on the other hand, the arms and munitions were despatched without further delay, he would use his personal influence to smooth matters over.

It may be necessary here to explain the situation which had been produced. It was obvious that Colonel Moscardó was in sympathy with the military revolt which had broken out in Morocco. But his actions up till now appear to have been strictly in accordance with his duties as Military Governor of the province. It was equally obvious that the General-in-Chief of the Guardia Civil was siding with the established Government; as indeed it was his duty to do. But he was in no way an immediate superior of Colonel Moscardó, nor were they in the same chain of responsibility. Thus, while he would have been perfectly within his rights in giving orders as to the disposal of the Guardia Civil within the province of Toledo, he was not acting within his rights when giving orders as to the disposal of munitions in the Toledo Arms Factory. And presumably he could have had no authority when threatening the despatch of troops and the bombardment of the town.

In view of these threats, all the Guardia Civil who were not at the moment on duty, were brought that night within the precincts of the Alcazar. Their families came with them.

THE TWENTY-FIRST OF JULY

It is now time that the situation of this garrison in revolt at Toledo, and of its commander, should be estimated. The news broadcast by the Government from Radio-Madrid and printed in such newspapers as had been allowed to circulate, was no doubt minimizing such few successes as the military revolt had had elsewhere in Spain. Nevertheless, making deductions for this, Colonel Moscardó must have realized that the coup d'état had failed in the capital and in almost every important garrison; that he was completely isolated; and that there was no help for him at hand. Nor could he have had any illusions as to whether the Government would carry out the threats made the day before. Toledo was only two hours by road from Madrid and, of the garrisons in revolt, it was by far the nearest to the capital. For the Government the matter would be one of prestige. Thus with an insufficient, miscellaneous and so far un-organized garrison he had to make rapidly what dispositions he could for the defence of Toledo, both against attacks from Government troops from Madrid, and against their armed supporters within the town.

Toledo is a walled town. Therefore it might be thought easy to defend. But the walls are those of the Middle Ages, and their length, more than three miles, could not be manned by the numbers available.

The forces of the garrison consisted of: —

The Guardia Civil, amounting to a little less than six hundred of all ranks;

The young soldiers attached to the Military Academy as grooms, officers' servants, etc., and none of whom had had any serious military training; [1]

The staff of the Gym School.

These two last-named contingents amounted together to between one hundred and fifty and one hundred and eighty men.

Such was all the garrison on the morning of July the 21st.

During the course of the day it was increased slightly, in various ways. For instance, a number of officers on the Active or Retired Lists reported themselves to the military commander. Seven or eight cadets of the Academy, some living in the district and others coming at risk to themselves from Madrid, did the same. Business men of Toledo, townsmen, artisans, workmen and peasants came into the Alcazar and offered their services, or asked for security for themselves and their families. But in the hours before dawn, when Colonel Moscardó had to make what dispositions he could, the forces at his disposal were under eight hundred strong.

With these he had to maintain a garrison in the Alcazar itself, to provide its defence and to carry on the routine duties essential in such a large establishment. Guards had to be provided for the city gates—of which some ten or twelve were important, and for the bridges across the Tagus—of which there were three. Piquets would be needed for the Town Hall; Toledo wireless station; the telephone and telegraph offices; several banks; the Cathedral (a national monument containing a vast store of art treasures and actual gold and silver); the bar-

---

[1] The exact numbers it is impossible at present to discover, for several reasons it may always remain so. For many of these young soldiers were on leave: it is uncertain which ones returned in time. Many of the documents dealing with the matter have been destroyed in various ways before or during the siege.

racks of the civil police; the electric power station; several other buildings of public utility within the town. But, after the safeguarding of the Alcazar itself, by far the most important and difficult task was the protection of the Arms Factory. For this two hundred of the Guardia Civil had already been detached—a quarter of all the troops available. And a detached post always has been, and always will be, a cause of weakness to a force, and of anxiety to its commander.

The Arms Factory was a particularly dangerous detached post. For it was outside the city walls and some three kilometres distant from the Alcazar; a third of that distance consisting of a maze of narrow alleys which offered ideal fighting grounds for armed roughs with a knowledge of the locality. It was clear that the garrison of the Alcazar and that of the Arms Factory could not count on support from each other, and must each ensure its own defence.

Moreover all guards on gates, bridges and buildings in the town must be strong enough to supply their own reliefs—for soldiers, like factory workers, must have rest and sleep.

The numbers available were utterly insufficient but what could be done was done. Parties were allotted to the various posts and were in their places by dawn. Only an hour later the Government troops were already in sight.

The Government forces, henceforward the "enemy," were first seen on the low hills northward of the town and about two miles distant. There the road from Madrid, which for leagues has traced its straight asphalt course over a naked plain, crosses the last ridge and sweeps down towards the gate of Visagra, by which it enters Toledo. The point where the high-road breasts the ridge is clearly seen from the Alcazar. On an early summer morning the air in Castile is almost always still and the light is extraordinarily clear and vivid. The slopes where the road is first visible are warm-tinted and dusty. The road is grey. To the left stands a line of tall dark slender cypresses.

The column of Government troops appearing on this road

was preceded by four large armoured cars, two of which were armed with light quick-firing guns mounted in turrets.[1]

Descending to levels which lie between these slopes and the town, the Government troops found their way blocked by detachments consisting of Guardia Civil and men of the Gym School. These had been posted in the Hospital of Tavera and in other substantial buildings which compose this northern suburb and flank the high-road from Madrid.[2]

The Government forces were large in numbers but consisted chiefly of the undisciplined militia of the Frente Popular stiffened and sometimes led by Regulars. Meeting this resistance they halted, consulted and finally deployed. Supported by their armoured cars and by machine-guns, they made some sort of attempt to attack the positions held by the Guardia Civil and force their way into the town. But finding that the men garrisoning the buildings commanding the road maintained their fire, the Government troops abandoned the attempt, and sheered off. Thereafter they took a north-westerly direction and, moving behind the trees of a little park, directed their way towards the Arms Factory.

Meanwhile other events had been taking place within the town itself.

At 7 a.m., with due solemnity, and with a detachment of the young soldiers of the Military Academy presenting arms, a proclamation was read in the great courtyard of the Alcazar, declaring a "State of War," in the town and province of Toledo.

The detachment with sloped arms and fixed bayonets then marched out of the courtyard, down the Cuesta (or slope) into the town. In the Zocodover, the main plaza of Toledo, the detachment was halted. It consisted of boys between seventeen and eighteen years of age. They wore khaki drill, with leather

---

[1] I.e. "cannon," not machine-guns.
[2] The Hospital of Tavera is a splendid and massive brick building of the mid-sixteenth century, having the general appearance of a large monastery.

equipment and khaki glengarries. They had had on the average some five months' service and looked not very different from the O.T.C. of an English Public School. The order to present arms was given and, while the idlers and peasants from the country stood listening, the captain once more read the proclamation.[1]

The proclamation was at the same time broadcast by the Toledo wireless station and all officers who were in the province, and all "well-disposed persons" who were able to, were asked to report themselves to the Military Governor.

Madrid must have heard this broadcast. There was now no possibility of turning back.

Yet another step was taken. Information had been furnished by the town police concerning the part played by the local extremists of the Left during the disturbances of the previous nights. An order for the arrest of several of their leaders was now given—this, since the proclamation of a "State of War," being within the power of the Military Governor. However, none of these leaders was to be found, excepting one, the schoolmaster of the local prison.

At 9.30 a.m. a Government plane appeared and dropped leaflets over Toledo. At the sight of this plane firing broke out in various districts of the town, this being chiefly directed against the Guardia Civil posted at various points.

The morning passed slowly. The Government troops taking a leisurely and roundabout way eventually reached the Arms Factory and partly surrounded it. Thereupon they sent forward a corporal to negotiate with the colonel commandant of the Factory.

The pourparlers which followed took place in the presence of several subordinate officers, some undergoing a course at the Arms Factory, others belonging to the Guardia Civil, a detachment of which had been mounted there the day before. These

[1] The scene can be perfectly realized by a glance at Plate 5.

officers, many of them young lieutenants, were so unfavourably impressed by the colonel's attitude, that they determined not to be bound in future by any orders he might give but to take what action seemed to them good. They therefore set about loading all the available small-arm ammunition into lorries. The loading of the lorries was carried out by some members of the technical staff and by young artillery officers who were undergoing a course of instruction at the Factory. The pourparlers between the corporal of the Government troops and the colonel commandant of the Arms Factory proved lengthy. So, while they were still in progress the lorries, under convoy, were sent off to the Alcazar.[1]

This done, the young officers went in a body to the colonel commandant and asked what steps he proposed to take for the immediate defence of the Factory. His answer seemed to them so unsatisfactory that they set about destroying as much of the plant as they could in the short time available. Then, dissociating themselves from the colonel commandant, they withdrew to the Alcazar, leaving two of their number to watch the course of events. This, at great danger to themselves, the two young men continued to do until the evening of the following day. Whether the Guardia Civil garrison withdrew before all this had happened does not seem clear.

Meanwhile at 3.20 p.m. another Government plane appeared, flew over the Alcazar and dropped bombs, causing some damage.

At 6 p.m. a flight of three more planes appeared and dropped twelve larger bombs on the Alcazar, killing a young soldier on duty on the Esplanade.[2]

---

[1] This accounts for the presence in the Alcazar of the immense supply of ammunition, barely half of which was fired away during the seventy-three days of the siege. The total amount of rounds at the beginning of the siege was, I believe, 1,500,000.

[2] The main upper terrace on the east side of the Alcazar. It looks down upon a lower terrace and upon the Tagus.

During both these air bombardments attacks were made from concealed positions upon sentries posted on the various important points in the town. The great majority of the population, however, remained indoors. The streets were deserted and business was at a standstill.

Another activity of that afternoon makes clear one of the straits to which the garrison of the Alcazar was later reduced. The water of Toledo had long been considered so bad for drinking purposes that all who could afford to, had been in the habit of buying water which was brought into the town and peddled from door to door. For this reason there was, among the several vehicles belonging to the Alcazar, a motor tank-waggon which was employed to fetch drinking-water from a spring on the other side of the Tagus. During the course of the afternoon, therefore, the tank-waggon under escort of two cars filled with Guardia Civil, drove down to the New Bridge, crossed it, filled up with water at the accustomed spring and returned to the Alcazar. But with so many to supply, this stock of drinking-water was exhausted in a few days. And for the rest of the siege the defenders depended upon wells within the grounds and rain-storage tanks, the water of which had been considered undrinkable. While as for washing, this was probably the last day on which anyone in the Alcazar was able to indulge in such a luxury.

Late that evening General Riquelme made a telephone call from Madrid and formally asked Colonel Moscardó his reasons for acting as he had. Colonel Moscardó gave them as follows. Firstly because the Government had ceased to be Spanish in policy and, to common knowledge, was controlled by Marxists who were using the country only as a pawn in a larger game; secondly because of his unshakeable confidence in the good judgment of General Franco; thirdly because handing over the arms of the gentleman cadets of the Alcazar to the Workers' Militia would be to inflict upon them an unthinkable indignity.

The first reasons are patently expressions of political bias. The last may sound fanciful. But it is the note to which the whole spirit of the defence of the Alcazar is in tune. And, later, a chapter will be devoted to this spirit, so foreign to our age in Western Europe.

Another less dramatic event of the morning had been this. The Civil Governor of the Province had been taken into custody—it would seem with his entire consent—and he and his family had been brought into the Alcazar.

During the course of the day various Army officers had come to the Alcazar and offered their services; some being officers on the Active List, others retired and on the Reserve. Some brought with them their families for safety. Various business men of the town also threw in their lot with the garrison. As for the rest of the population of Toledo the great majority, as the recent elections had shown, would probably have mildly favoured the cause, but they were unorganized and unarmed. The Extremists of the Left, on the other hand, who formed but a minority, had been organized and armed, perhaps in view of the expected Communist revolution. During the day their position had been strengthened by the arrival of Government troops outside the town. And, though most of the Government's militia-men remained as a formed body, and in the neighbourhood of the Arms Factory, it seemed likely that some of them had filtered into the town and swelled the ranks of the local extremists.

THE TWENTY-SECOND OF JULY

At 7 a.m. three planes arrived from the direction of Madrid and bombarded the Alcazar.

At 9 a.m. a battery of 105-cm. guns which the Government

forces had brought into position on the low hills two miles north of the town, opened fire upon the Alcazar with high-explosive shells.[1]

At 10 a.m. the three Government planes returned and dropped bombs upon the town, causing fires in the south-eastern district. And at about the same time an unknown person telephoned to Colonel Moscardó saying that the Government had appointed him, in place of the Civil Governor who had sided with the garrison. He stated that he spoke on behalf of the Provincial Assembly, which body by the order of the Government had now been purged of the four-fifths of its members who had represented the parties of the Right. He demanded the surrender of the Alcazar within two hours.

Upon this Colonel Moscardó called a meeting of the senior military officers and of the civilian elements in the Alcazar. A vote was taken and by a large majority a refusal was decided upon.

The day was excessively hot. During the lunch-hour and the hour of siesta which followed it, all was quiet.

At 4 p.m. a large Government plane arrived and began a bombardment; firstly on the Alcazar and secondly on the Hospital of Tavera (a building outside the town and still held by a detachment whose fire had diverted the Government troops on the previous day). Some damage was done and a fire was started among the buildings on the Zocodover and on the Cuesta (the sloping roadway which led up from the plaza to the Alcazar and formed the main approach to it).[2] The fire proved extensive and destroyed a considerable number of houses to the northwest of the Alcazar, and under the shadow of its terraces. This pleased both sides. For the Government forces seem to have been anxious to raze these house, so as to facilitate assaults upon the north façade of the Alcazar; while the be-

---

[1] The spot from which this battery fired is known as the Dehesa de Pinedo. It will be referred to by that name.

[2] It is seen in Plate 5.

sieged were equally anxious that these houses should be levelled in order that their field of fire might be clear. The houses were burnt and fell into a confusion of ruins. Thereafter the north side of the Alcazar—till then hidden—was visible from the Zocodover.[1]

During this air bombardment enemy rifle-fire was opened from various points upon the windows of the Alcazar. The guards, also, mounted upon important buildings in the town, were attacked. On previous days firing in Toledo had been with revolvers or automatic pistols, now it was with rifles. This proved that the local extremists had been reinforced by some militia-men of the Madrid column, who during the hours of darkness had somehow filtered into the town.

All outlying detachments were thus in danger of being cut off. This was realized by their commanders, and the officer in charge of the Hospital of Tavera garrison (outside the Madrid gate, and guarding it) took stock of his situation. His force had not been seriously attacked since the previous morning, but his communications with the Alcazar were now threatened. Moreover, the enemy possessed artillery, armoured cars, aircraft and enormous superiority in numbers. He could hear heavy firing from the direction of the Arms Factory. What this indicated he did not know, and such reconnaissance parties as he sent out did not return. He therefore decided to retire to the Alcazar. The civilians with his force were first dispatched, protected by an escort. This movement took the enemy by surprise and was accomplished without loss. But the subsequent withdrawal of the main body proved difficult. It had to fight its way back, yard by yard. The distance is not more than three-quarters of a mile, yet it took this detachment nearly six hours to cover it. And, even then, the later stages of the withdrawal were helped by the fall of night. Actually the enemy fire, though it hampered movement, was extremely inaccurate;

[1] Among the houses so burnt was the Inn of Cervantes which stood to the left rear of the arch seen on Plate 15.

and thanks to this, known casualties were not heavy. But during the retirement the following disappeared:—one military doctor, one civilian doctor; one sergeant-major; two sergeants; three military craftsmen; four soldiers; one bugler. Whether these were casualties from enemy fire, or whether they deserted, was not known.

Meanwhile in all parts of the town pressure on the posts of the Guardia Civil had been so heavy that all had been withdrawn, excepting those of the Radio-Toledo station and the Bank of Spain. Throughout the twilight and during the first hours of darkness these isolated detachments made their way back to the Alcazar. And before midnight the two artillery lieutenants who since the evening before had remained in the neighbourhood of the Arms Factory to watch events, came in.

Despite the amount of rifle and automatic pistol fire the known casualties of the day amounted to only one dead and twelve wounded. But to these must be added the thirteen who were "missing" during the withdrawal from the Hospital of Tavera. The day's losses thus amounted to twenty-six.

A matter of much concern was that the artillery bombardment, though not heavy, had damaged the electric cables and cut off the supply of electricity to the Alcazar and all its dependent buildings. Despite all their efforts the garrison never succeeded in tapping any alternative supply of electricity. Throughout the siege they remained practically without light and for many weeks without a means of using such wireless apparatus as they had.

THE TWENTY-THIRD OF JULY

At 4.30 a.m.—not long after daybreak—a Government plane made a lengthy reconnaissance over the Alcazar and its outbuildings. It then flew back in the direction of Madrid.

Now occurred an incident which was typical of what was happening all over Spain. But, because it was typical, it may help us to understand how this struggle came later to be conducted with terrible ruthlessness. At 10 a.m. Colonel Moscardó was called to his office, as the chief of the local Workers' Militia wished to speak to him over the telephone.

I know the room in which he received this communication. Being on the south face of the Alcazar it had not suffered greatly from shell-fire and, when I first saw it, was much as it must have been on that July morning.

The room was low, hung with torn terracotta wallpaper. It was ugly but full of character; part of a reconstruction undertaken after a fire in the 'eighties. There was a vast knee-hole desk, a revolving chair; the uninspiring equipment of a Government office. Hiding one corner was a built-in settee, the back of which, carried to some height, formed a screen. It was L-shaped and above the imitation leather upholstery were chestnut-wood panels, each of which enclosed an enlarged photograph of some past colonel-commandant of the Academy. In a building so palatial and so magnificently furnished this room seemed forlorn and neglected, out of place. The photographs of the colonel-commandants were faded. In romantic shakos and ill-fitting tunics, hands on sword-hilts, they had all the sadness of the recent past. A few of the earlier ones wore whiskers. These had given place to heavy silken moustaches; these to ones the points of which had been greased. Towards the very end the moustaches had been clipped.

The leather of the settee was bullet-holed and torn. By the windows was a knee-deep pile of empty cartridge cases. The inkpot, still lying where it had fallen, had spread a wide black stain across the floor, visible here and there amidst the dust and wreckage. The glass was all gone from the window; the remnants of some blind or curtain chattered in the wind. With innocent but reproachful eyes the dead colonel-commandants surveyed the unimaginable untidiness of this room which in turn had belonged to each of them.

On the morning in question Colonel Moscardó was very busy but, on receiving this message, he crossed the courtyard and went into his office.

The chief of the Workers' Militia was still on the telephone. He informed Colonel Moscardó that he had his son in his power, and that unless the Alcazar were surrendered within ten minutes he would have him shot.

On receipt of the message Colonel Moscardó asked to speak to his son, so as to be certain that he was indeed in the hands of the enemy. The young man was called to the telephone and for a few moments the father and son spoke together. Then the chief of the Workers' Militia took his place and repeated his threat. Colonel Moscardó at once told him that there could be no purpose in waiting for the ten minutes to elapse, as in no circumstances would he ever surrender the Alcazar, of which a sequence of unexpected events had placed him in charge.

The line was cleared.

A few minutes later Colonel Moscardó was again called to the telephone and informed that his son had been shot.

These are the bare facts. The following version of the conversation between Colonel Moscardó and his son is current everywhere in Spain. I have not taken the only means of confirming or disproving it, but I give it here, for what it may be worth. According to this version the boy asked what he should do. To which his father replied, "All you can do is to pray for us and to die for Spain."

To which the boy is reported to have said, "That is quite simple. Both I will do."

The incident became known to the garrison, and the above version, which is theirs, may be true.

It seems that during the afternoon detachments which had been on guard at the Toledo Radio Station and at the Bank of Spain managed to make their way back to the Alcazar.

PLATE 7

THE "CATACOMB ROAD"

It ran under all four sides of the Alcazar. The light on the right comes through the doorway of a breached classroom. The barricade was built to prevent shell splinters entering this, the main lines of communication.

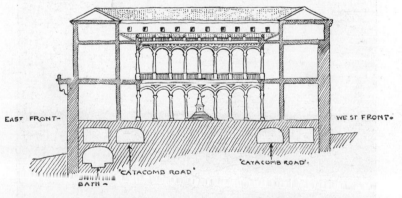

SECTION OF THE ALCAZAR

Showing the position of this "Catacomb Road," of the classrooms on the outer sides of it, and of the Swimming-Bath in a sub-basement.

PLATE 8

THE ALCAZAR FROM THE SOUTH

Following the roof lines from left to right there are:—The
Alcazar; the Capuchinos; the dining-hall; the Quarters-of-the-
Soldiers (sheer above the slope). Across the gorge of the Tagus
is seen the Castle of San Servando.

A COURTYARD IN THE CONVENT OF
LA CONCEPCION

This was less than 100 yards distant from the outworks of the
Alcazar. Trench mortars and a field-gun were used from here,
but some of the nuns, though forced to wear lay clothing, were
allowed to remain.

The moon had been new only five days before and the night must have been dark. But the Tagus in the gorge below seems always to throw back some starlight towards the Alcazar. It was this reflected light, perhaps, that enabled a big three-engined plane to fly over the Alcazar and drop fifteen bombs.

THE TWENTY-FOURTH OF JULY

The position of the garrison of the Alcazar was clearly a serious one. The refugees and their families had brought the population within the building and its grounds up to some eighteen hundred persons, almost a third of whom consisted of women and children. There were, too, among the men some too old to take part in any fighting and others who, though young, had had no military training. The cadets being on their holidays, the stock of food was small and would not suffice now for more than a few meals. Nor was there any means of knowing how long a siege the garrison would be called on to withstand. Almost everywhere else in Spain the supporters of the military revolt had been defeated. Some had fled: some, hard pressed, were on the point of surrender. In Spain the coup d'état, of which Colonel Moscardó's action had been but one small and local echo, had clearly failed. It was certain that the garrison could not be relieved in the immediate future; and that it might never be.

In view of this Colonel Moscardó decided upon a sortie in force, for the purpose of collecting food. At 12.30 p.m., an hour when it was calculated the free and undisciplined Workers' Militia might be at their midday meal, two simultaneous sorties were made by companies of the Guardia Civil; working, of course, under their own officers. One of these parties made its way out by the Stable Approach and passing under the arch of La Sangré entered the plaza Zocodover, which is lined with

cafés and provision shops. The other cutting westward across
the calle del Comercio, the main thoroughfare of the town,
attempted to raid a street some distance away, in which there
were a number of provision stores. Both raids failed. The companies of Guardia Civil were met by sustained rifle-fire from
barricaded upper windows. They suffered casualties, and after
attempting various detours, were forced to return to the Alcazar. Indeed the only result of those sorties was the accidental
capture of one of the local Extremist leaders who, with some
male members of his family, was brought in and held prisoner
in the Alcazar during the entire length of the siege.

At 2 p.m. that afternoon a three-engined Government plane
first bombarded the Alcazar and then "spotted" for the "105"
guns which were now established near the battery of "75's", on
the low hills north of the town. So aided, these guns kept up a
slow and methodical bombardment for an hour, after which
the plane flew away. But at 5.30 p.m. it returned, repeated its
bombing of the Alcazar and then once more "spotted" for the
same guns.

Considering that the number of shells fired at the Alcazar
had not been great, the damage done was considerable. But
the fire had been deliberate and well directed by aeroplane
observation, while the gunners had worked in ideal conditions;
for, though for artillery the distance was a short one, the gun
position had been out of range of any weapons possessed by the
defence. The guns in question having been on the north of
the town the damage done was exclusively to the north façade
of the Alcazar, in which the main gateway of the building was
situated and which offered in the enemy's eyes the most favour-
able point for an attack.

On this occasion the gateway and many of the rooms around
it were damaged, and a fire was started in the north-west tower.
Some shells, which fell wide, hit the church of La Magdalena,
standing about one hundred and fifty yards to the west of the
Alcazar, and thus on lower ground.

The casualties of the day were three dead and nine wounded. The dead were buried after midnight in the south-western corner of the riding-school. There was no priest to perform the service and this was done always by one of the officers, whose exalted and religious spirit proved of inestimable help to the defenders.

THE TWENTY-FIFTH OF JULY

At dawn on this day it became clear that the Alcazar, together with its grounds and outbuildings, was now so closely invested that a state of siege had begun.

On the east side the grounds stretched down to the river. Across the river—which here runs through a gorge—are cliffs. These are some four or five hundred yards distant from the Alcazar itself and they formed the nearest line which the enemy could take up on this side. On the three remaining sides, however, the houses of the town closely hemmed in the Alcazar. Thus on three sides the investment was a very close one, and on the fourth it was effective.

All buildings looking upon the Alcazar had been occupied in the course of the night by the enemy and had been put in a state of defence. Everywhere doors and windows had been sand-bagged and loopholes had been made. The roofs of Toledo are invariably of pantiles and of so low a pitch as to be almost flat. Thus, while safe and easy to walk on, they have just enough slope to offer concealment for rifle-men. All roofs from which the Alcazar could be seen were therefore already occupied. And wherever the tower of a church or monastery rose above other buildings, it had been put to use as a nest for machine-guns or snipers. Thus, as soon as there was light enough to see, rifle and machine-gun fire was opened from all sides upon the Alcazar and its dependencies.

At 5 a.m. the "105" guns opened fire. The fire was steady and was directed, as before, entirely against the north façade of the building. Some damage was done and a motor-coach—one of those in which the Guardia Civil had been brought in eight days before and which for lack of garage space had been left in a corner of the north terrace—was set on fire. The shelling by these guns continued steadily until 8 a.m. While this bombardment lasted there was little rifle or machine-gun fire from the loopholed windows and roof-tops, and it was presumed that the enemy's rifle-men were watching the novel sight of bursting shells. As soon, however, as the artillery fire ceased the machine-gun and rifle-fire from the houses began again. The men occupying these belonged in all probability to the Workers' Militia, which formed a larger and non-technical part of the besieging force. They were new to their work but they set about it with zeal. And, though their fire was inaccurate, they kept it up with the enthusiasm of the first morning of a holiday. Some at least must have done their year of army service but of late their only military training had been endless marching in political processions and perhaps a shot or two in riots and street-fighting.

At 12 p.m.—an hour when in Spain even Regular troops are apt to rest, especially during the hot weather—the battery opened fire again and, with a half-hour break at 4.30, continued its fire till midnight.

This slow but steady bombardment throughout the day proved to be part of a general scheme. For at dusk three planes flew over the Alcazar and dropped a shower of pamphlets, which pointed out to the garrison how helpless they were against artillery fire and called upon the rank and file to mutiny or desert.

At 9.30 that night a captain of the garrison was despatched on a secret and dangerous mission. He was to make his way through the enemy's lines and out of Toledo. He was then to go across country and find General Mola, whose column was believed to be somewhere in the Sierra de Guadarrama, a vast range just visible on the horizon when the air was very clear.

The revolt of General Mola had been among the few in Spain which had had local success. He was believed to have drawn to himself a number of supporters and Colonel Moscardó was anxious to let him know that the revolt in Toledo was still holding its own and that the Alcazar, though besieged, had not surrendered. To give him this information had become essential, as Radio-Madrid had announced that the Alcazar had already surrendered and the Madrid newspapers (some had been captured during the sorties of the day before) had printed a detailed description of how the garrison had marched out.

As far as anyone inside the Alcazar knew, General Mola's column was the only force upon which the garrison could ever possibly count for its relief. And, if he were to believe that the Alcazar had already surrendered, there could be no chance of his marching to its assistance.[1]

There was indeed within the Alcazar a movable wireless transmitting set, which was part of the equipment of the Guardia Civil and which they had brought in with them. But it was one constructed for normal conditions and for use with mains supply of electricity, and the bombardment having already cut the electric cables there was no such supply available.

During the day the Alcazar had been bombarded for fourteen hours by a battery of four guns firing at short range and using high-explosive shells. But in accordance with an adopted plan, the defenders, throughout the seventeen hours of daylight, had made no reply to the continuous rifle and machine-gun fire levelled against the windows at close range. Thus, except for the many necessary observation posts, there had been no need for the garrison to expose itself. This was as well, as they also were new to their work.

They had much to learn. Later they evolved a drill which

[1] Actually General Mola's advance southward, though rapid at first, was held up and his force remained stationary for several months.

enabled them to evacuate any portion of the building while it was being shelled; and yet to remain ever ready to re-occupy it the moment that the artillery fire ceased, or when there was any likelihood of an infantry attack. But as yet they had had no such training and thus the casualties of the day were heavier than they would have been when their special methods had been perfected and become a matter of routine. As it was the losses of the day amounted to one dead and twelve wounded.

THE GARRISON

The siege of the Alcazar had now begun. But before proceeding further with the story, it is necessary to do two things; first to describe the numbers and arms of the garrison, and secondly to give some description of this building which, built as a palace, proved to be of such great strength that it was able to withstand nine weeks of bombardment and the explosion of three gigantic mines.

The fact may seem curious, but it is difficult as yet to ascertain the true combatant strength of those who by one chance or another came to make up the haphazard garrison of the Alcazar.

THE CADETS

The number of cadets of the Academy had fallen to such an extent that during the summer term of 1936 there were but a hundred and thirty of them. And, as July is a holiday month in Spain, the cadets were away and only eight of them managed to return and take part in the siege.

SOLDIERS ATTACHED TO THE ACADEMY

But, for those who were stirred by reading of how the Alcazar

was being defended by its cadets, there is comfort in knowing
that the young soldiers attached to the Academy did sustain
some of the most desperate and hardly credible episodes of the
siege, and were in fact a year or so younger than the cadets
themselves would have been. The average age was probably
not quite eighteen.

SOLDIERS OF THE GYM SCHOOL

To these must be added the staff and pupils of this School.

GUARDIA CIVIL

These formed the largest group within the garrison. There
were some six hundred of them—of all ranks. They served
under their own officers and their own commander. There are
some, indeed, who attribute to him the brilliance of the defence. They may be right. Perhaps to Colonel Moscardó belong only the determination, the faith, the devotion, by which
the Alcazar was held.

THE CORPS OF OFFICERS

There were, also, some one hundred and fifty Army officers;
a few being officer instructors of the Academy; others being reserve officers, or active officers on leave. Amongst them was the
captain who had been sent from Morocco to warn Colonel
Moscardó of the intended coup d'état. His presence was provi-
dential. He was the only engineer officer of the garrison. It was
he who was able to determine the points at which the enemy's
mines would explode.

THE CIVILIANS

There were, too, a number of civilians. Most belonged to one
of the several political parties which are described below.

The Falangistas. This political party, modelled on the Fascists
of Italy, had come into existence only a few months before.
They were at the moment much "in the news," but it is under-

stood that there were not more than ten thousand of them in all Spain.

Renovacion Española. There were some members of this party. Its aim was the restoration of the ex-king, Alfonso XIII.

Carlists. There were, too, a few members of this political party, known more correctly as the Traditionalists.

Peasants. There were, too, some peasants, craftsmen and labourers, who for one reason or another threw in their lot with the garrison.

THE WOMEN AND CHILDREN

Some twenty of the women were wives or relatives of officers of the Academy, or were ladies of Toledo. The greater part, however, were wives of the Guardia Civil, or mothers of the young soldiers.

APPROXIMATE STRENGTH

Officers	150
Cadets	8
Young soldiers	160
Guardia Civil	600
Falangistas	35
Renovacion Españolas . . .	25
Carlists [1]	10
Peasants and workmen . . .	40
	1,028

[1] The Carlists, till the Civil War, had consisted of an ancient and extremely Conservative organization. They had had their origin in, and still based themselves on, support of the legitimate Carlist line which had been displaced exactly one hundred years before. During that century these Carlists had fought two protracted and bitter civil wars against the royal house which in their view had usurped the throne; and to which the ex-King, Alfonso XIII, had belonged. But, though a claimant of their own was still a pretender to the now non-existent Spanish throne, their views appeared to outsiders to be more an affirmation of loyalty to the past than any form of practical politics. The Carlists properly have their home in the north-west corner of Spain and

The number of non-combatants was made up somewhat as follows:—

Men—too old or unfit	.	.	.	100
Women	.	.	.	.	520
Children	.	.	.	.	50
					670

THE ARMS OF THE GARRISON

As for arms, the garrison possessed ample stock of rifles and bayonets, and some ten to twelve machine-guns. But none of

the existence of any in Toledo must have been accidental.

Three months of civil war completely changed their position. By their readiness to serve and by their stability they became the mainstay of General Franco's cause, and the "power behind the throne." The Nationalist Government of Burgos (the northern portion of General Franco's Insurgent cause) found itself unable to take Irun, the all-important railway centre near the French frontier. The legionaries who with difficulty had been spared from the southern front made gallant but fruitless attempts. One bandera of it went into battle with some nine hundred men and thirty officers and came out with under three hundred men and no officers at all. It was essential that Irun should be taken and the Burgos Government had no fresh troops with which to renew the attack.

At this point the Carlist organization came forward with an offer of forty thousand of its followers, all of whom had done their army service and had lately received training in the Carlist detachments. They came, these Requetes, as they are now called; paid out of their own subscriptions at a standard rate of one peseta (fourpence) a day for all ranks, from private to colonel. They took Irun.

They came of a tough, hardy, somewhat dour race. But the young men are cheerful, at any rate while fighting. They hold to the traditions of the past, their officers being sons and grandsons of those who fought in the Carlist wars. I have met one distinguished old gentleman who took part in the fighting at Irun. He wore the dark brown lumber jacket and breeches of the Carlist, and their scarlet tam-o'-shanter. He had a white patriarchal beard and steady eyes. Three of his sons and one of his grandsons had fought at Irun in the same battle as himself. Two sons had been killed. The old gentleman, when last I saw him, was in a town just behind the Madrid front and was waiting to be drafted into one of the Carlist battalions in the trenches.

the latter were less than fourteen years old, and two were reputed to have been through the Melilla wars. Beyond this they had been used for the instruction of half a generation of cadets. Some of them, from having been kept for stripping and reassembling practice, were apt to come to pieces when in action. There were a few sub-machine guns—these being instructional samples.

Thanks to the young artillery officers and the technicians of the Arms Factory, who had brought in all the small-arm ammunition they could find, there was an inexhaustible supply of it in the Alcazar: some give the amount as one-and-a-half million rounds. Indeed, although the siege lasted for seventy-three days the defenders on the day of their relief had not used over half the stock available.

There were two light guns; one a mountain gun, for which there were a dozen or so rounds; and the other a still smaller piece, for which there were so few rounds that its use was hardly contemplated. Owing to the almost total lack of ammunition for them, these guns could not be used in the defence. They were placed, one inside each of the two principal gateways; to be used only in the last extremity, should the enemy succeed in breaching the gates. One was never fired at all, but was buried beneath a sudden fall of masonry.

The other, the smaller piece, remained behind the door of the southern façade—ready for an emergency that never arose.

There was also in the Alcazar one small trench-mortar. It had been used for the instruction of cadets and for it there were several dozen rounds. These were too precious to be used except at a crisis. Actually it was fired with great skill on two or three occasions, to the delight of the officer who had been the instructor of trench-mortar fire, and of those who watched its bombs exploding on the targets.

HAND BOMBS

There was a stock of bombs, freshly brought in from the Arms Factory, and of the "jam-tin" type. But the number was very limited and, even in the most critical moments, strictest economy in their use was necessary.

The two little guns with their dozen rounds of ammunition can be disregarded and it can be said that the defenders of the Alcazar had no artillery.

Against the machine-gun and rifle-fire, the trench-mortar bombs, the hand-bombs, the flame-throwers, the tanks and armoured cars of the besiegers, the garrison had but their rifles, their few worn-out machine-guns, and an utterly insufficient stock of hand-bombs.

Against the enemy's artillery and bombing planes they had no means of reply.

THE STRENGTH OF THE ALCAZAR

The Alcazar was held by a thousand men and boys, always short of rest and sleep, and starving for the greater part of the time. It was held in spite of artillery bombardment, air attacks, the explosion of three enormous mines, and eight separate general assaults delivered by overwhelming numbers. How was this possible?

It was possible, in part because of the qualities and the faith of its defenders; in part because of the cool yet sometimes reckless skill by which all they did was directed; and in part because of the extraordinary character of the building itself.

And for the understanding of what follows some description of the Alcazar is necessary.

Inevitably the story of such a siege is woven round things in themselves inanimate; round some doorway which became of more importance than those who gave their lives defending it; round a broken tower, the fall of which seemed to the defenders a humiliation transcending military defeat; round a vault far underground, which in the last days was both hospital and chapel, and where by the light of one mule-fat dip some men lay dying, while others, in their moments off duty at the loop-holes, came to pray.

Without the stones, the bricks and mortar, the defence would not have been possible. Without some description of their form and purpose, the story of the siege cannot be understood.

THE ALCAZAR

ITS STRUCTURE

The Alcazar of Toledo, a vast, high, rectangular building, stood upon the slopes above the Tagus and dwarfed the whole town. Inside it was a very large paved courtyard, surrounded by two storeys of arcades. At each corner was a square tower, surmounted by a steeple.

The east and west sides of the Alcazar dated from the Middle Ages. And, though in later days they had been pierced by a few grandiose windows, the walls on these two sides remained those of a fortress. The other two sides, those at the north and the south, were built as façades of a palace; and, though solid and massive, they were in no way constructed for defence.

The building had been gutted several times by fire; the last occasion being in 1886. So, though the shell was everywhere the original one, woodwork had been largely suppressed and beams replaced by girders. Thus in 1936 the Alcazar had the best of the two epochs of construction; walls from the days of splendid masonry, roofs and floors from the age of steel.

But what enabled it to harbour its garrison, after the explosion of the mines had split and thrown down its walls, was not the strength of its various parts, but the unusual nature of its planning, brought about by the different levels of the ground on which it stood.

If the reader will look for a moment at Plate 39 he will notice that the north terrace, that on the right in the sketch, is at least a storey higher than the "Esplanade" terrace in the foreground. He may be able to appreciate, also, that the ground at the south end—that on the left of the sketch—would be on a still lower level. There were, in fact, three different levels on the four sides of the Alcazar.

The level on the north side was that of the main gateway and of the courtyard of the palace. On the east and west, therefore, the small windows below this level were those of basements.

On the east side, the one invisible in the sketch, there was another gate leading into the Alcazar and named the "Waggon Entrance." This led directly into the basement. A waggon could enter by it and drive round under all the four sides of the building, in a subterranean vaulted roadway, which is called in this story the "catacomb road." In the original design of the palace this roadway had provided stabling for some four or five hundred horses. It was almost as dark as a railway tunnel, but on the outer sides were classrooms for the cadets, lit by barred windows. On the inner side of the rectangle formed by this "catacomb road," and actually under the central courtyard, were large vaulted chambers. They had practically no means of light or ventilation, but during the worst periods of the siege they formed safe places for the women and for the other most precious possessions of the garrison.

This "catacomb road," with the chambers off it, formed another and subterranean world beneath the Alcazar. And, on the south and east sides, there was even a sub-basement.

These underground portions of the Alcazar proved of immense importance during the siege, but this was not at first realized by the garrison and it seems that it never was by the besiegers.[1]

THE DEPENDENCIES OF THE ALCAZAR

A palace cannot be converted into a military academy for a thousand cadets without the addition of subsidiary buildings. The Alcazar had many such. They proved vitally important during the siege and provided on three sides an outer line of defence. It was they that stood the real brunt of most of the attacks. Without a description of them the story could not be understood. Though there were many of them, they can be treated as constituting three groups.

The first was a building standing to the north-east of the Alcazar, on lower ground, falling away towards the river. From its use in some bygone epoch it was known as the House-of-the-Military-Government. It consisted of a long, low, wedge-shaped block dating from the turn of the eighteenth century. It was faced with stucco, was two storeys high and without ornament. Within it were several pleasant little courtyards, with trees and plants in tubs. Architecturally this block of buildings had a gentle and retiring grace. It seemed content, lost in a backwater of life.

It stood above a wide, unimportant road which sloped down somewhat steeply towards the river. As a result of this difference of levels one end of the building was low and rose directly from the road; while the other end was high and raised upon a plinth-like basement. Running almost the whole length of this basement was a vaulted stable, lit by an occasional barred window. This, Stable No. 4, was defended by the youngest of the

---

[1] In an appendix at the end of this book there will be found an appreciation of the architecture of the Alcazar. It has not been introduced here, lest the thread of the story be broken.

garrison and was the scene of some of the most desperate fighting. Behind the building was a narrow lane, known as the Stable Approach; which was of no importance, except that at all costs it was essential to deny the enemy entry into it.

Opposite the House-of-the-Military-Government stood a famous convent-like building called the Hospital of the Santa Cruz. A little lower down the hill was the Convent of La Concepcion. Both these buildings were from the beginning in the hands of the enemy.

The second important group of buildings is that seen on the left in Plate No. 39, and formed the outer defences there. The buildings had been constructed on the terraces which descended from the Alcazar towards the river, like two giant steps. All dated from the rebuilding of the Academy during the 'eighties.

Of these buildings the one nearest the Alcazar was known as the Capuchinos; after a monastery which had once occupied the site. It rose high above the rest, was mostly of three storeys, and contained living-rooms and bedrooms of the Academy.

Below the Capuchinos was the dining-hall of the cadets, and close to the dining-hall was the riding-school.

South-eastwards of the riding-school stood a big irregular-shaped building, known as the Quarters-of-the-Soldiers. In it were lodged in normal times the soldiers and grooms attached to the Academy. It was of red brick, machicolated, in a Hohenzollern mock-Gothic. Though it had somewhat the appearance of a tin soldiers' toy fort, it proved to be of exceedingly solid construction. Its eastern face rose sheer from the precipitous slopes above the Tagus.

Another feature of consequence on this side was an outside corridor, known as the Curved Passage.[1] Through it communication could be kept up under cover between the Alcazar and

[1] On Plate No. 39 the Curved Passage is clearly seen on the left, leading from the base of the big tower.

all buildings on this side. Were it to be destroyed—as in fact it was—the only means of reaching them would be by crossing the open.

There remains but one more outwork to describe. From the plaza Zocodover a wide formal street, known as the Cuesta, led up to the Alcazar. On the east side this road was overshadowed by a high terrace which frowned down upon it.[1] The side of this terrace was hollow and in the thickness of its walls were three storeys of little rooms. Above these ran a long, dank passage, the windows of which are clearly seen in the photograph. During the siege these were occupied and fire from them prevented the enemy from approaching the Alcazar by this, the normal approach. The windows were too high above the road for bombs to be thrown into them; and were, also, in a position almost impossible for the enemy to shell. The darkness and length soon gained this passage the name of the "Simplon."

The reader will find the story of the siege far easier to understand if he has fixed in his memory the positions of:—

The House-of-the-Military Government,
The Quarters-of-the-Soldiers,
The Capuchinos,
The Curved Passage,
The "Simplon."

THE BESIEGING FORCE

What were the numbers of the Government force which besieged the Alcazar and of what was it composed? It is not yet

[1] This terrace is clearly seen on left of Plate 5. "Cuesta" means "the slope."

PLATE 9

THE ALCAZAR FROM THE WEST

On the left is seen the North Terrace and below it the windows of the "Simplon." Until the explosion of the mines, no attack was launched against this side of the Alcazar, on account of lack of space for troops to deploy.

THE SAME VIEW, AFTER THE SIECE

The church tower will be recognized.

PLATE 10

THE GREAT COURTYARD OF THE ALCAZAR

In the middle is the statue of the Emperor Charles V and, in
the spandrels between the arches, his Imperial eagles.

THE SAME COURTYARD AFTER THE SIEGE

The walls and gallery which divided it from the Hall of the
Great Stairs have been demolished and one of the twin stairways can be seen.

possible to give any exact answer to these questions; perhaps it never will be.

The Government in Madrid was working under endless disadvantages. The Army, or a large part of it, was in revolt. The Government, finding itself deprived of the armed forces upon which authority in all countries ultimately depends, distributed arms to the population; or rather to its own supporters. In all countries the steady and reliable members of every class are the last to rush to arms, and thus it was the extremists among the Government's supporters who now found themselves with rifles and ammunition in their hands. Wild with political enthusiasm, delighted with their new weapons and with the power these suddenly gave them, they promenaded the streets and made demonstrations. Sometimes they indulged in looting, in the burning of churches and convents, and acts of private or class vengeance. The regular police, far outnumbered and unable to keep control, practically disappeared from view. That was the state of the capital in which the Government was trying to establish its control.

Nowhere, perhaps, was there such confusion as at the Ministry for War. The majority of such senior officers as the Frente Popular Government had not superseded, had thrown in their lot with the military revolt. Many of the clerical staff who had not done this, had nevertheless been dismissed for their supposed political opinions. Within twenty-four hours, no less than three different persons were appointed as War Minister. Thus it is likely that the War Ministry did not itself know what bodies of troops had been sent, or had gone on their own initiative to Toledo; and it is quite possible that it never afterwards knew what was the number of those taking part in the siege.

During the first fortnight the War Ministry must have been at its wits' end. With a military revolt in several of the barracks of Madrid, it was expected to crush similar revolts in half of the

garrisons of the country. All that it did would have to pass the
distrustful scrutiny of the Communist, Syndicalist, and Anarchists supporters of the Government. Immediate results were
demanded and it had no organized forces at its disposal. It
acted not so much with energy, as with frenzy. There was no
time for reflection or, perhaps, even for the routine docketing
practised in any State department.

Decisions might have been taken to send to Toledo this or
that "battalion" of the Red Militia, now rechristened the
Milicias Populares. But, unless these decisions were in agree-
ment with those taken by the various parties of which the
Frente Popular was made up, it was unlikely that they would
have been carried out. Some companies might have been despatched by bus, but having thought of some objective more to
their mind, might have gone elsewhere. Other companies,
destined for other fronts, might have preferred Toledo. Some
of these companies had organization of a sort, others had none.
A few may have kept records, but the practice had been that of
the old regime and would have quickly become suspect.

Another difficulty which will face those trying to discover the
strength of the besieging force, is that food was generally commandeered or looted. It is unlikely that any requisitions for it
were made, and it will therefore not be possible to discover the
ration-strength, and so from that calculate the number of troops
fighting on the Government side.

Some things, nevertheless, are certain. One is that, of all the
centres in which the military revolt had not been crushed,
Toledo was the nearest to the capital and the easiest to reach.
Moreover, the stupendous silhouette of the Alcazar was as well
known in Spain as the Round Tower of Windsor Castle is in
England. Its capture, therefore, would have been both spectacular and impressive; and must have seemed easy. Thus it
can be taken for granted that the Government did all it could
to achieve this, and that the forces at Toledo must have been
considerable.

Of the artillery and technical staff engaged we know more. The number and calibre of the guns which the Government troops brought to bear were noted down by the garrison. And from the same source we know that the besiegers had several armoured cars, and on occasion two or three tanks; that they had flame projectors, mortars, and a very large number of machine-guns. Presumably the artillery-men lived near their guns and well outside the town. Their numbers can be roughly calculated from those normal in a battery.

But in estimating the number of Government forces who lived within Toledo, and who can be regarded as infantry, the recollection of the inhabitants of the town is almost all there is to go on. Some place the number as low as four thousand: some give it as eight thousand: some believe it to have been ten thousand.

There is also the evidence of an Englishman who was in Toledo on the morning of September 18th—the day on which the mines were set off. In his opinion there were at least two thousand militia-men in or about the Zocodover, waiting to deliver the assault which was to follow the explosion of the mines. He was informed that there was another and equally large force on the south of the Alcazar, to deliver a simultaneous attack on that side; and he gathered that there was a third body ready to move up from the river upon the east side of the building. Beyond these assault columns there must have been machine-gunners and rifle-men to keep up the fusillade from the cliffs across the Tagus, and there must have been men on technical and special duties. According to these calculations the strength of the Government militia-men in the town on that day cannot have been less than seven or eight thousand.

How were the forces of the Government organized? That, again, is hard to know. They consisted of volunteers from the various political parties which made up the Government. They left the evidence of this upon the buildings they occupied. Scrawled upon the walls, surmounted by the hammer and the

sickle, are the C.N.T., the U.G.T., and F.A.I., of their parties.[1]
A proportion of these men must have done their year's compulsory military service and must have learned to shoot. They had many rifles and unlimited ammunition; and after the first week they had many machine-guns. They had ample opportunity to practise marksmanship. As time went on their skill at arms must have improved. But skill at arms is not enough.

In open warfare such troops would have stood no chance. They hated discipline. Their officers were elected, and no doubt often dismissed by their men. Even in siege warfare it cannot have been easy to persuade such troops to stay on the particular roof-top where they were needed. It must have been harder still to marshal them for an assault, to induce them to keep under cover until the pre-determined moment, and then to launch them in a charge. But they were keen enough and brave enough, they had learned how to shoot, and for sniping and for street-fighting they were probably the equal of regular soldiers.

Most of them were fervent, some were perhaps inspired. They were fighting for something they understood; for the destruction of tradition, of privilege, of wealth, of religion. The Alcazar seemed the symbol of all these things, and to destroy it they were ready to give their lives.

THE TWENTY-SIXTH OF JULY

With Sunday, July 26th, the second week of the siege opened.

At 6 a.m. the battery in its old position on the Dehesa de Pinedo, northward of the town, fired a few practice rounds. At 6.30 a.m. it began a steady fire, while a plane circling overhead was either "spotting" for the gunners or making a protracted reconnaissance.

[1] C.N.T.—Syndicalists. U.G.T.—Socialists. F.A.I.—Anarchists.

At 8 a.m. the battery ceased fire. But throughout the day there was rifle-fire upon the Alcazar and its dependencies. It continued until evening, with no other development.

The enemy's detachments had now established themselves firmly on all sides, in windows, on roofs and towers facing the Alcazar and its grounds.

On the north they held the Hospital of Santa Cruz, and the Convent of La Concepcion, both of which were very solid buildings and had courtyards where troops could be massed.

On the west they occupied all houses which faced the Alcazar and, behind them, such houses and church towers as overlooked their roofs.

On the south the towering façade of the Alcazar looked down, across a diminutive plaza, upon a terrace of little three-storeyed houses. The windows of these must have seemed unpleasantly close to those of the Alcazar, and, though the enemy detachments sometimes entered them, they did not occupy them.

On this south side, but nearer the river, they occupied the gardens and houses which overlooked that empty space known as the Corralillo.[1]

Thus the Alcazar itself could be assailed by point-blank rifle and machine-gun fire from three sides. And on this day the enemy began to establish himself in strength upon the cliffs on the farther side of the Tagus. Here there was an old Moorish castle called San Servando, and straggling along from it the walls and one-storey cottages of the village which bears the same name. From that side of the river the range to the Alcazar did not exceed four or five hundred yards, and to its terraces the distance was considerably less.

At 6 p.m. the battery in the Dehesa de Pinedo once more

---

[1] Corralillo is a diminutive of corral, a place where horses and cattle are rounded up.

opened fire and continued until daylight failed.

At dusk another enemy plane appeared and made a lengthy reconnaissance.

The casualties of the day amounted to only two wounded. It had been a Sunday, the first since the garrison had been invested. No Mass had been celebrated, as there was no priest within the building. Nor had any shots been fired from its windows. To the men who had come from Madrid for its capture the Alcazar must have seemed silent, aloof and disdainful.

THE TWENTY-SEVENTH OF JULY

Monday was very hot. As a result the enemy's rifle-fire was slack. At 8 a.m. a plane appeared, hovered over the Alcazar, was fired at by squads in the courtyard, and withdrew towards Madrid.

Thereafter the chief concern of the garrison was the problem of food. The bread supply was now exhausted and baked corn was served out as a substitute. But even of corn there was not much. The population of the Alcazar consisted of some seventeen hundred men and women, and the store of corn in hand amounted to six thousand pounds—this having been intended for the horses. There was a considerably larger supply of oats. There was, too, a very small quantity of mixed groceries.

The last of the meat had been finished at the midday meal on Sunday and on this day it became necessary for the first time to kill some of the horses and mules in the stables for food.[1]

---

[1] The figures from various sources are conflicting. In the summary issued officially after the relief of the Alcazar, the number of horses and mules given was ninety-seven and twenty-seven. But one hundred and seventy and twenty-nine are from a source that is at least as official and seems to me more likely to be correct. Actually, eighteen of the horses and mules died of disease during the siege, or were so badly wounded that they could not be used for food. There were on the day of relief one horse and five mules left. Thus one hundred and sixty beasts were actually killed and eaten.

The first to be sacrificed was Pistolera, an ill-tempered mare who had kicked half the grooms in the stables. Several came to see her shot. Her nameboard was taken down and no one mourned her.

Of water for drinking—a matter of even greater importance than food—there was plenty in the various wells and rain-water storage cisterns within the precincts; though the quality was mostly bad.

For washing there was none. For during the first aerial bombardment the pumping machinery, used to raise water from the Tagus, was damaged beyond repair.

There was in the Alcazar a sufficient supply of medical requirements and there were three doctors. But there were no anæsthetics and any amputations necessary would have to be performed without them—and were.

Yet on the whole, a survey of the stores within the Alcazar was not too discouraging. There was food of a sort for at least another week. Cooking was still being done in the normal kitchens; despite the rifle bullets slashing at the metal sheeting of the roof and sometimes finding their way through a chink between the sandbags in a high window. On that night, too, a concert was held.

The day remained remarkably hot and the afternoon passed quietly. To the besiegers' fire not a shot was returned.

After nightfall it appeared that the enemy in the various houses facing the Alcazar had been relieved by others, for the volume of his rifle-fire noticeably increased.

The casualties of the day amounted to two wounded.

THE TWENTY-EIGHTH OF JULY

During the hours after midnight fires had been noticed in various parts of the town and, when the morning came, it was seen that several churches had been set alight and gutted.

The day passed quietly. But in several of the barricaded windows and loopholed walls which faced the Alcazar, machine-guns had taken the place of rifles. These at first were handled gingerly but as soon as the gunners mastered their initial difficulties they played with them ceaselessly, like new toys.

To this fusillade the defenders of the Alcazar made no reply; in part because there would have been no purpose in making any; in part because within the Alcazar the garrison was being organized. Men who could shoot had been allotted to different posts in the building. A system of reliefs was being arranged, with equal strength for night and day; for soon the moon would be full and the chance of night attack therefore greater. It was arranged that the men should work, as far as possible, in relays of six hours on duty and six hours off.

The surplus officers—for of them there was a disproportionately large number—were told off for special duties. For example, the garrison having no active means of replying to the enemy's artillery fire, a scheme was prepared by which during every minute of daylight his gun positions were kept under observation by at least two separate and distinct posts, stationed in the towers. These were furnished with the best field-glasses and the moment that the enemy's gunners were seen to approach their guns the "Take Cover" was sounded and was repeated in every part of the Alcazar.

So perfect did this system presently become, that on not more than four or five occasions during the whole siege did a shell reach the Alcazar before the garrison had been warned. The same did not apply to mortars which, being used from behind cover, could not be observed.

For the old and infirm, and for boys, duties were found. But some of the young and healthy were needed for the routine duties and fatigues; the feeding and watering of horses and mules; the killing and cutting up of those needed for food; the grinding of the corn; the baking of the bread; the preparation and distribution of meals; the sanitation of this overcrowded building, now without water; the carrying of ammunition and stores.

For experts, too, there was work. To give an example, there were in the Alcazar the field-transmitting wireless apparatus of the Guardia Civil, and also several small receiving sets, property of officers. All these were dependent upon mains supply of electricity, which was no longer obtainable within the Alcazar. For some time, therefore, sorties were made to tap some cable of the town supply. But, when all these attempts proved unsuccessful, the amateur wireless experts succeeded with the help of parts from various sets in devising first a receiving set, and eventually a transmitting set.

A daily news-sheet was hectographed and distributed. It followed the lines of such official military sheets in the Great War: its news was excessively optimistic and it had heavy jokes.[1]

For the women there was no work. Such is the Spanish attitude towards their sex, an attitude of which the women themselves appear to approve. They had their children to look after, they had little else to do but talk. Yet their lot was not an easy one. They were confined in whichever happened at the moment to be the safest part of the building. The safest was often the darkest, the dankest, the stuffiest, the most evil-smelling. But though no official tasks were found for them to do, the women did in fact greatly help their men. They helped them to sustain their courage and it will be seen that on each occasion when the question, either of surrender on terms, or of the evacuation of the women and children was raised by the enemy, the women were as definite in their refusal as were the men. At a critical moment, when hope seemed gone, they announced

---

[1] It was called "The Alcazar." Copies of it, reproduced on the original duplicating machine and by the original staff, can be obtained. The price of the complete set was, in October 1936, fifteen pesetas—plus postage. It could then be obtained from the Secretary, EL AJUNTAMIENTO (Town Hall), TOLEDO, SPAIN. The profits, I believe, are given to charities concerned with the dependents of those who endured the siege.

themselves ready to take their turn at the loopholes, should the time come when there would not be men enough left.

Their presence strengthened the determination of the defenders in another way. As time went on, the Alcazar became for all, not only the symbol of the traditions and glories of their race, but also their actual home. It was, too, the one place left in Toledo where prayer could still be offered before an altar. Thus, with the women and children at their sides, the men felt, in a way scarcely ever literally true in modern times, that they were fighting for their God, their country, and those they loved.

This day saw one small triumph over the mechanical difficulties of the garrison. Those to whom the matter had been entrusted, contrived an apparatus for grinding the corn. It consisted of various mincing-machines from the cadets' kitchen coupled to the engine of a motor-bicycle.

The day was a quiet one. There were no casualties.

THE TWENTY-NINTH OF JULY

Another quiet day, except for persistent fire from the enemy's newly acquired machine-guns. To this again no reply was made.

The garrison was being taught not to expose itself unnecessarily at the loopholes, to avoid dangerous corners, to take the safest and not the shortest routes between the Alcazar and its various dependencies. There was need enough of caution even on a quiet day. If only four hundred of the enemy were distributed in the windows, on the roofs and in the towers which faced so large a target as the Alcazar; if each fired only one shot every three minutes during the hours of daylight; then more than an eighth of a million rounds would be fired. Actually the fusillade was often kept up by night as well as by day; and many of the snipers' nests now held machine-guns, which fire ten times more quickly than it is possible for a rifle to do. So on a quiet day, such as this one, anything from a fifth of a million to a third of a million rounds must have been fired at the windows of the Alcazar.

Certainly the walls were thick and many of the windows had iron grilles, which made easy the building of sandbag barricades behind them. But a stream of bullets, especially from a machine-gun, will chip away stone, however hard it be; and in time will cut through iron bars. There are in the now ruined Alcazar, places where the walls which frame the windows are eleven feet thick, but where the stone has been pounded away by rifle-fire; others where brick and mortar of Roman hardness have been reduced to the appearance of nibbled cheese.[1]

Added to this, a bullet striking slanting stone or metal will ricochet. It may hit a ceiling or a chandelier and, with its nickel envelope split and jagged, go whistling down a passage far away from the window through which it entered. Gay shots aimed at a weather-vane or guttering may once in a hundred times hit it, and once in a thousand times glance off, go spinning through the air and into the fancied safety of the courtyard a hundred feet below.

Thus, even on these quiet days, there were casualties and on this one two men were killed and three wounded. Two less to feed; but perhaps five less to man the loopholes.

At 5.45 p.m. a plane coming from the direction of Madrid made a reconnaissance over the Alcazar. At 6 p.m. another did the same.

An hour before midnight the enemy rifle and machine-gun fire became suddenly intense and remained so for two hours. The reason for this was not clear, but in these early days of the siege the garrison took rapid fire as a likely prelude to an assault.

[1] For examples see Plate 17.

THE THIRTIETH OF JULY

Another quiet day; rifle and machine-gun fire, to which no reply was made.

The weather was very hot. Some of the garrison were suffering from stomach troubles, due to the bread made of unleavened wheat, only partially ground and with the husk on it.

At 5 p.m. a plane appeared from the usual direction, made a cautious reconnaissance and flew away.

At 7 p.m. the enemy's battery of "75's" opened fire upon the Alcazar.[1] This battery had been lately brought into position in the Dehesa de Pinedo, on the low hills north of the town; and near to where the battery of "105" guns was already established. Its fire was directed upon the north façade and the main gateway, which even with the naked eye must have been easily seen from the enemy's gun position. After a time the battery turned its attention to the kitchens and serving-room. This shelling was continued for some time by moonlight.

The early night was calm and unusually still, and the only sound to be heard was that of the river below, rilling over its weirs. But close upon midnight machine-gun fire was opened from the old Moorish castle of San Servando and the loopholed walls of that hamlet, both on the cliffs across the Tagus.

The casualties of the day amounted to one dead.

THE THIRTY-FIRST OF JULY

Another quiet day. The rifle-fire against the Alcazar was slight. It was believed that the enemy must be short of artillery ammunition and was waiting for a supply from Madrid.

[1] Field-guns, which in Spain as a rule fire high-explosive shells.

There was no change in the position and there were no casualties.

THE FIRST OF AUGUST

The morning and lunch hour were quiet. But it seemed that the enemy had secured a supply of artillery ammunition. For at 2.45 p.m. the "105" battery in the Dehesa de Pinedo opened a fairly rapid fire upon the riding-school, the dining-hall, the serving-room and the kitchen, the Quarters-of-the-Soldiers, and the officers' rooms in the Capuchinos.

The riding-school and the dining-hall, it will be remembered, were large but lightly constructed buildings; with walls of brick and glass, and roofs of metal sheeting laid on planks and carried on steel girders. The effect of shelling them was at once apparent and must have been encouraging. The bombardment continued all through the afternoon and evening. It ceased at 7 p.m.; after the riding-school had been set on fire. The roof proved too high to be easily reached by the antiquated and meagre fire appliances belonging to the Academy. Even when the shelling had ceased, efforts to extinguish the flames failed. The fire continued throughout the first part of the night, the planking of the roof was consumed and the metal sheeting slid off and fell to the ground, making much noise. The girders of the roof twisted and hung where they were, or collapsed inside the building, which since the beginning of the siege had been used as a burial-ground.

Casualties of the day were eight wounded.

THE SECOND OF AUGUST

At 12.30 a.m., and while there was still a glow within the rid-ing-school, the enemy's "105" battery recommenced its fire, and with a half-hour break for lunch continued till 4 p.m. the following afternoon; targets being the same as on the day be-fore.

At 2 p.m., while this shelling was still in progress, a big enemy plane appeared and dropped a number of bombs. They fell wide of any important target. Beyond setting fire to a motor lorry and making holes in the Esplanade, they did no harm.

During the afternoon the rifle and machine-gun fire was unusually heavy, especially upon the House-of-the-Military-Government. Indeed, so persistent did it become that it was thought necessary to prevent the impression that the defenders had been mastered and could not man the loopholes; thus a heavy return fire was developed for a quarter of an hour. The enemy was worsted in this duel and for some time remained silent.

At 7 p.m. the heavy battery, which had been resting for three hours, opened fire again; this time on the Esplanade, the Quar-ters-of-the-Soldiers and upon the Curved Passage—that vital corridor which linked the Alcazar with the dining-hall. The enemy seemed to have realized early in the siege that practically the whole defence of the south and south-west sides was pro-vided by the Quarters-of-the-Soldiers; and that, if once the cor-ridor leading to it were destroyed, it would become extremely difficult for the defenders to hold this south-east corner of the grounds.

The shelling was continued until after midnight and then ceased for a few hours.

The casualties of the day amounted to one dead and four wounded. It was understood that the women and children were suffering from want of sleep, owing to these night bombardments.

THE THIRD OF AUGUST

Soon after midnight the "105" battery and the "75" battery commenced their daily shelling. And at the same time heavy rifle-fire was opened from the old castle of San Servando across the river; from the loopholed walls and houses near it; and from several positions in the town of Toledo itself.

The moon was at full and the light of it seemed almost as clear as that of day. The slightest movement on the Esplanade or other terrace could be seen by the enemy; thus the normal distribution of food and ammunition, the moving of the wounded and like duties—usually performed at night in comparative safety—had now become hazardous. For instance, it was no longer feasible to use the little iron footbridge which joined the upper storey of the House-of-the-Military-Government with the Esplanade. Instead, the only safe way from there to the Alcazar was now across the corner of the riding-school terrace, up the ramp, or sloping road, which led along the face of the wall of the upper terrace, and so into the Curved Passage. The first portion of it, also, had become to some extent dangerous. A barricade from the stable doors (under the House-of-the-Military-Government) to the commencement of the sloping road was therefore built. From the end of this barricade a trench was then dug in the ramp. This enabled those passing up it to keep their heads below the parapet on their left. But even when this work had been completed and this route was comparatively safe, it remained a long and inconvenient one, and many a man preferred to take the risks of the footbridge above.

Before dawn the enemy field battery closed down but the

"105" battery kept up a slow and deliberate fire throughout the remainder of the night, throughout the morning and the early afternoon.

During the late afternoon the fire was taken up by field-guns.

At 11 p.m. another battery of "105's" opened fire from a position which does not seem to have been located by the garrison that night. Its shells were aimed at the north façade of the Alcazar, at the Esplanade, the Capuchinos and the Curved Passage. This bombardment was kept up until 12.30 a.m. Much damage was done. Many of the rooms in the Capuchinos were wrecked. The Curved Passage was holed in several places, and as it was essential to the communications of the defence, it was necessary to build barricades to block the holes in it, even while the shelling was in progress.

Once again the women and children had been denied the night's rest.

The enemy's artillery had now been firing upon the Alcazar for thirty-eight hours out of the last fifty-eight. The women in the basements had suffered considerably from the strain—not so the children. Terrified as they had been at first, they soon grew accustomed to the crash of bursting shells and the thud of falling masonry. They learnt to distinguish between the sharp explosions of the "75's" and the deeper ones of the "105's." They discovered means to imitate these sounds, and also the typewriter-like clatter of the machine-guns. Indeed after a few days the bombardments appeared almost an amusement to the younger children.

During the course of this day Colonel Moscardó received a confidential message of the greatest importance. It informed him that a large quantity of wheat, property of the Bank of Toledo, had been stored some weeks before in a small building on one of the roads between the river and the foot of the riding-school terrace.[1] The road was a private one belonging to the

[1] Who made this communication to Colonel Moscardó, or how it was made, I have not discovered. In official documents there is no further infor-

PLATE 11

THE NORTH FAÇADE OF THE ALCAZAR

Showing the main gateway and the North Terrace. The obvious entrance being here this side of the Alcazar was the first to be shelled, and was reduced to the state seen below.

This photograph was taken from almost the same spot as the one above it. The north façade had by now become "the great breach on the north."

PLATE 12

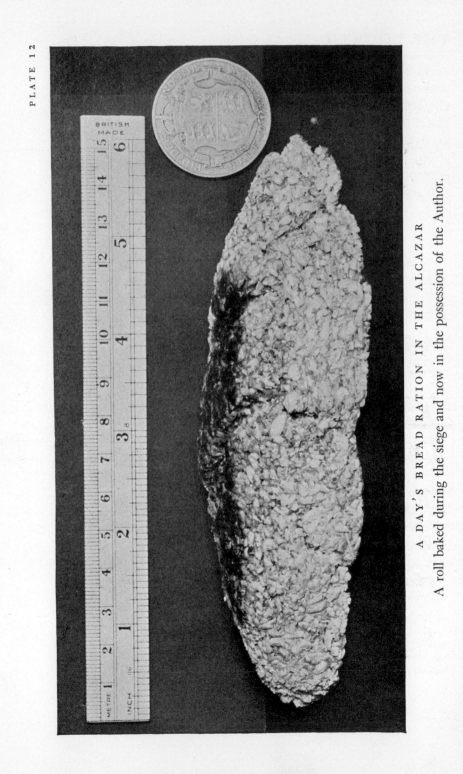

A DAY'S BREAD RATION IN THE ALCAZAR

A roll baked during the siege and now in the possession of the Author.

Academy. Indeed, though actually it was outside the defences and on a lower level, this wheat store was technically within the grounds of the Alcazar. Nevertheless, anyone descending the slopes of the riding-school terrace and entering this granary by daylight would be in view of the enemy.

It was a night of full moon but the necessity of obtaining food was immediate. Detachments of Guardia Civil and Falangistas were drilled for the purpose and during the night carried out a sortie. Twenty-five sacks, each of which contained one hundred and eighty pounds of wheat, were brought back.

On this the improvised grinding machine was at once set to work. In normal circumstances this machine would have been too small to grind for the needs of so many. But the ration of wheat was so limited that the plant was just capable of providing one roll a day for each person.

THE FOURTH OF AUGUST

At dawn it was seen that the new battery of "105's" had been firing during the night from a position near the Mocejon road (Mocejon being a village east-northeast of Toledo). From this position the enemy were able to see and bombard both the east side and the north side of the Alcazar. But not a shell was fired by the enemy's guns during the entire day.

The hours passed quietly, except for the habitual rattle of machine-gun fire and rifle-fire. On this day again the defenders did not reply with even a single shot.

At 11 p.m. the new battery of "105's" began to shell the Curved Passage, which from their new position must have been clearly visible by the light of the full moon. After a time the

---

mation, nor can any survivor of the siege that I have met throw any light upon the matter. The building can be seen in Plate 39, standing below the north-east corner of the riding-school terrace.

gunners turned their fire upon the dining-hall and the Capuchinos; and finally upon the main gateway and the north façade. The damage done was serious, especially to the Curved Passage, the importance of which the enemy gunners certainly realized.[1]

The casualties for the day had been only one wounded; and for the day before one dead, and two wounded.

THE BEGINNING OF PRIVATIONS

It was now a fortnight since the proclamation of the "State of War" had been read, since the first air bomb had been dropped; and it is time to make a survey of what has happened within the Alcazar.

During this fortnight the number of casualties had not been great; twelve dead and sixty-five wounded. The artillery and air bombardments had not been severe. The enemy's rifle and machine-gun fire had seldom been returned. Thus there had been little need for the men of the garrison to expose themselves. Indeed many of the casualties—two killed and twenty-three wounded—had been the result of street-fighting before the garrison had been withdrawn within the precincts of the Alcazar. Yet the casualties since then—ten dead and forty-two wounded—had probably been heavier than they need have. The garrison had been "shaking down," learning their work, evolving and perfecting the methods and expedients which later

[1] According to stories persistent among the women who were in the Alcazar, the enemy gunners during these first days deliberately aimed too high, so as to miss the Alcazar and hit the Arms Factory, by then of course in Government hands. This being discovered, the gunners were tried and shot, the direction of the artillery being given to a Russian lieutenant, who was afterwards taken prisoner and executed. I cannot find any confirmation of such stories. The infantry investing the Alcazar were largely Workers' Militia, brave but ill-disciplined and unskilled in arms, but the artillery-men were experts; being gunners who had remained faithful to the Government.

enabled them to put up the resistance they did.

And while they had been picking up the tricks and technicalities of loophole fighting and of the defence of buildings, they had also been learning to face privation. After the first few days the normal foodstuffs had been exhausted. There had been no more meat; they had eaten horse-flesh and mule-flesh. There had been no more bread; they had eaten baked wheat instead. Sugar which had been reserved for the children was now all gone. There was no coffee, no rice, no chick peas—so beloved of Spaniards—no fruit or vegetables. For some time now there had been no salt.

One horse or mule was killed each day and its flesh, served as a stew, had to feed the whole garrison. I have asked many who survived the siege how much meat this allowed to each person. The answer seems to be this: that the meat ration amounted to two, or sometimes three, strips of meat, each the size of a man's little finger.

So much for meat. Beyond that there was only bread.

The daily ration of this amounted to a single roll, very heavy, very gritty, very hard, and weighing about five ounces. These rolls were weighed and equalized carefully, for on such rations each grain counted. They were brown, singed black at the top and bottom. So small were they that one of them, a day's ration for a man or woman, could be completely covered by a cupped hand.[1]

---

[1] The following incident will make clear the quality of this bread. Some three weeks after the relief I and two young troopers, who had formed part of the garrison, were clambering upon the ruins of the Alcazar. Here, frowning down upon the terrace far below were rifle-pits. These were nearly knee-deep in empty cartridge-cases. Turning them over with his hand one of my companions picked up something which might have been a blob of dry cement.

He showed it to his friend.

"A bit of bread one of our lot must have lost somehow."

"It is a dog's doings."

"It is a bit of the bread, I tell you."

"No."

"Taste it."

Of all things necessary for the garrison, drinking-water was the most important. Of this there was for each man, woman or child, one litre a day; that is one large wine-bottleful.

The lack of salt seems to have been a greater hardship than might be imagined. Instead of it, some tried using crushed plaster from the walls. That gave a little savour but the taste lingered on after the meal and produced thirst. The young men suffered much, also, from lack of any sweet stuff and at least one lost his life in a sortie to raid bananas from a shop near by.

But of all the privations the greatest for the men seems to have been the lack of tobacco. Cigarettes in Spain cost little and the young soldier thinks the day sad on which he cannot smoke his twenty or so. Of cigarette paper there was an ample store. For, as any Spaniard who can afford to, re-rolls his cigarettes in better paper, there was in the cadets' canteen a huge stock of such, printed with the arms of the Academy.

But what was there to be smoked? The leaves were stripped off acacias upon the Esplanade; off the eucalyptus trees up on the Zig-Zag, and below the dining-hall; off the Virginia creeper which covered the romantic trellised bower on the terrace of the riding-school; off the weeping willows in the little garden of the colonel-commandant, where to-day iris and Madonna lilies thrust their way up between the fragments of broken shells. They set upon the trees and smoked their every leaf. They tried the ground-up bark of the eucalyptus trees; the bark of acacias; stable bedding; dried grass mixed with Army Forms. Sometimes they could not wait for night-time, lest others might get there first. Then, breaking most stringent orders, they would crawl out on to the open terraces and climb the trees, in full view of the enemy. They were sniped at. Several were hit. One is said to have been killed.

A pause. . . . "It is bread."
"Give it me."
Another pause. . . . "You're right."

Acacia leaves made the best substitute for tobacco. Lime leaves were not too bad, at any rate for the first few puffs. The leaves of the eucalyptus tree seemed medicinal and were by far the worst.[1]

There were ten prisoners in the Alcazar during the siege who had been taken in raids and sorties. They were given the same rations as the garrison. Why as much? Because on less they could not have remained alive.

THE FIFTH OF AUGUST

During the morning there was nothing to report. Rifle and machine-gun fire was continued from all sides. This, when well-directed, necessitated the frequent rebuilding of window barricades which had to be kept in serviceable condition, for the repelling of any possible infantry attack. The afternoon also was quiet. Soon after 5.30 p.m. the enemy's "155" battery near the Mocejon road, and his battery of field-guns in the Dehesa de Pinedo, opened fire upon the main gate. The results were not important.

At 6 p.m. an enemy plane appeared and circled overhead, either to "spot" for the gunners, or to reconnoitre. The sight of this plane produced the usual results and the machine-gun and rifle-fire blazed out and for some time remained intense.

At dusk it slackened and the guns ceased fire.

The casualties for the day amounted to ten wounded.

[1] I have tried them all, leaves that have re-sprouted upon the mangled branches and from the shattered trunks. I confirm the above opinions.

THE SIXTH OF AUGUST

The day was quiet. There was no artillery fire. As a result of this several daylight sorties were made by the garrison; the object in all cases being to obtain food. Many houses were entered but the enemy had cleared most of them and the results were poor. Some fruit, tinned milk and sweets were brought in and given to the children. A few hundred cigarettes were found and divided. But although these foraging sorties had produced little, they were a relief, after two weeks of inaction; and the garrison was delighted.

The casualties of the day were one dead and two wounded.

THE SEVENTH OF AUGUST

On this day, also, there was no artillery fire. The air was very still and the heat intense. An order was published limiting the distribution of drinking-water to one single issue a day; a lamentable necessity. The heat seemed to have reduced the energy of the besiegers, their fire was half-hearted, and there were no casualties among the garrison.

THE EIGHTH OF AUGUST

At 7.45 a.m. a big three-engined plane flew over the Alcazar and its dependencies, dropping sixteen bombs. Some of these, piercing the roof and exploding inside the building, completely wrecked the Capuchinos. The floors were destroyed: the roof fell in: the wreckage caught fire. Some of the garrison were killed and their bodies lost under the pile of ruins.

In the wake of this plane came another which dropped tear-gas bombs. Some of these greatly hampered the work of the rescuers in the Capuchinos. Others fell in the courtyard of the Alcazar. But as a drill had been evolved to deal with such eventualities the inconvenience caused was not great. The bombs were covered with sand, petrol was then thrown on them and set alight; this being the best way to hasten evaporation of the gas.

Owing to the complete wreck of the Capuchinos it was not possible to use this method among the ruins, and as a result the tear gas much hampered the stretcher-bearers.

The Guardia Civil forming the garrison of the Capuchinos were reinforced and the rearrangement of the defence was set in hand. But never for a moment had the survivors in the ruins of this building ceased to reply to the rifle and machine-gun fire which was poured upon it, after it had been wrecked by the aeroplanes' bombs.

The day's casualties amounted to eight wounded and four dead, all of whom lay buried beneath the ruins of the Capuchinos.

THE NINTH OF AUGUST

With the first light, rifle and machine-gun fire was intensified to a pitch not before experienced. This was especially noticeable from the houses over the west side of the Alcazar and from the Santa Cruz.

At 5 a.m. the enemy's artillery sent over some ranging shots, registered, and then ceased fire.

Soon afterwards a large bombing-plane appeared and dropped

heavy bombs on the north-west and north-east corners of the Alcazar. Thereupon the enemy's riflemen and machine-gunners gave rapid fire. This was continued so long that the garrison of the Alcazar expected an assault; probably on the north, and either from the Zocodover, or from the Santa Cruz and the Convent of la Concepcion. Loopholes were manned; the reserves stood to arms: for a long time the enemy's fire was returned with vigour. The assault was expected from one moment to another but nothing happened and after some two hours the enemy's fire slackened to its normal rate.

After that the day passed uneventfully; the enemy's lunch interval and hour of siesta being quieter than usual.

At 6 p.m. an enemy plane appeared, made a lengthy reconnaissance, especially over the wreck of the Capuchinos. It then flew away towards Madrid.

In Evening Orders twenty of the Guardia Civil were mentioned for bravery in the Capuchinos during the previous day.

The casualties for this day amounted to two dead and seven wounded.

THE TENTH OF AUGUST

It was found at dawn that during the previous night two corporals and seven young soldiers, all belonging to the establishment of the Academy, had left their posts in Stable No. 4 and had deserted.

To prevent a repetition of such an event all the buildings on this lower terrace were constituted as a detachment and placed under the command of a lieutenant-colonel.

The day was quiet. The work of clearing the Capuchinos was carried on. After many difficulties the body of one of the Guardia Civil was recovered from under the ruins.

Once more the stock of tinned milk, lately increased by

foraging raids, was so low that the issue of it could be allowed only to children of under three years of age.

During the day one of the observation posts, which was provided with powerful glasses and kept the enemy's position under constant scrutiny, had noted through a window of a house several large bunches of bananas. The house being one which it might be possible for a sortie party to reach, a raid was made soon after dusk by men of the Gym School and some Falangistas. The only results were that one of the sortie party was killed and the bananas, when brought in, were found to be rotten.

THE WOMEN IN THE ALCAZAR

For those who have read any Spanish history it may at first seem strange that the women of the Alcazar were not manning the barricades. For in no other country have the women such a record of military achievements. From the days when the Romans laid siege to Numancia, to the present time, the Spanish women have been found fighting beside their men. Dozens of Spanish towns can tell such stories. One, which I knew well when a boy, had been defended by its women and old men against a raiding Moorish army, when the fighting men of the town had marched to the attack upon Granada.

It is said that a few weeks after the relief of the Alcazar there were companies of women among the Government forces defending Madrid. Indeed during the siege itself women were sometimes seen among the militia-men of the besieging force. It is said that some lived permanently with the Government artillery in the Campimento and used to work with the gunners.

Yet within the Alcazar no task of the defence was entrusted to the women. They were not allowed to cook, they were not allowed to nurse the wounded. It is certain that they would have been ready to do these things, and the explanation for why they were not permitted to, is probably as follows.

The martial deeds of Spanish women have been performed among irregular troops. The defence of the Alcazar was a defence by Regulars. Yet, though the women were not allowed to share in the duties of the garrison, they were, as has been explained, of immense help to the men morally and, had they not been there, it is well possible that the defence could not have been sustained.

None were killed, none were wounded. Yet in some ways they suffered worse than the men. Almost from the first they were kept in dark corridors and vaults. During the last weeks of the siege none of them saw the light of day, and the rooms in which they lived were cold, dark and smelt abominably.

One of the vaults they inhabited measures ten yards by five. Its ceiling is very low. It has a single door leading into the "catacomb road." There was no other ventilation and no light, except sometimes a mule-fat dip. In this room ninety-four women and children lived for three weeks. None of them had washed for more than two months. Few had changed their clothes since the siege had begun.

I know one of the women who endured the siege. She gave me her recollections of it. Hers are no doubt typical.

Her name is Doña Carmen Aragones. She is of a good family and a resident in Toledo. She is, I suppose, thirty. She had been married to an Army officer who had died in Morocco some five years before the Civil War. Since his death she and her two children had lived in Toledo with her father. They were close friends of Colonel Moscardó, and when the events of July 1936 made a decision necessary, she, with her children, her father and two of her brothers, went up into the Alcazar.

For the first three or four days she lived in the House-of-the-Military-Government; then in a room in the south-west tower. Then, as conditions became more dangerous, she was moved down into the basements. During the last three weeks she lived in the vault just described.

When Doña Carmen came into the Alcazar she was wearing a black-and-white cotton frock. In that she lived throughout the siege. When her stockings wore out she gave up wearing any. Soon she abandoned shoes, for with high heels it was impossible to move about in semi-darkness over cobbles, litter and general destruction. She had no hat. She had no coat. During the last weeks she suffered much from the cold.

At first she used to keep perhaps an egg-cupful of water from her daily ration, for washing purposes. But there was no soap and no towel. The weather was very hot then and a litre of water was barely enough to quench thirst. Soon she gave up washing. She had a comb, she kept her hair combed back. Sometimes she tried plaster off the walls for face powder.

Doña Carmen has an almost childlike warmth and generosity of nature, and everyone who knew her during the siege has spoken of her extraordinary gaiety and courage.

At first she suffered much from hunger. But after the first ten days she did not feel hungry any more. What physically troubled her most was lack of sleep. During bombardments of the courtyard there were but two or three feet of stone between the low vaulted roofs and the paving of the courtyard on which the shells were bursting. She says that each shell seemed to burst against the back of her own head. But more terrible than the shells was the earthquake rumble and vibration, caused by the falling columns of the arcade. The size of them is seen in Plate 22, where Doña Carmen is seen sitting on one of them, when I persuaded her to enter the Alcazar for the first time since the siege.

As days went by the stench within the vaults became more and more terrible. Towards the end the smell of bodies buried, of necessity, within the building, made it almost impossible to keep down any food. Even weeks afterwards the reek of putrefaction in the swimming-bath was hardly bearable.

As the siege continued Dona Carmen grew thinner and thinner. She could put her two clenched fists into the hollow of her stomach. After the relief she went into a hospital and under doctor's orders began to feed up. She tells me that in the first fourteen days she gained twenty-two pounds in weight.

She had her children with her and for her the worst part of the siege was watching their failing strength. One of her brothers had always been a semi-invalid. But she, her father, her two brothers and her two children, all came through the siege alive.

At night the men for duty used to come down into the basement to visit their women and relations. Often the women would give them morsels of food they had saved from their own meals.

At the close quarters at which they lived none suffered alone. For a peasant woman mourning her lost son or husband would fill the vaults with her lamentations for hours on end. Death was always near them. One thought never occurred to them, the thought of surrender. And, when for weeks it seemed impossible that any relief force could ever reach them, the women, even more than the men, took the death of themselves and of the whole garrison as the only possible ending to the siege.

THE ELEVENTH OF AUGUST

The desertion of six more young soldiers of the Academy was reported at dawn. This inevitably spread a sense of despondency and of insecurity. The deserters had been stationed in or near Stable No. 4, and several of them being grooms, doubtless knew ways of getting in and out, other than the normal ones.

There does not seem much reason for believing, as the garrison afterwards did, that these boys joined the enemy. Their average age did not exceed eighteen and their average service six months. It seems more likely that, having got clear of the town, they made for their homes.

Another quiet day enabled the work of clearing the Capuchinos to be continued. During this the body of a second Guardia Civil was recovered from under the ruins.

The population of the Alcazar had not yet become used to the indigestible nature of the bread; nor, perhaps, to the smallness of the rations. Indigestion and stomach trouble seem to have been general and on this day one of the old ladies died; a natural death, of which unsuitable and insufficient food may well have been a contributory cause.

The question of diet had now become so serious that a sortie for obtaining some other food was decided on. It was carefully planned and was made by a volunteer detachment of Falangistas. They found their way blocked by obstacles and all windows held by enemy rifle-men, who raked the alleys with a considerable, though inaccurate, fire. The sortie party succeeded in reaching a big provision store and forcing an entrance, only to find that the contents had been looted or removed.

After midnight another sortie was made, this time by volunteers from among the Renovacion Española. The object of this one was to find some electricity supply cable and to tap it. If this could have been done without the enemy's knowledge, and had the electricity obtained never been used for light purposes, the linking up of the Alcazar and the town supply might never be detected; while the electric current would enable the field-wireless set to transmit messages, and the grinding plant to have been driven without the use of petrol, the stock of which was small and was urgently needed for other purposes.

The calle del Carmen, the street beneath the windows of Stable No. 4, was chosen as the best site for this raid. In the upper part of the street, between the Zocodover and the terrace of the "Simplon," were a number of shelled and burnt houses. It was hoped in the ruins of these to find an undamaged mains cable, and concealment enough for the tapping operations to be carried out. The sortie was made and experts searched everywhere. They found no cable of any use and at length had to withdraw. This proved the fourth depressing incident of the day.

To guard against further desertions drastic steps were taken. The casualties for the day amounted to one killed, in a sortie; and one natural death.

THE TWELFTH OF AUGUST

The day was quiet. Machine-gun and rifle-fire, which always began soon after dawn, slackened earlier than usual. The enemy's inaction began to seem suspicious but as yet the garrison of the Alcazar had no inkling of what the besiegers were planning.

During the noon-day heat a sortie by Falangista volunteers was made into those houses on the calle del Carmen which faced Stable No. 4 and the House-of-the-Military-Government. The houses in question were those in which the sortie party had been looking for an electric cable during the previous night. Though carried on in daylight and in partial view from the windows of the Santa Cruz, the sortie party went out and returned without loss. They found little worth bringing away.

At 5 p.m. the enemy's batteries opened upon the north and east façade of the Alcazar. The damage done was slight.

THE THIRTEENTH OF AUGUST

Once again the morning was quiet.

At 12.30 p.m. all the enemy's batteries opened fire upon the same targets as on the day before, and continued till 1.30. And during this time the machine-gun and rifle-fire which had been desultory all the morning increased in volume.

Perhaps because the sortie party of the day before had been seen entering the houses in the calle del Carmen and opposite Stable No. 4 the enemy, under cover of artillery bombardment, sent parties into these houses and set them on fire; or so it appeared to some of the garrison's observation posts; others holding that the houses had been fired by a chance shell.

In any case some of the enemy were seen in one of the houses soon after the fire had been observed. The garrison of Stable No. 4 therefore opened a heavy fire upon them, as the defenders of the Alcazar were anxious that the houses in question should not be destroyed; for the following reasons: that the houses were at point-blank range and the garrison of the Stable considered that they could with rifle-fire prevent enemy snipers from establishing themselves in their windows; that, as long as these houses were standing, they hid the Stable from the Convent of la Concepcion; that, if once the houses were demolished, the Convent, which offered many positions for machine-guns and snipers, would dominate the Stable at some eighty or a hundred yards—a range at which the besiegers seemed to consider themselves safe enough to keep up a constant fire.

For some long time the fate of these houses remained undecided and meanwhile a heavy fusillade was kept up between the enemy and the garrison of Stable No. 4. Eventually the houses were burnt, but not so completely as they might have been. While as a result of their having been partially burnt

the enemy afterwards found it difficult to set them on fire or
to demolish them. In fact their walls continued to stand and
till the end hid the greater part of Stable No. 4 from the enemy
in La Concepcion.[1]

At 7.30 p.m. the enemy's batteries again opened fire upon
the north side of the Alcazar and maintained it for half-an-hour.

While this bombardment was in progress and was absorbing
the attention of such enemy as could watch it, a sortie was
made by a strong detachment of the Guardia Civil from the
opposite side of the Alcazar. This party crept out from the
Capuchinos and succeeded in getting some way before being
noticed. They then drew upon themselves some enemy fire,
but this in the half-light was very wild and inaccurate. In fact
they were able to enter the lower storeys of several houses, the
upper storeys of which the enemy was holding. This raid
proved reasonably successful and a quantity of eatables was
brought in.

At nightfall a surprise was sprung upon the garrison, when
from the upper windows of the Zocodover, searchlights were
trained upon the Alcazar. Thenceforward, on almost every
night throughout the siege, the Alcazar was kept floodlit on
this side by the enemy. This enabled him to keep up machine-
gun and rifle-fire upon it; even on a night such as this one,
when the moon was in its last quarter and darkness would
otherwise have given the defenders some measure of rest. This
in another way also added to the difficulties of the garrison.
For the stream of bullets, hour after hour, and day after day,
rendered possible by this flood-lighting, soon ate away the
sandbags or stones with which the windows were barricaded.
These now needed more frequent renewal and the repair of
loopholes was always done at a risk.

Soon after midnight, despite precautions taken, two more
young soldiers belonging to the staff of the Academy deserted.

The casualties of the day, mostly due to the continued fusil-

[1] Their ruins can be seen in one of the photographs on Plate 30.

PLATE 13

NORTH FAÇADE OF THE ALCAZAR IN 1550

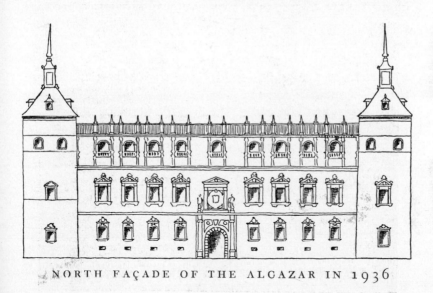

NORTH FAÇADE OF THE ALCAZAR IN 1936

Drawn by Miriam Pearce

PLATE 14

DOÑA CARMEN ARAGONÉS
A survivor of the siege.

lade of the morning when the garrison and enemy had been disputing as to the fate of the houses opposite Stable No. 4, amounted to eight wounded.

As for several days there had been no sugar or coffee left, and as breakfast without these pleased no one, the number of meals was reduced from three to two; the first being at 11.30 a.m. and the last at 5.30 p.m. A further reason for changing the hour of meals was that the increasing enemy activity at certain times suggested that the meal hours of the garrison might have been betrayed by deserters.

THE FOURTEENTH OF AUGUST

This day showed a revival of enemy activity. All the morning his machine-gun and rifle-fire was heavier than during the past week.

At 12.30 p.m. his "105" batteries started to shell the north façade; and later the Esplanade. This bombardment lasted till 4.30. Some material damage was done and one of the coaches on the Esplanade was set on fire and burnt out. But lessons had been learned and the system of giving the "Take Cover" had been so perfected that an ordinary bombardment seldom worried the garrison.

Machine-gun fire from the enemy's lines on the other side of the river had of late become both more frequent and more accurate, and now made it dangerous for anyone to show himself upon the Esplanade or riding-school terraces. This greatly hampered working-parties and made the necessary maintenance and repair work difficult.

At dusk, as often, there was a pause. But once daylight had faded the searchlights again floodlit all the north side of the Alcazar.

At 7.30 p.m., by the light of these, the "105" batteries and the "75" battery began shelling the gateway. This was continued for an hour and a half.

There followed a short period of quiet. Then the enemy from the Santa Cruz made a surprise attack upon the detachment guarding the Stable Approach—(which, it will be remembered, branched off the calle del Carmen and ran behind the House-of-the-Military-Government). This Approach led to both the Stables and, by way of the Zig-Zag, up to the north terrace. It was narrow and was protected on one side by detachments in various coach-houses which bordered it, and by the west corner of the House-of-the-Military-Government on the other. Some twenty yards along it, and hidden from view of the enemy in the Santa Cruz, were some iron gates which were kept closed. These, though flimsy, would at any rate have hindered an enemy rush. But had he been able to force a way down this passage the results would have been disastrous. For it would have been possible to mass large numbers of men on the dead ground about the Zig-Zag. From there the distance to the gates was but some forty yards.

This enemy attack, the first he had made, took the garrison by surprise. Till the moment of it there had been no more than the usual desultory fire from a few of the loopholes of the Santa Cruz. Suddenly there broke out a concentrated fusillade from as many rifle-men and machine-gunners as its windows would hold. The fire was rapid, the range a stone's throw.

After a few minutes of this intense fusillade the searchlights on the Zocodover were suddenly turned out and, before the eyes of the defenders had had time to become accustomed to the darkness, the gates of the Santa Cruz were thrown open and a large number of the enemy appeared. Pouring through the gateway and rushing across the Santa Cruz terrace and the roadway, they began to spray with petrol all the doors and windows, and all the ground surrounding the Stable Approach. They then attempted to set fire to this, at first with flaming rags and then with hand-bombs.

But the eyes of the garrisons in the corner of the House-of-the-Military-Government, and in Stable No. 4, had by now become accustomed to the darkness and they delivered a terrific fire upon the enemy at point-blank range. To this the enemy replied with hand-bombs, thrown from the street, and with a covering fire from the upper windows of the Santa Cruz. All attempts to set fire to the petrol failed. The attackers could not maintain their position. Dragging their wounded and dying with them, they made their way as quickly as possible back through the gateway of the Santa Cruz.

After a considerable pause a further attempt to set fire to the petrol was made, but this time only by bombs and lighted torches thrown from the windows across the street. The distance (forty yards) was too great for this and the attempts were abandoned. The enemy's rifle-fire then died down and presently the searchlights were turned on again.

Once more all the northern side of the Alcazar was illuminated and the normal intermittent rifle-fire began. An hour later a fresh searchlight was turned on. This one had been installed so as to throw its beam at right angles to the rest; through the arch of La Sangré and so down the whole length of the calle del Carmen. Thus it lit, from this end, the entire north front of the House-of-the-Military-Government, which included the windows of Stable No. 4. The beam was so directed that the Santa Cruz on the other side of the street was in comparative darkness. Thus the windows of the defenders could be seen by the enemy, while the loopholes occupied by his sharp-shooters could at times only be detected by the flash of rifles.

During the past fortnight the wireless experts and amateurs of the garrison had been trying to build up a set from pieces of the various ones they had. At first they had intended to depend upon a mains supply. But, it having been impossible to obtain this, they had now evolved another type of set. With this they now succeeded in picking up Radio-Madrid and hoped presently to reach other stations. The news which Radio-Madrid happened to be broadcasting was both contradictory and fantastically untrue. This Government-controlled station gave out during the course of the evening: first, that the Alcazar had at last surrendered; and, later, that this appeared to be an exaggeration, as part of it was still being held by some hundred famished madmen who had their families with them and would not let them go. The absurdity of this seems to have encouraged the garrison, as it depicted the state of muddle and improvisation in Madrid.

The day had been a fortunate one, following one of disappointments. There had been no casualties: a raid had brought back some food at last: the enemy's first determined attack had been repulsed: the first wireless touch had been made with the outer world.

THE FIFTEENTH OF AUGUST

The day started quietly. Then at 9.40 a.m. the enemy's batteries began a bombardment of the Curved Passage.[1] Later the gunners turned their attention to the spot where, since the wrecking of the kitchens, the cooking of the garrison had been done. This raised again the unpleasant suspicion that the enemy's shelling was being directed in accordance with information given by deserters.

While this shelling was in progress a large three-engined plane appeared, circled overhead and dropped incendiary bombs on the Curved Passage and on both the old and the improvised kitchens. Two more of the motor-coaches on the Esplanade were set alight and burnt out. As usual, the artillery

[1] The Curved Passage, it will be remembered, formed the only covered communication between the Alcazar and its outworks on the south-east, and was therefore extremely important.

bombardment ceased just before the lunch-hour. After that, and throughout the afternoon, a slow and steady machine-gun fire was kept up by the enemy; especially from across the river. This, being directed against the Esplanade and riding-school terrace, hindered the repairing of damage done to the Curved Passage.

At 7 p.m. the enemy renewed the bombardment, with both the heavy and field batteries: and with a 50-mm. mortar, which always proved vexatious.

It appears that the enemy in the Santa Cruz had been busy during the day, cutting a hole, from the inside, through the wall at the south-east corner of the upper storey.[1] Soon after dark the last stone was pushed out, and through the hole so made a high-pressure pump began to spray the House-of-the-Military-Government and Stable No. 4 with petrol. The garrison of the Stable, acting in accordance with the procedure already decided upon, withdrew; themselves set fire to the petrol; waited till it had burnt out; and then returned to their posts.

There were no casualties on this day. And this, considering the hours of shelling and the incendiary bombs, was proof that the garrison were becoming adept in keeping under cover.

THE SIXTEENTH OF AUGUST

On this day the siege entered upon a new stage and the anxieties of the garrison became greatly increased by the discovery that the enemy was driving a mine-shaft towards the Alcazar, with a view to blowing it up.

At 7 a.m. the heavy battery took up its fire upon the Curved Passage and the surrounding portion of the Esplanade. But by 7.45 shelling ceased, and as the rifle-fire was slight, the garrison

[1] Just visible on Plate 24.

was able to hear for the first time unusual subterranean sounds. The grave importance of these was at once realized by all. The actual sounds were not loud but their dull vibrations could be felt rather than heard.

Consultations followed, various experiments were made, and it was deduced that a mine-shaft was being driven towards the south-west tower. However, the experts were able to add that, as the Alcazar was built upon extremely hard virgin rock and the mining was being done by hand, the progress of it would be slow.

The food problem had again become acute. For several days there had been a small quantity of chick peas, or of rice, or of dried beans to add to the stew. The supply of these was again exhausted and small quantities of baked wheat were substituted. This, though indigestible, could be absorbed. But, as it was noted, "the change did not appear to please many."

The afternoon passed with nothing to report.

At dusk a flight of three planes was seen far away in the south-eastern sky, where the evening before one of the observation posts had reported planes. These aircraft were very distant and invisible to the naked eye.

Largely to divert the thoughts of the garrison from the mining which was being carried on, a sortie was ordered. It was made some time before midnight, by men of the Gym School. They did not succeed in finding any food but brought back many packets of chocolate, which were given to the Hospital and to the children.

During the two previous nights bombing and flame attacks had been made against Stable No. 4 and against the narrow entry to the Stable Approach. For the better protection of this corner, barricades were constructed and swung out into position, blocking the entrance.

That night the garrison was much encouraged, as those responsible for the wireless succeeded in tuning-in both Portuguese and Italian stations. The false reports broadcast by

Radio-Madrid were thus exposed. Representatives of all ranks and from all the groups which made up the garrison, were called in to listen to this wireless reception.

The casualties of the day were only two wounded, and these had been the only ones during three days.

THE SEVENTEENTH OF AUGUST

The morning was tranquil, without even rifle-fire. Thus in many parts of the Alcazar the sound of mining could be heard. The garrison was therefore kept busy on repair work which the absence of the usual fusillade made easy.

At 11.45 the enemy's "105's" and "75's" opened fire. The dining-hall, kitchens, Curved Passage, were their targets. Several high-explosive shells burst in the kitchens, doing great harm and further damaging the machinery which had been adapted to grind wheat. Such of the apparatus as could be moved was rescued under shell-fire and taken elsewhere. But it became clear that in future no use could be made of the kitchens.

Presently the guns changed their target and began shelling the main gate and north façade. This was a relief, as no essential service was now carried on above ground on that side of the building.

At dusk a sortie to fetch wheat was made by the Guardia Civil, men of the Gym School and some Falangistas. Thirty large sacks were brought in.

As soon as it became dark it was noticed that the alleys opposite the south-west corner of the Alcazar were floodlit and had been wired and barricaded. The garrison took this to mean that the six sorties they had made during the past six days had got on the nerves of the enemy.

The only casualty of the day was one man wounded.

THE GARRISON AND THE WHEAT

The sortie made on August 17th to replenish the wheat supply brings up a question for which there seems no easy answer.

The house in which this wheat was stored, though not within the defences of the Alcazar, could be reached easily enough; as is proved by the number of successful expeditions made to it. Yet, should the enemy come to know of this granary, they could certainly prevent the garrison from reaching it.

It was now a fortnight since the existence of this wheat had been known. Yet only on two occasions had foraging parties been sent out to bring in wheat. For the past week there had been little moonlight; indeed the 15th had been a night of the new moon.

Why had no other attempt been made until this night? The diminishing food supply must have caused even greater anxiety than the enemy's mining operations. Yet, till the very end, the wheat was brought up at infrequent intervals and, apparently, only to supply the needs of the next few days.

Much indeed was never brought up at all. It lay there in the granary, outside the doors, scattered over the rough precipitous trail which led up to the riding-school terrace. Later, in the last critical days of the siege, the Workers' Militia occupied all this quarter. They traced their sickles and hammers on the walls: they scrawled up the initials of their political parties, and "Viva Rusia."

The relief force drew near. It arrived. The besiegers slipped away. The wheat remained, a dry, hard, beady heap, still filling the whole end of the granary.

The rains came. Inside the broken doors the wheat sprouted and pushed up spears of pale viridian. For a time small boys came with sacks to fill them here. Then someone set the grain on fire. It smouldered for several days. Its sharp odour drifted up to the terrace, where it mingled with the stench of dead bodies.

Why was the grain left there?

The care with which the garrison had prepared itself against each immediate contingency was remarkable throughout the siege. Take for instance the day when the first tear-gas bombs had been dropped. A procedure, already worked out and rehearsed, was at once adopted. Take for instance the first time that Stable No. 4 was sprayed with petrol. For that danger, too, they were prepared. A dozen other cases speak of forethought. Why was not all the wheat brought in?

Can it have been that, though the problem of the food shortage was always there, it was never more urgent at one moment than at another? Can it have been an extreme example of the doctrine of mañana? [1] Or can it have been that the garrison and their commander had so perfect a trust in divine intervention, that the question of taking thought for the morrow did not exist?

This last alternative could be so easily dismissed; it appears so illogical, so preposterous, fitting in so ill with the precautions they took, that I hesitate to offer it. Yet knowing the spirit that filled that strange, starved garrison, and knowing how in those last days it was only the completeness of their faith which saved the Alcazar, this is the explanation I myself accept.

THE EIGHTEENTH OF AUGUST

Once again the morning was quiet. The bursts of machine-gun fire were chiefly from across the river and so demanded no reply.

[1] Mañana, of course, means to-morrow. And it is often suggested that this should be the motto of any Spanish Government.

At 2 p.m. the observation posts reported two big guns, later identified as "155's," being man-handled in the Dehesa de Pinedo, on the low hills to the north of the town, where the battery of "75's" and one of the "105" batteries were already in position.

The temporary position of the kitchen seems to have been betrayed once again by its smoke. Much fire was directed upon it and cooking became unduly dangerous. It was therefore removed into the sub-basement, which existed under the south façade, and was a whole storey lower than the catacomb roadway. A bread oven was now built here and was used throughout the rest of the siege. It will be remembered that the south façade of the Alcazar was carried on an arcade, not unlike that of the Ritz in London.[1] The smoke from this bread oven was led through a pipe, up into the roof of this arcade. There it spread and dispersed into the outer air through the tops of the various arches. Thus it was not seen, and the enemy never thenceforward knew where the cooking of the garrison was done.

At intervals during the afternoon the enemy sent over large mortar bombs. These were found more annoying than the shells of the artillery.

At dusk all firing ceased.

Survivors of the siege recall how calm these evenings were; how at such times they used to listen to the surge of the Tagus in the gorge below, as it poured over its weirs; and how they used to forget the dull thud-thud of the enemy's miners, cutting their way through the virgin rock.

[1] See Plate 31.

THE NINETEENTH OF AUGUST

The morning was quiet, though at each moment it was expected that the enemy's new guns, his "155's," would open fire. Several times the gunners were seen to take up their positions, as though for coming into action. Yet not a shot did these "155's" fire throughout the day.

During the previous night the news picked up from various wireless stations had spoken of the columns of General Franco's army which, having crossed from Africa, were fighting their way northwards. These reports made it seem possible that the unknown aeroplanes twice seen in the western sky, might belong to his army.

Therefore, as the enemy's new "155" guns constituted a fresh danger to the Alcazar, appropriate ground-screens were spread on the terraces, so that any friendly plane might be informed of these guns' position and might bomb them.

After his midday rest and siesta the enemy began to bombard the Esplanade with large bombs from a mortar. This proved galling. The mortar remained active until dusk.

Then, rifle and machine-gun fire having ceased and the evening being very still, the garrison became once more aware of the sounds of mining.

Late at night a sortie in force was made on to the Cuesta and into the passages beyond. This was not easy, as many of them had been wired and blocked with obstacles, and most were floodlit. However, by opening a heavy fire on anyone showing at the upper windows, the sortie party penetrated some way into this maze of narrow streets. They reached the house in which it was calculated that the mine was being sunk, soused it with petrol and set it on fire. They waited till it was well alight and then retired.

This seems to have made a considerable impression upon the

enemy. For he cut off the electric light in various districts of the town and sounded alarm bells. Soon afterwards the battery of "75's," no doubt informed by telephone, opened a rapid fire upon the Cuesta and its surroundings, so as to cut off the raiding party or to prevent others from leaving the Alcazar.

The result of the raid was discouraging. The sound of mining still continued and it was soon realized that the house burnt could not have been the one from which the miners were working.

The rest of the night passed without event. The casualties for the day had been two wounded.

THE TWENTIETH OF AUGUST

The machine-gun and rifle-fire, which as usual began at dawn, slackened soon after.

At 7.30 a.m. the battery of "75's" opened fire upon the north and east sides of the House-of-the-Military-Government. A heavy mortar soon joined in, throwing bombs which at once began to do serious damage.

The damage to the east stables had been considerable. Several horses and mules had been wounded. Therefore, as soon as the fire ceased, orders were given to transfer the rest of them to some safer spot. They were brought cautiously into the harness-rooms, and thence taken at top speed across that corner of the terrace, up the ramp leading to the Esplanade, and so into the swimming-bath. None of these movements could be seen from the position where the enemy's "75" battery was established, and the garrison counted that the enemy's observation and communications would not be good enough for the battery to learn of all this, until the operation had been completed. The task was a difficult one; it was performed with spirit and without loss.

The transfer of the horses had been done after the morning's shelling had ceased. But, while it had been actually in progress, an incident took place which to an Anglo-Saxon seems extraordinary. The shell-fire, which on the night before had followed the sortie by the garrison, had set alight one of the houses on the Cuesta. The fire, after smouldering all night, had been fanned by the morning's wind, and was now blazing. It happened that one of the adjoining houses belonged to someone who was a friend of many of the officers in the Alcazar. This house was now seen to be in danger. Volunteers were called for, a sortie was made, and most of the furniture in the rooms was removed and brought up into the Alcazar. Actually this was done without interference.

Some time after 4 p.m. the long-expected happened, and the enemy's "155's" opened fire. Their fire, as had been anticipated from their position, was directed upon the gate and the north façade. The damage done by these large high-explosive shells was startling. Fragments of the cornice, balustrading and ornaments on the roof, began dropping like icing from a cake. The first was accurate: the shells burst well; none failed to explode. As the evening progressed the rate of fire was increased. Great blocks of masonry, loosened during the early afternoon, began to fall. The guns continued to fire until the late dusk.

Thereafter all was quiet, except that from the southwest corner of the Alcazar there came the rhythmic tapping thud of the miners at their work.

At 11 p.m. several new searchlights were turned on. One from the castle of San Servando, across the river, directed its beam upon the New Bridge; though why this was done no one in the garrison could imagine. Another in the church tower of La Magdalena, and another in the chapel of the Paso de la Barca, lit the southern and western walls of the Alcazar.

During the bombardment of the evening a baby had died, though of natural causes.

THE TWENTY-FIRST OF AUGUST

The morning opened with violent machine-gun and rifle-fire.

At 7 a.m. the big "155's" began a slow and deliberate fire. The range was an extremely short one for such guns, nevertheless it was beyond reach of the defenders' rifle-fire. The enemy gunners had other advantages. Their forward observation posts could find cover in houses overlooking the Alcazar; and, had they needed it, could use the town telephone service to direct the fire of their guns. As a result of all this, the shelling was extremely accurate. Much damage was done though the bombardment did not last for more than an hour.

At 11 a.m. it was resumed. The walls of the north side of the Alcazar, though very thick and solidly built, were pierced by the main gateway and by twenty or thirty windows. These powerful high-explosive shells soon, therefore, began to knock down large sections of unbroken masonry. Sometimes the entire stonework between two windows would fall in a single piece.

It had been found that during a bombardment the enemy's sentries and rifle-men were in the habit of watching the shell-bursts, instead of keeping their attention on their own front. Taking advantage of this, a sortie was made into the Cuesta while the shelling was actually in progress. The object was to bring in anything useful from another house which was on fire. Bales of cloth were found, many of which were brought back and handed over to the store-rooms.

At the same time, while the second bombardment of the day had been in progress, the observation posts high up in the towers had seen a flight of three planes, very far away, in the direction of Talavera de la Reina. It seemed possible that these belonged to the Nationalist columns, fighting their way up from the south and from the west. It was, therefore, considered that they might be closer than had previously been believed. The garrison were elated. Wireless aerials, already prepared, were rigged up and an attempt was made to tune in the field wireless of the Nationalist High Command. These efforts were not successful.

Soon after 4.30 p.m. the "155's" began their third bombardment and fired more rounds than during the previous ones. That section of the northern façade nearest to the river was in part demolished. Both the outer walls and the inner walls collapsed and, falling in a huge mass of rubble, filled the wrecked rooms on the ground floor. The debris spread in avalanches; some extending across the terrace which faced the gate; some invading the arcades and overflowing into the courtyard itself.

At 7 p.m. the battery of "75's" and the big mortar began a bombardment of dining-hall and kitchens.

Soon after dark the enemy from the upper windows of the Santa Cruz sprayed the narrow end of the House-of-the-Military-Government, and the posts on the Stable Approach, with petrol. They then attempted to set light to this; at first by throwing hand-bombs; later by sending out parties of men, covered by machine-gun fire. The hand-bombs fell short, and the men sent out were driven back by the garrison's fire.

THE TWENTY-SECOND OF AUGUST

This day was a decisive one in the siege of the Alcazar.

At 5 a.m. a plane was seen in the south-west. It circled for some time and then retired westward. No markings had been seen upon it and the garrison continued to dispute as to whether it was friend or enemy.

At 7 a.m. the machine-gun and rifle-fire increased to considerable intensity.

Soon a large mortar established inside the courtyard of the

Santa Cruz began to lob bombs over the roof. These fell with fair accuracy upon and around the House-of-the-Military-Government; the distance being not more than sixty or eighty yards. Placed where it was, this mortar was safe from retaliation. The explosion of such bombs is severe. Much of the interior of the House-of-the-Military-Government was wrecked and set on fire. The garrison of the vital Stable No. 4 were forced to withdraw from their loopholes. Keeping low and close to the walls they escaped injury, though two sentries who had to remain in exposed positions were wounded. The barricades at the windows, built of sandbags filled with stone rubble, were torn and displaced and the work of rebuilding them later, in view of the enemy just across the street, was both slow and dangerous.

At 10 a.m. a big three-engined bomber, escorted by a pursuit plane, circled over the Alcazar and dropped a dozen incendiary bombs. It attempted to fly low but the reserves of the garrison opened fire upon it from within the courtyard and it was forced to rise higher. After that most of the bombs fell wide, and the fires caused by them were quickly put out by the parties which were always ready to deal with such situations.

While this aerial bombardment was in progress the "155's" again opened fire. The shells bursting upon the breach in the north façade added to the difficulties of those who were extinguishing the fires caused by the incendiary bombs. Notwithstanding, the work was carried on as planned. The success of these methods, so often rehearsed, increased the confidence of the garrison.

Meanwhile, as on the other occasions when aeroplanes had bombarded the Alcazar, intense rifle and machine-gun fire was directed on it from all sides. Barricades had been erected at the ends of passages to prevent stray bullets entering them. Yet it often happened that bullets, glancing off angles of stonework, found their way round corners to an extent which would have seemed impossible. At such times there were few spots in the

PLATE 15

THE ALCAZAR FROM THE PLAZA ZOCODOVER

The street ahead is the Cuesta, which was the main approach
to the Alcazar, but was subsequently blocked when the nearer
of the two towers fell across it.

SEVEN WEEKS LATER

This photograph was taken from the spot where, in the one
above it, two men are standing. The houses between them and
the Alcazar have been demolished. The north-west tower has
fallen and blocked the road, but the other three are still intact.

PLATE 16

AFTER EIGHT WEEKS OF SIEGE

Two towers are still standing, though the one on the right is just out of view. The leaning column in the foreground of this photograph can be made out in the two below.

THE AFTERNOON OF SEPTEMBER 18TH

The mines had exploded that morning and the south-west tower has gone. Only the south-east one remains.

AFTER THE RELIEF: All the towers are gone.

Alcazar which were perfectly safe.

Towards the close of day the event took place which made this date memorable in the history of the siege. In the stillness of the evening a plane was seen rushing out of the southern sky. Flying very fast and low it headed directly for the Alcazar and passed just above the towers. And, as it cleared them, it let fall a square object, much larger than any bomb. This landed with a crash among the shell-holes on the Esplanade. A party was sent out, and cautiously approaching found it to be a large tin trunk which had been smashed to fragments by its fall and had scattered its contents far and wide. Everything that could be found was snatched up and brought under cover; and only just in time, for the arrival and passing of this plane produced almost at once an enemy bombardment.

The contents of the trunk proved to be tins of food and packets of sweets and chocolate. These had been so well wrapped up that only a few had been spoiled. It was at once realized that this was probably the plane seen in the distance early that morning, and that it belonged to the columns of the Nationalist army.

But, if there had been any doubt as to whether the plane was friend or foe, this would have been dispelled by the great volume of enemy rifle and machine-gun fire directed upon it from every corner of the town, directly it had passed over the Alcazar. It was soon lost to sight, and then those of the enemy who could see the men rescuing the contents of the shattered trunk, opened fire on them. However, the light was bad and the shooting extremely wild.

The appearance of this plane stirred the enemy to action. The "155's," the battery of "105's" and of "75's," all commenced a bombardment of the Alcazar at their highest rate of fire. This however did not last long. For there was no moon and soon the night closed in.

During the day the observation posts had reported that the enemy were withdrawing the battery of "75's" from the posi-

tion it had always occupied in the Dehesa de Pinedo. Now
from the flashes seen in the twilight it was clear that the battery
had taken up a position on the Campimento de Alijares, two
miles away, across the river and in a grove of olive trees just
below the sky-line of some low hills. Thus the enemy's artillery
bombardment was being delivered from two sides. And to this
a big mortar in the castle of San Servando had added its fire.

Meanwhile the tins and packages were being unpacked before a delighted crowd of women, children, and of those men
who had not been recalled to their posts by the bombardment.
Yet the possibility of this being a ruse of the enemy and an attempt to poison the garrison, could not be ruled out. A few
samples were subjected to analysis. All the results were satisfactory.

The artillery fire had ceased but the big mortar in the castle
of San Servando still kept up its vexatious bombardment. The
castle was within rifle range. Thus there was offered the first
opportunity of replying to an enemy bombardment. Moreover
the garrison was in high spirits, both on account of the visit of
the aeroplane and of the provisions which had been dropped.
It was decided, therefore, to teach the enemy a lesson. The windows of the east façade and the old Arab battlements which ran
along it, were manned. The one trench mortar of the garrison,
which till now had never been used owing to the shortage of
ammunition, was set up, and several rounds were allotted to it.
Then at a given order rapid fire was opened upon the San Servando castle by several hundred rifles, a few machine-guns and
the mortar. This was maintained for fourteen minutes. Then
the "Cease Fire" was given and complete silence followed. So
great had been the moral effect that not one answering shot
had been fired from San Servando, and never again was bombardment by any mortar from an exposed position attempted
within rifle range of the Alcazar.

The casualties of the day were officially noted as being: one
killed, eight wounded; one natural death. But, when the in-

tensity of the day's bombardment is remembered, it is not easy to dismiss the thought that "death from shock" might well have been a truer diagnosis.

Yet time is merciful, the memory of man is strange, and those who endured the siege say that of all their recollections, one of the most vivid is the joy of the children, the women and the young soldiers, when that night a small ration of sweets or jam was doled out to them.

THE MARCH TO BADAJOS

At dusk on Saturday the 22nd August an aeroplane, dropping a tin trunk of food upon the terrace of the Alcazar, brought hope and encouragement to the hard-pressed garrison.

It had long been realized that General Mola's column, on which the garrison had depended for any chance of relief, had failed in its march from the north, and had been held up ever since in the Sierra de Guadarrama. To what army, therefore, had this aeroplane belonged? The story of that army and its march towards Toledo is so extraordinary as to seem fabulous.

Until about the 10th of August no one had heard of it. There had been rumours, hard to check; wireless broadcasts, by partisans, and mostly lies. For weeks no war correspondent had been within a hundred miles of where the army was; nor, if one had, would he have had means of sending out his "story."

The facts became known to the Press only after they had lost their "news value." Thus they obtained but little space, and so the public knows little of this army or of what it did.

There has not been, so far as I know, any authentic account of its exploits. And no more is claimed for this one, than that it was compiled on the spot from what sources were available; and that it will give the reader some idea of how the Alcazar ever came to be relieved; which is after all essential to this book.

A sequence of events, therefore, with no claim to do more than that, is here set down.

On the 16th and 17th July the military revolt broke out in Morocco, and was immediately successful. On the 18th, 19th and 20th July similar revolts broke out in Spain. These were successful only in the north-west.

As a result there remained two rebel armies; one, under General Mola, in the north-west of Spain; and the other, under General Franco, in Spanish Morocco. Between the two lay all the southern half of Spain, and also the Straits of Gibraltar, which were controlled by the Government's fleet. And, even should a way be found to smuggle troops across from Africa, they would have to land in Andalusia. Now the Andalusians are very different from the Castilians. They are light, lazy, excitable, unstable, easily fired by political propaganda. Except for the towns of Cadiz, Jerez and Cordova, Andalusia is said to have been entirely on the side of the Frente Popular.

On about July 19th—that is two days before fighting started in Toledo—there arrived near Seville a certain General Queipo de Llano, commander of the Carabineros regiment then stationed in Madrid. It is said that he came from Morocco, by air; and with him came a handful of officers. Outside the city he collected various soldiers and some men of the Guardia Civil; making up a force of one hundred and eighty all told. He commandeered lorries, drove with his supporters to the Radio-Sevilla wireless station and seized it. He then began a series of broadcasts, most of which, though wildly untrue when issued, he proceeded to transform into facts.

His announcements were:—that only Madrid, Barcelona and a few other industrial towns remained in the hands of the Government; that in the rest of Spain the coup d'état had succeeded; that he himself, with the advance guard of a large army, had seized Seville; that the army, consisting of forty thousand legionaries and Moorish regiments, had landed on the coast and were marching upon the city; that all soldiers—Guardia Civil, ex-soldiers, and those who cared for the ancient glories of Spain—should rally to him, and so greet the (wholly non-existent) army which was now approaching the town; that he would expect all such during the course of the afternoon at a rendezvous he named outside the city.

Leaving a small garrison to defend the wireless station, he put the rest of his force back into lorries. He then managed, by appearing several times and from various directions upon the main squares of the city, and by asking whether other of his columns had passed that way, to create the impression that his force was indeed many times larger than it was. The Government authorities in the city called upon the troops but they found them in many cases unwilling to act. Old soldiers, Guardia Civil and others, hastened to the rendezvous. The armoury of a barracks was occupied and arms distributed.

Thereupon, according to hearsay, the Government commander, fearing that the barracks might be cut off from one another by a rising of the population, withdrew from the city with all the troops who would follow him.

His forces were probably a hundred times more numerous than the followers which General Queipo de Llano had by now collected, but he was completely blinded by the audacity of his opponent. Instead of recapturing the Radio-Sevilla wireless station, or putting it out of action by shell-fire, he arranged for another, and far weaker station, to commence broadcasting, and to give itself out as "Radio-Sevilla."

This station then announced that the insurrection had been quelled without difficulty and that all was once again quiet in the city. The "Rebels," with their far more powerful station, permitted these broadcasts to be made, then contradicted them, and then smothered any further broadcasting by the station in the hands of the Government commander.

The coup d'état had succeeded brilliantly. But Seville is a city of some two hundred thousand inhabitants. Outside it were large Government forces, equipped with artillery, armoured cars and cavalry; while this "Rebel" leader who had seized the city, in theory only, had not even now at his disposal more than two thousand men. Indeed he could not possibly have maintained his position, had it not been for the unconnected, yet somewhat similar exploit, of another supporter of General Franco's cause.

Faced with the difficulty of crossing the Straits a certain Colonel Castajón,[1] commanding a force in Spanish Morocco, embarked one evening in a small sailing-boat, taking with him thirty-five picked officers and men from his own command. Evading the warships which patrolled the Straits, he landed upon the coast of Andalusia with his handful of men, amongst whom was a squad of Moorish soldiers. He entered the nearest town, commandeered motor transport and with his little band of followers set out upon the conquest of Andalusia.

The landing of Colonel Castajón, and the speed with which his little column moved, created just the incidents necessary to confirm General Queipo de Llano's broadcasts. From the mayors of widely separated towns and villages came telegrams and telephone messages reporting the passage of legionaries and Moorish troops, and asking for instructions. Rumour travels fast and by the evening Seville believed in the imminent arrival of that phantom army of forty thousand men. Soldiers deserted and joined the Nationalist leader. The Guardia Civil came to him in complete units. The Government continued to announce from all its wireless stations that it still held the

---

[1] The "j" in Castajón is pronounced as an "h" and the accent is on the last syllable. The Colonel, now a General, is just over forty and I believe was then the youngest Colonel in the Spanish Army. He is round-faced, dark-eyed, buoyant and gay. Some weeks later, when he was on his march to Madrid, I lunched with him. He had by then a mixed column of legionaries and Moors, admirably equipped with field-guns, howitzers and technical units. His soldiers had one especial cause for pride; that, since their commander and his thirty-five men had landed, his force had never indented for a gun, a rifle or a single round of ammunition; everything they possessed having been taken from the enemy in battle.

city and that its feeble wireless station was Radio-Sevilla. But the facts were against it and the broadcasts did it more harm than good. Indeed, as the truth leaked out, the mere daring which the Nationalists had shown soon brought the fickle Andalusians to their side.

By the 22nd of August, that is some three days after Colonel Castajón had landed, the Nationalist broadcasts from Radio-Sevilla claimed that the whole of Andalusia had been won.

Seville had been taken, much of the south brought over to General Franco's cause; but none of this made any more possible the transport of "The Army of Africa" to Spain. General Franco thereupon decided to despatch at least some reinforcements by air. He had few planes. Some were shot down by enemy warships. But the distance was not great and the work was continued and developed. Gradually and by driblets further detachments of "The Army of Africa," together with guns and stores, were brought across the Straits by air.[1]

The troop-carriers were escorted by pursuit planes. These on occasion, to draw away enemy fire from their convoy, found it necessary to swoop down and engage the warships at close range. Made bold by their success at this, they took to attacking warships whenever seen. As a result it was considered that the experiment should be made of sending across surface transports, escorted by aircraft.

About the 5th of August two mail steamers of the trans-Mediterrana line were camouflaged and extra funnels added. Crowded with legionaries and Moorish regulars these transports set out, escorted by aircraft, an armed trawler, and one obsolete gunboat, the crew of which had thrown in their lot with the "counter-revolution." They were intercepted by a large and modern Government destroyer, armed with five four-inch guns. But engaged by aircraft and by the ancient gunboat the Government warship withdrew, and the troops were duly

[1] The questions of foreign aircraft and secret intervention may here be raised, but I do not propose to deal with them in this book.

landed at Algeciras. Slowly the command of the sea was wrested from the Government warships, which in most cases had put their officers to death and were controlled by a Soviet of seamen.

But the Nationalist forces which had first reached Andalusia had not waited for reinforcements before moving northwards. It was on speed and on daring that they had depended, and if the beleaguered garrisons of Toledo, Huesca and Oviedo were to be relieved there was not an hour to be lost.

By the 7th of August the advance troops had reached Zafra, a town which by road is some 110 miles north-west of Seville.[1]

About the 8th of August they were at Almendralejo, more than twenty miles farther north.

About the 9th or 10th they had occupied Merida, the important road and rail junction, yet another twenty miles farther on their way. Here they were able to get in touch with General Mola's forces in the north, by telephone and radio and, however precariously, a junction had been effected.

But at Merida they were faced with a new problem. The Government, to stop this advance, had thrown a large force into Badajos, some forty miles away upon their flank. To continue their advance and leave it in their rear would have been madness.

The decision was made. The column had been advancing at the rate of more than twenty miles a day, overcoming Government detachments at almost every village on the way. Yet no rest was given here. The column turned west and rushed upon Badajos.

On the 11th of August—it is said at the hour when they first sighted it—they announced the capture of the town. Till then they had followed with remarkable success the policy of announcing victories first, and winning them afterwards. But Badajos was fruit that would not fall for the shaking.

[1] This date at least is certain, for I know two British ex-officers who joined the force at this place and on this date.

The town was a strong one, having once been a frontier fortress and having in its time endured many sieges. It had walls, it had gates. The Government forces in the town are said to have been three times as numerous as the Nationalists; and to them was added a large number of countrymen who, having lately seized land, killed some landlords and imprisoned others, were fearful of what might happen. Crowding into the town, these men had been armed by the Government commander. Angered by this, or taking advantage of the approach of the Nationalist columns, the Guardia Civil refused to act. It is said that the Government commander then turned machine-guns on these recalcitrant Guardia Civil, mowing them down to the number of between two and three hundred. It is said, also, that the imprisoned landlords of the district were then massacred.[1]

On the 11th or 12th of August the Nationalist columns arrived before Badajos, heard of what was said to have happened in the town, attempted to rush the gates and were driven back with heavy loss.

What happened during the next two, or even three, days is still largely a matter of doubt. But by the evening of the 13th or 14th of August, after a short and light bombardment with the one battery of field-guns they possessed, the Nationalist forces took the town by storm.

A night of street-fighting and of "cleaning up" followed. It was said that any of the Workers' Militia or other Government supporters found with arms in their hands were turned into the bull ring (there being no prison large enough to hold them) and were shot in more or less cold blood.[2] But how true or not these stories were is discussed in the next chapter.

[1] For these statements, however, there are only the reports of the Nationalist columns.

[2] It may be that the climate of the Badajos district induces ferocity. The following account of the storming of the town, given I believe by an eye-witness, suggests something of the sort.

"Now commenced that wild and desperate wickedness which tarnished the lustre of the soldiers' heroism, for hundreds risked and many lost their

ASIDES

The exploits of the Army of Africa have raised at least two questions of which the writer, and perhaps the reader also, is acutely conscious. The questions are:—the alleged massacres after the storming of Badajos; and the employment of Moorish troops in Spain.

The question of the alleged massacres at Badajos is important for this reason. There have been many proved atrocities committed by members of the Frente Popular but there have been hardly any attributed to the Nationalists. The supporters of the Madrid Government, therefore, have always referred to what is said to have taken place in Badajos after its capture on August 14th.

Frankly at the time, when I read in the French and English Press accounts of what was supposed to have happened, I believed them. Later I met the actual troops who had captured the town and, having seen them, I could no longer believe what I had read. That was but a personal impression. Yet it was so strong that I went to a good deal of trouble to discover what the truth had been.

Wishing to hear the worst that had been said against the Nationalist forces and their actions in Badajos, I wrote to the

---

lives in trying to stop the violence. But the madness generally prevailed. And as the worst men are the leaders here, all the dreadful passions of human nature were displayed. Shameless rapacity, brutal intemperance, savage lust, cruelty, and murder, shrieks and piteous lamentations, groans, shouts, imprecations, the hissing of fires bursting from the houses, the crashing of doors and windows, and the reports of muskets used in violence, resounded for two days and nights in the streets of Badajos. On the third, when the city was sacked, when the soldiers were exhausted by their own excesses, the tumult rather subsided than was quelled. The wounded men were then looked to and the dead disposed of."

The troops in this case were British and their commander the Duke of Wellington. The paragraph is from Napier's History of the Peninsular War.

Spanish Embassy in London, explaining that I was writing a book and that I was anxious to hear what they could tell me about the alleged massacres. After some delay I received a most courteous letter which gave me three "stories," and the source from which they had been drawn. The letter was written by the Assistant Press Attaché, at the direction of His Excellency the Ambassador. I take it that it represents the case as the Madrid Government sees it.

Three "stories" were given in the letter:—

An "eye-witness" account which had appeared in the Paris edition of the New York "Herald Tribune," under the name of N. Reynolds Packard, United Press Correspondent.

An account which had appeared in the Paris "Populaire,"— Havas Special Correspondent.

An account which had appeared in "Le Temps," from their own Correspondent.

I knew all about these three reports. They had been repeated or copied in various forms all over the world.

I will deal with these stories in the order in which they have been given.

First comes that of Mr. Packard. I quote the relevant portions of it:—

"With the Insurgent Armies near Badajos, August 15th.

"Following the troops into the suburbs of Badajos to-day, I witnessed guerilla street-fighting, etc. etc. etc.

"Most of the defenders were entrenched in the old castle, which made Badajos one of the best defended cities in Spain. As fast as they were captured, the defending loyalists were executed in mass killings."

The answer to this is:—that Mr. Packard had never been in Badajos in his life, nor anywhere near it. This, I presume disposes of the report appearing under his name.

Anyone wishing to verify this, can find the evidence in an appendix to this book.

· · ·

Next comes the Havas Correspondent whose account appeared in "Populaire." The relevant part of his story reads:—

"On the Ajuntamiento Square, in particular, are lying numerous partisans of the Government who were lined up and executed against the walls of the Cathedral. Blood has poured in streams from the pavement. Everywhere you find clotted pools. In one of them, against the palace of the military authorities, you can see caps and membership cards of the Left parties."

I have investigated how this story came to be written. The correspondent was a M. Marcel Dany. He was, it appears, a permanent correspondent of Havas, but neither of the Havas correspondents with General Franco's army knew of his existence there. In company with a Portuguese journalist, Señor Mario Neves, who acted as guide, he left Lisbon by car at 2 a.m. on the 15th of August. They reached the Spanish frontier and ultimately obtained permission by telephone, from the Nationalist Commandancia at Badajos, to cross the frontier and to visit the town. In company with the Portuguese journalist and another French journalist, M. Dany spent some hours there.

To set against the story that M. Dany wrote, I have an account of what the Portuguese journalist, who took him round, saw and described. He makes no suggestion of any indiscriminate killing but states that there had been hours of bitter street-fighting and subsequently some executions. The relevant portions of his account can be found in the appendix.

M. Dany returned to Portugal the same day and sent off his "story" from Elvas that evening. He sent off one more story on the 16th, and another on the 17th, of August. According to Havas' telegram, given at the end of this book, he then left Portugal and it is presumed did not return.

.   .   .

Next comes the story from the Correspondent of "Le Temps." This was a M. Jacques Berthet. He visited Badajos on the same day, with his compatriot M. Dany, with Señor Neves acting as guide.

The relevant portion of the story which he sent, and which was published in "Le Temps," runs:—

"*Militia-men and suspects arrested by the insurgents were immediately executed. At the present moment about twelve hundred have been shot on the charges of armed resistance or grave crimes. I saw the pavement outside the military commandancia covered with the blood of those executed, and still strewn with their caps and personal objects. The cathedral, in which numerous families had taken refuge, is in disorder, but has not been damaged. Two militia-men captured in the choir were executed facing the high altar, before which they are lying in their blood. The arrests and executions en masse on the plaza de Toros (bull ring) continue.*"

(Some portions have been underlined for reference.)

Now the account of the Portuguese journalist who showed these two Frenchmen round, tells a very different story. He also mentions that there was blood on the pavement, but he points out that there had been heavy street-fighting everywhere. As to the two militia-men "executed before the high altar," he reports that the cathedral had been used by the Government troops as a machine-gun nest and that there were some dead bodies lying in the nave. As for the executions en masse in the bull ring, he states that the bull ring had been shelled several times and that there were some corpses lying about.

This French journalist also returned to Portugal the same evening, with his compatriot, and with Señor Neves. I do not know how many more cables he sent or how long he stayed in Portugal, but I have it on the authority of the Havas Agency that he was thrown into prison and then expelled from the country.

I think that this disposes of the three stories given me by the Spanish Embassy in London, as representing their case in this matter.

.   .   .

Now for the other side. I know two British subjects who actually did enter the town with the Nationalist forces. One was an ex-captain of the Indian army, the other had served as a subaltern in the Brigade of Guards. They were not there with the permission of the War Office and I am not entitled to give their names. They both told me that there was no massacre of any sort. They said that, on the entry of the Nationalist forces, hundreds of the inhabitants rushed to the Command and denounced various of the prisoners, as having been responsible for the atrocities which had been committed during the Anarchist-Syndicalist reign of terror, which the arrival of the Nationalist troops had ended. Trials were held and there were many executions. But, more than all else there had been street-fighting for many hours. One of these officers added, "It was a rough night, you know, street-fighting everywhere. The troops behaved most decently."

I have also a letter from another British subject, a Mr. F. G. Sturrup, who has long had a business in Badajos. With his permission I quote three paragraphs from the letter he wrote to me on the subject.

"1. *I was in Badajos two weeks after the capture by Franco.*

"2. *There were no massacres at all. But the street-fighting was terrible. Badajos being one of the towns where the assassination was greatest, Franco set up tribunals and shot many*

Communists, but all after fair trial.

"3. Foreign correspondents, who often could not speak Spanish, witnessed some of these shootings but did not know that those being shot had been tried and sentenced for crimes committed."

The last evidence I would quote is that of Captain Francis McCullagh, a British war correspondent. He wrote as follows:—

"I went thoroughly into that question and satisfied myself that no Red who surrendered in Badajos was shot. . . . I have been unable to find any Englishman or American who saw with his own eyes any shooting of unarmed men by the Nationalists."

      .   .   .

I hope it may not be thought that my desire to dispel the stories about Badajos is intended as an attack upon Mr. Packard or either of the two French journalists. Mr. Packard has stated most emphatically that he did not write the story which appeared under his name and that he knew nothing about it. I have gone into the matter carefully and I entirely believe what he says. As for the two French journalists, if they believed what they wrote, they were misled. As far as I know, I have never met any of these three journalists.

Heaven knows, I have no wish to throw doubt upon the word of war correspondents. In Spain I lived with many of them and, honestly, I was astonished by the care that most of them took to verify each story or impression that they got; and even more by the way in which they helped each other; and by their kindness to each other and to me.

      .   .   .

The second question remains, the employment of Moorish troops in Spain. To this I offer the answer which I believe a soldier of the Nationalist armies would give.

"We brought our Moorish troops from Africa. Admittedly the Moors are a backward race. But their civilization is older than any existing European one. They have their religion and they respect ours. They respect both women and traditions. They are not savages. They are well behaved, dignified, quiet and polite. Their religion forbids them to drink. Our Moorish soldiers are highly disciplined and steady troops. They are at least the equals of any Indian troops put into the field by England against other Europeans in the world war. They are incredibly above the Sengalese who in peace time garrison Southern France and who are called out against strikers, when the need occurs.

"We have not the colour feeling of the American and the Englishman. In our army a Moor can rise to be an officer and can command Spanish soldiers, and Spanish officers junior to himself. This often happens. And in any unit Spaniards and Moors serve side by side. As for using Moorish troops in civil war in Spain, there is nothing new in this. The first occasion on which it was done was by Señor Azaña, the actual President of the Madrid Government against which we were fighting. The second occasion was when a government of the Left, faced with the revolution of Anarchist miners, called in Moorish troops to crush them.

"We saw our country reduced to chaos, its ancient traditions destroyed, our religion suppressed. We came ourselves; and with us we brought the Moorish regiments, our comrades of long standing in peace and war. Will you, you others, think how you would have acted had you been in our place?"

THE TWENTY-THIRD OF AUGUST

With the first light, search-parties were sent out on to the Esplanade to look for any letters which the tin trunk might

PLATE 17

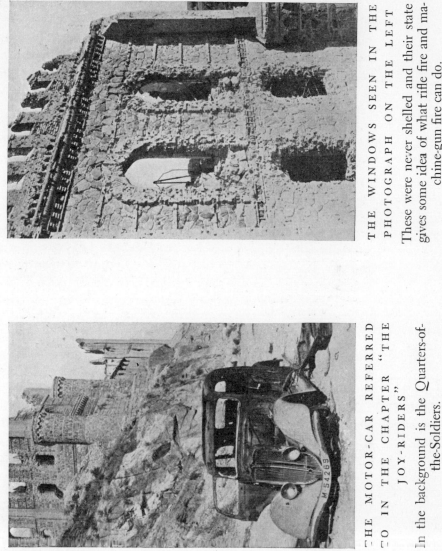

THE WINDOWS SEEN IN THE
PHOTOGRAPH ON THE LEFT

These were never shelled and their state
gives some idea of what rifle fire and machine-gun fire can do.

THE MOTOR-CAR REFERRED
TO IN THE CHAPTER "THE
JOY-RIDERS"

In the background is the Quarters-of-
the-Soldiers.

PLATE 18

20th OF AUG

CUESTA

3rd OF SEPT.

CUESTA

8th OF SEPT.

CUESTA

18th OF SEPT.

CUESTA

After explosion of the mines

22nd OF SEPT

CUESTA

After last tower had fallen

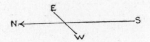

N ← E / W → S

THE ALCAZAR
IN VARIOUS STAGES
OF DESTRUCTION

have contained. Two were found and brought in, before it was light enough for the enemy to open accurate rifle-fire. At the sight of these the spirits of the garrison, already high, rose higher. Signal screens were spread in the courtyard, to let friendly aircraft know that they had been safely received. Meanwhile the letters were taken to the Headquarters Office and opened.

Across the left corner of each sheet of paper was a band of the red-yellow-red of the old régime. One letter was headed with the Holy Cross, the other with the armorial bearings of Spain.

The first letter to be opened read:—

"From the Commander of the Army of Africa and of the North.

To the brave defenders of the Alcazar.

We are well aware of your heroic resistance and we are bringing you all possible help. Count on it, we shall soon reach you. Meanwhile, at whatever cost hold on. We are sending you some help (the provisions). Viva España!"

The note was signed and rubricated, General Francisco Franco.

The other, headed with the armorial bearings of Spain and with "Viva España!", read:—

"All ranks of the Army salute the brave defenders of the Alcazar. We are hastening to your aid. Rushing every obstacle, overcoming all resistance, advancing columns are pushing on to your aid. Viva España!"

This on behalf of all ranks was again signed and rubricated by General Franco.

The second letter—and soon afterwards a copy of the first—was posted up in a spot where all in their turn could read it in safety.

The garrison seemed to have been particularly pleased that these notes were at once exhibited; this making it clear that nothing of importance was being kept back. Each, after reading the letters, went at once to the chapel, to pray to Our Lady of the Alcazar, and to offer thanks for the great mercy of God. For a chance of delivery now for the first time seemed possible.

At 7 a.m. the mortar, which had been moved to another and safer position, commenced a bombardment of its favourite targets, the dining-hall and the Quarters-of-the-Soldiers.

A quarter of an hour later the "155's" joined in, once again upon what remained of the north façade. These heavy pieces did much damage, bringing down more walls and further wrecking the arcades which surrounded the courtyard. After an hour and a quarter the fire of all guns ceased. The mortar, however, continued its bombardment, off and on, all the morning.

Shortly after noon a big bomber, with a pursuit plane up on high as escort, appeared from the north. Both flew over the Alcazar and dropped many large metal containers, six of which fell into the courtyard. These on landing burst and deluged everything with petrol; incendiary bombs being then dropped to set this alight. And, while anti-fire squads were dealing with these conflagrations, the "Take Cover" was sounded and almost at once a heavy bombardment was begun by the "155's"; by the "75" battery, installed in its new position across the river; by the mortars hidden in the courtyards of the Santa Cruz, and from the large mortar installed on the farther side of the Tagus.

This bombardment was so heavy that for some time a general assault by the enemy was considered likely. Everyone stood to arms. It was believed that the enemy's most probable points of attack would be either the Ziz-Zag on the north, the Capuchinos on the south-west, or the Quarters-of-the-Soldiers on the south-east. The detachments near the Zig-Zag, and near the dining-hall were therefore strengthened—the latter being a convenient central spot from which the garrison of either the Capuchinos or the Quarters-of-the-Soldiers could be reinforced. As yet there was no likelihood of direct attack from the east or west. For on the east the enemy were still on the farther side of the river, while on the west the houses and narrow alleys made enemy deployment impossible.

The rifle and machine-gun fire continued on all sides but the bombardment by the batteries and mortars slackened and ceased.

The knowledge that there were columns of Nationalist troops within perhaps eighty or a hundred miles, and that some of these at any rate were striving to reach Toledo, made even yet more careful observation necessary. Extra observation posts were therefore stationed in the towers, with orders to keep up a ceaseless watch in every direction and especially upon the southern and south-western horizon. In so clear an atmosphere and from such a height the roads could be seen many miles distant, tracing their way across the plain.

For once an official task was found for the women. It was clear from the paper of General Franco's letters that the Army had adopted once again the traditional and royal red-yellow-red of Spain. The women were now therefore set to make rosettes, consisting of five concentric bands of these colours, and an order was issued that as soon as these were ready all the garrison should wear them.

At dusk the rifle-fire and machine-gun fire grew spiteful and, as it became dark, increased in intensity, especially against the defences on the north side. It soon became evident that fresh machine-guns had been installed in the windows of the Santa Cruz, from which at intervals they had engaged the defenders of Stable No. 1, day and night, for the past week. One of these new machine-guns, more accurate in its fire than any yet observed, had been installed in the hole which the enemy had knocked in the wall at the south-west angle of the Santa Cruz. (This hole can be seen half-way up the corner of the wall on the left of Plate No. 24.) This gun was evidently handled by an expert who, instead of "traversing," directed his fire always at a single spot. Thus the sandbags were soon cut to pieces, the rubble inside trickled out, and a gap was made. Only by constantly moving from one side to the other of the threatened window, could the man at it save himself. And, as the minutes went by, it became increasingly difficult for him to do so.

Some time after nightfall the enemy searchlight which floodlit the empty street, which lay between Stable No. 4 from the Santa Cruz, was suddenly turned. At the same instant the gates of the Santa Cruz were thrown open and great numbers of the enemy rushed out. These dashed across the road and towards the entrance to the Stable Approach; only to be checked by the concentrated fire of the defenders. Some, however, did succeed in reaching the wall of the House-of-the-Military-Government and, keeping close under it, were hidden from the defenders at the loopholes overhead. From this position, they hurled hand-bombs round the corner at the posts guarding the Stable Approach. To counter this the defenders in the windows above them were obliged to show themselves unduly, and this in their turn exposed them to the fire from the windows of the Santa Cruz, only forty or fifty yards away.[1]

Almost all the defenders of Stable No. 4 were the young soldiers attached to the Academy; though they had been stiffened by a few Guardia Civil.[2]

Now one of these had taken up the defence of the window already mentioned which, on account of the expertly handled machine-gun in the hole in the wall opposite, had become

[1] See Plate 24.

[2] As far as I can discover, the garrison of the House-of-the-Military-Government at first consisted of some ten officers, some forty-five young soldiers and eight men of the Guardia Civil. Beyond their rifles they had one submachine gun and some bombs—but so few that these were to be used only in extreme emergency. I gather that, as the young soldiers gained experience, the number of officers and of the Guardia Civil was reduced. There were never any Falangista or "civilians" here. This was a little corner of the Regulars.

especially perilous. This man now realized that, on account of the volume of enemy fire directed against them, the young soldiers farther down the Stable could no longer stand up to their task at the loopholes. While, if they were unable to show themselves at their loopholes, those of the enemy sheltering close beneath the wall were free to do as they liked. Seeing that the situation was a desperate one, he abandoned his duel with the machine-gun which was picking away at the sandbags of his own window, and began to engage, one after another, the loopholes from which the enemy's rifle-fire was being directed against the Stable. Being an excellent shot he was able to keep down the enemy's fire. But the machine-gun opposite him, freed from his attention, could proceed with a systematic cutting away of the stones and sandbags which protected him.

This proved a slow process, for now and again he would abandon his rifle and start repairing his barricade. But a machine-gun can fire forty shots to one a rifle can. Moreover, as soon as this Guardia Civil had provided some protection for himself, he began to spread his fire over all windows of the Santa Cruz. It would have been impossible, of course, for this single man to have engaged a machine-gun for so long and at such short range had it not been for the darkness which made the flash of his rifle alone show the whereabouts of his window. For him the situation may have been less difficult. For, while for lack of any means of lighting it Stable No. 4 was always in darkness, the enemy having less discipline and knowledge than the besieged, often kept the gallery of the Santa Cruz lit at night, thus disclosing the positions of their loopholes. Nevertheless the duel soon proved too unequal and he was hit. He went on fighting. He was hit again. His barricade started to crumble but he kept up his fire.

Meanwhile the attack from under the wall and round the corner of the building swung to and fro. The enemy with bomb and sub-machine gun made many attempts to round the corner and rush the short distance which separated them from the Stable Approach. But each time they were driven back; by the frontal fire of the posts at the entrance to the Stable Approach; and by the enfilade fire of the young soldiers, who thanks to this action of the Guardia Civil at the farther end of the Stable, were able to show themselves at their loopholes. Petrol containers were thrown against the iron gates (flimsy affairs, just within the Approach itself and thus hidden from the Santa Cruz): the petrol was set on fire: both sides were forced to withdraw: it burned out: the defenders rushed back to their posts: and a little afterwards the enemy came on again to the attack.

And while this was going on, up at the narrow north end of the House-of-the-Military-Government, the fire-fight between the one Guardia Civil at the farther end of the Stable, and the machine-gun in the corner of the Santa Cruz, continued.

Struggling to keep down the enemy's fire he had been once more wounded. He went on fighting. From time to time he tried to rebuild his sandbag barricade and, as he fought, he went on shouting "Viva España! . . . Viva España!"

Presently, wounded again, he slipped from the window. He recovered himself and scrambled back into his place again. Once more he was hit and was forced back. He made another attempt, reached his window, went on firing and shouting. At last he slid down and was unable to rise again.

They got him on to a stretcher and carried him out. The way from there to the hospital, up in the Alcazar, was long and difficult. They took him through the darkness of the other stable which ran southward and at right angles to the first. From there the way lay through the door on to the terrace; behind a barricade which hid this dangerous corner from the enemy across the river; and so up the long straight communication-trench, scored into the ramp which led up to the terrace of the Esplanade. They reached the top of the road, turned

into the Curved Passage and carried the stretcher down into
the vaulted sub-basement of the Alcazar. They put him down.
There, surrounded by the wounded of other days, he lay shouting, "Viva España! . . . Viva España!"; and proclaiming over
and over again how happy he was to be dying for his country.

That basement is very large and lofty. Overhead there runs
a vaulted roof. There was no light except that of a single
mule-fat dip. The place, so lit, was full of swinging shadows.

The volume of rifle-fire was slackening, for the attack from
the Santa Cruz against the Stable Approach had failed; this
perhaps he may have realized. There was nothing to be done
for him. They let him go on shouting. Presently he was dead.
He had eleven wounds. His name was José Serrano and he was
a private of the Guardia Civil.

THE SPANIARDS

What manner of men are these? Was José Serrano unique
among his people? Or can it be that our conception of the
typical Spaniard is not well-founded?

What do we really know of this race which for a century
and a half dominated Europe; which discovered, conquered
and moulded half the New World? We do not read their
literature. We do not see excerpts of their newspapers. We
do not know their films. They and we are very far apart. Their
ideals are not our ideals: their vices are not our vices: nor are
their virtues ours.

There are, perhaps, two causes which prevent us from understanding the Spaniard.

The first is a word—"Dago." The word Dago is said to be
a corruption of Don Diego, and the "Don Diegos" were those
valiant but unbending Spanish viceroys who did their best to

counter the free-and easy pirate sailors of Elizabethan England.
But words are loose things and this one has come to apply to
the half-Spaniards of the Americas. The average citizen of the
United States may know the Mexican but he does not know
the Spaniard. The average Englishman is more likely to have
met the Argentino of Paris bars than the Castilian of old Spain.
So the Anglo-Saxons are apt to imagine that the Spaniards re-
semble those Spanish-speaking peoples they have seen.

The other cause which perhaps prevents us from understanding the Spaniard is that high-coloured noisy vision of the bull-
fight, swirling skirts and castanets. This too gives a misleading
picture.

There are many races in Spain. There are the Catalans, who
are near to Marseilles; the Andalusians, who are near to Africa;
the Basques, who are apart from any other race on earth; there
are the Castilians—the unifiers and makers of Spain. The
Castilian delights in a bull-fight and looks upon swirling skirts
and castanets as suitable entertainment for an occasional evening of leisure. But in his ordinary life he is grave, quiet, tem-
perate and sober.

It is said that the Spaniards are lazy: but is lazy the word?
I offer the following story.

A Spanish merchant whose brandy is known throughout
Spain and whose sherry is sold the world over, told me this
story.

He was, he said, a Liberal. No longer young, he lived in
Madrid and interested himself very little in the family business
he had inherited. Then one day, looking at his passbook, his
conscience pricked him. He took the train to Jerez and called
together the managers and shop stewards of the bodegas where
his wines were mixed and stored. He explained to them how,
owing to the fall in the value of Spanish currency, he had been
making more money than he felt entitled to. So, instead of
an average wage of (say) five pesetas a day, he intended to pay

his men eight. He went back to Madrid.

On the first day of the new conditions, he was called to the telephone by his Jerez manager. Everything there was in confusion. Soon after three o'clock, the shop stewards had appeared in the office of the manager.

"What," they asked, "do you make it that we have earned to-day so far? We calculate it must be at least five pesetas already."

The manager considered. "That is about what it works out at."

"Well," said the shop stewards, "if we've made our five pesetas, we're off!"

Is that laziness? Or is it that the Spaniards have a philosophy which puts leisure before gain?

What else?

They are proud. But there are many forms of pride. The Spaniard's form of pride does at least give him something which we lack. For he is not impressed by size, by wealth, by pretensions. That another should think more of himself because he is rich seems to the Spaniard as childish, as that he should think more of himself because he is fat. He does not value a house more because it is higher than others, or cost more to build. For him it is a house, convenient or inconvenient, good to look at, or ugly.

There is a grievous form of pride which makes a man arrogant and overbearing. This form is rare among them, for the Spaniards are a polite race.

They put leisure before money. They are proud. What else?

They are intolerant; that seems not to be denied. They have suffered for it. They continue to suffer for it. There is no sign that they will ever cease to do so.

They drove out the Moors who were the foundation of their industries; the Jews, who had built their commerce. They made the Holy Inquisition, which was neither Spanish nor necessarily cruel, a name which stands for cruelty. Slack in administration, in matters of the spirit they had a fanatic zeal. Speculation of any sort became dangerous. Mental inaction was safe. They remained inactive. The world swept on and left them.

Yet this intolerance may have had its origin in singleness of heart. The Spaniard is literal. He says that for this cause he is ready to die. That is what he means. He has no second meanings, no mental reservations. His standards seem narrow and unadaptable. To him our own standards seem in some matters so loose as to be hardly standards at all. He may fail to live up to his ethics but they will not bend and suit themselves to his actions. In one way, at least, this singleness of heart has proved ruinous to him. Faced with conflicting interests we look for compromise. He cannot conceive it. What was right remains right. Talk cannot change moral values! For him expediency has no meaning; at least no decent meaning. Believing this or that true, how can he in honour compromise? He cannot. Thereby he is incapable of the elasticity upon which good government is based.

The history of Spain is the history of a people who had singleness of heart, often purity of heart, and who have suffered endlessly because of it. So in Spain politics have ever been dominated by religion; that is her history. In England, religion has ever been dominated by politics; that is hers.

They put leisure before money. They are proud. They are intolerant. They have singleness of heart. What else?

They are cruel. They set little value on life; on the lives of others, or on their own. That cannot be denied.

What else?

They are sober, sober in all material things. During many weeks just behind the line of battle, in towns where young soldiers had come out for a breath of life, I only saw two men who had too much to drink.

They are sober in manner. They are sober in dress; even when, as in extemporized uniforms, the colour is bright.

They are gentle-voiced. To be loud-voiced, to be assertive, to talk down others, would seem to them, in all classes, distasteful.

In their buildings, in their manner of life, all classes are sober and polite.

What else?

They are ignorant. Education has been neglected and for this the Church may be to blame. The new schools—and they say, "of late years it has rained schools"—have not yet had their effect. The people of the countryside are ignorant even in their farming. The people of the towns have been allowed to grow up uncared for and most that they have been taught has been bad for them.

Yet a people who live the life of their fathers and grandfathers, who are not impressed by size or speed or wealth, have a wisdom of their own.

They are devout. Even those Spaniards who proclaim themselves Red and atheist, have not ceased to credit the existence of a God; it is that they are in revolt against Him.

They have one other outstanding quality; one which brings us back to this soldier of the Guardia Civil. They are brave.

We may not know much of the Spaniard of to-day but we know something of his history; and the Spaniard is still the same.

Pizarro conquered Peru with his hundred and eighty-three men. Cortez conquered Mexico with seven hundred infantry, eighteen caballeros and a few small pieces of artillery. Gonsalvo de Cordoba, cut off in the toe of Italy and almost without supplies, fought the French, who had immense advantages in numbers, to a standstill. He invented the discipline on which, ever since, the armies of the world have been organized. For a century and a half the army he had made remained invincible.

The English may remember the Spanish flagship at Trafalgar, masts gone, on fire, fighting to the last. The Americans may remember the slow rusty out-of-date cruisers which, with blasting-powder for their guns, and boilers fired with wood and coal dust, sortied out of Manila to meet the whole armada of the United States.

The world has swept on and left them but the Spaniards remain the same.

I would not have set these things before the reader, had I not believed that, if he has weighed them in his mind, he will better understand the story of the Alcazar.

The world has swept on. Can the reader who wishes to understand this story step back a little, and see the defenders of the Alcazar with Elizabethan eyes, in their pride, their bravery, their ruthlessness, their singleness of heart, their knowledge of the presence of God?

THE TWENTY-FOURTH OF AUGUST

The attack upon the Stable Approach had lasted far into the night and after it had been finally repulsed the enemy had continued a desultory machine-gun fire. There was a lull before dawn. Then as the sun rose, the spatter of the fusillade increased.

At 7.30 a.m. the "155" guns opened fire, as always, upon the north façade. They began to widen the breach already created through the upper storeys, between the gateway and the north-east tower. The tower itself suffered. The walls near it were cut away, down to the level of the gallery which surrounded the courtyard. Of the palatial rooms of the first floor, and of those above them, nothing remained. They had been knocked into fragments which now filled and hid the ground-floor rooms below, and spread in avalanches of dust and debris, outwards over the terrace and inwards across the courtyard. Where this part of the north façade had stood, there ran a long heap of broken masonry which formed a barrier somewhat like the rampart round a child's sand castle. Thus the enemy in his efforts by his shell-fire to widen the gateway had blocked it; and where he had breached the walls, had created a mountain of rubble, steep enough and loose enough to prove a serious obstacle.[1]

Yet, though this rubble heap formed some sort of protection it was not one quarter the height of the walls of which it was the ruins; and thus from this side the courtyard of the Alcazar was open to the enemy's view and shell-fire.

While this shelling of the north façade was in progress, the big mortar from its position on the farther side of the river, and a smaller mortar from within the courtyard of the Convent de la Concepcion, began a bombardment of the House-of-the-Military-Government.

At 3.30 p.m. the "155's" opened fire again and began widening the breach in the north façade still further by shelling the part of it which was on the other side of the gateway and which had not yet been much damaged. Later the mortars and the battery of "75's" began to bombard the dining-hall, and afterwards the House-of-the-Military-Government.

During the day parties of the enemy had been reported working along the slopes between the terraces of the Alcazar and the river. This caused anxiety, in part because they might discover the existence of the wheat store, and in part because their presence might indicate the enemy's intention to sink a mine-shaft on that side, in an attempt to blow up the House-of-the-

[1] Plate 11 shows this breach from outside.

Military-Government. Other parties had been seen in the neighbourhood of the New Bridge (a river bridge just below the terraces of the Alcazar). It was thought possible, therefore, that the enemy might desire to cross the river in force and establish his line on the Toledo side of it; thereby closing in upon the Alcazar on this side. For these reasons special observation posts were established, to keep ceaseless watch on the cliffs and slopes between the defences and the river.

There was, too, another and greater cause for anxiety. For the sounds of mining by the south-west tower had changed in tone. The work was no longer being done by hand but with pneumatic drills. Thus there were now two sounds; the rapid but muffled rattle of the drills upon the face of the virgin rock, and the panting of the motors which drove the compressors. The drilling was unquestionably nearer but it was as yet impossible to locate its position.

In the orders of the evening the Guardia Civil, José Serrano, who the night before had given his life in the defence of Stable No. 4, was mentioned for "very distinguished conduct." The artillery officers and the buglers of the observation posts were also commended for their vigilance. For thanks to them the "Take Cover" had always been sounded in time for the garrison to seek shelter.

THE TWENTY-FIFTH OF AUGUST

The morning opened quietly, and this enabled the salvage squads to reduce somewhat the chaos in the courtyard. Paths were cleared through the rubble so as to enable the garrison to move from one place to another without having to climb over fallen columns and blocks of masonry. The barricades protecting those doors which opened upon the courtyard were repaired. For many had been knocked over by the concussion of the heavy shells and in some cases the doors behind them had been blown in. Some of the stones which protected the few lights of the basement had been displaced; these were put back in position. The stairways were cleared of the wreckage.

This work had not been completed when at 10 a.m. the "Take Cover" sounded and a few moments later the "155's" fired a single round each. But, apparently satisfied that they still had the range, they fired no more. Shortly afterwards, however, the battery of "75's," firing from their new position across the river, began to bombard the north façade. Their shells were light and normally could do no great damage but now they were able to take the breached façade in enfilade. Thus their shells, entering the remaining rooms through the partition walls, did considerable damage.

At 2.30 p.m. a big three-engine plane came droning out of the sky and dropped heavy bombs, some of which fell in the courtyard and shook down two of the columns.

At dusk a new attack was made from the Santa Cruz. This time none of the enemy showed themselves outside the building, but from the window deluged the Stable Approach and the positions near it with petrol, afterwards throwing bombs to ignite this. These attacks continued for a long time.

Somewhat after 9 p.m. another method was tried. Two high-pressure pumps were brought into play from the Santa Cruz. When they had sprayed all the surroundings of the Stable Approach with petrol, some parties of the enemy sortied from the gates, and covered by heavy machine-gun fire from the upper windows, rushed across the road and attempted to set the petrol alight. Their success was only partial and no great damage was done. They withdrew, leaving several dead on the road.

At 10 p.m., at 11 p.m., at midnight and at some time after 1 a.m., these attacks were renewed.

The casualties of the day had amounted to only two wounded; and on the day before to one dead and four wounded.

During the night the sound of mining was nearer and more persistent than before.

TOLEDO DURING THE SIEGE

What was happening in Toledo while its Alcazar was being besieged? The answer is in two parts. Outwardly, from the point of view of an airman passing over and glancing down, there was little change; few ruined buildings, little sign of war. Here and there a church had been burned by irresponsible supporters of the Government. But guards must have been mounted upon the cathedral and upon many other precious places. For little structural harm was done to most of them. In some cases, these national monuments were pillaged. But this may have been during the last days, even hours, when the guards had been withdrawn and the way lay open to anyone bent on theft or sacrilege. The Virgin's famous cape of pearls was stolen, half of the great gold monstrance has disappeared; saddest of all, for some of us, the St. Francis of Alonzo Cano has gone. Endless other things have disappeared from the cathedral treasury and from other sacred buildings. Yet for none of this can the Government, working at such a disadvantage, be held directly responsible.

In lesser churches and in the convents, filthy things were done. Altars were broken up. Grecos and Ribéras were slashed or carried off. Bodies of long-dead nuns were disinterred and thrown about, or left lying, mute and yellow, amidst excrement and torn missals, and lace altar-cloths used as toilet-paper.

As for the conditions of life in the town, these were in many

ways like those in Madrid itself. Churches had been closed by
order of the Government. Religious services of any sort were
forbidden. No baptisms, marriages or Christian burials were
permitted.

As for the clergy, their lot was a hard one. There were, it is
said, just over six hundred priests resident in Toledo when the
siege of the Alcazar began. A few may have escaped. Seven are
said to have survived, and the rest were killed.[1]

Yet it must not be thought that all the supporters of the
Government behaved as this suggests. For instance, in the
Convent of la Concepcion, which formed part of the actual
"front line" against the Alcazar, no violence was offered to the
inmates. Its many chapels and shrines were horribly dese-
crated, but the nuns were permitted to go on living in the
rooms round several of the little courtyards of the Convent;
and there they remained throughout the siege.[2]

In the industrial cities of Valencia and Catalonia big businesses, native or foreign, had been confiscated, and were run
on Communist principles.[3] But in Toledo there were no industries worth syndicalizing and nothing of the sort occurred.

In some districts even the smallest businesses had been taken
over by the "Workers," and the peasants, stirred up by agitators
from the towns, had seized the land. In a few small places
money was "abolished" and life arranged—until food disappeared—upon Communist lines. But the townspeople of Toledo, and the country people of the province, were conservative
and had no desire for such things, so in many respects this
ancient city escaped lightly.

---

[1] Up to the time of writing this book the official figures for Toledo have
not been published, and those given here are those current in the town.

[2] On Monday, December 7th I listened to the Government-controlled wireless station, Radio-Madrid, making a long discourse containing obscene jokes
on the subject of the Immaculate Conception, it being the even of that
festival.

[3] The works of Ford and General Motors in Barcelona may be quoted.

There was a reign of terror, just as there was in other towns. Each street was combed and practically all the well-to-do were shot. The rough rule appears to have been this: that anyone who had employed a servant in his house or more than two workers in his business, had merited death. There were exceptions; not many.

The purpose of this book is to describe the defence of the Alcazar and only to give such information as may be necessary for the understanding of the story. Yet, as it must give some picture of events in Toledo during these weeks, two cases, in different classes of society, are here recorded; both being typical and both being known to the author.

Señor Mariano Miedes was one of those Toledans who threw in their lot with the military and so became part of the garrison of the Alcazar. He came of a well-known Toledan business family. He was a man in the mid-thirties. His father was a Traditionalist. One of his sisters had helped to organize concerts for that party. His four brothers did not interest themselves in politics.

During the siege of the Alcazar members of the Frente Popular, in uniform, called at his father's house and asked him what were his political sympathies. The old man, who had strong views but only a feeble voice, replied that he stood "For God. For King. For Country." [1] He was taken into the street and shot.

The ration cards of his family were then taken away. For some time they starved, for no one dared to give them food. Then the sister went to the Government Food Control office. There she met her death in a way too horrible to be described. At intervals of a few days her four brothers were shot.

When I met him some three weeks after the Alcazar had been relieved, Mariano Miedes had not then recovered from

[1] This being the well-known motto of the Traditionalists, or Carlists.

starvation and what he had been through, but was about to leave for the front. He was one of those who helped me with the material for this book. I have his permission to publish these details.

The other example is from a very different sort of household.

In the early 'eighties a young peasant and his wife opened a little restaurant on the low ground outside the town. After many years they had saved enough to rebuild their venta. Three years before the summer of the siege, the Venta des Aires celebrated its fiftieth anniversary; two years later the family bought a motor car, to fetch provisions from the town.

The military revolt broke out. The Workers' Militia came in their buses from Madrid. They learned their way about the town. The old lady has told me often how "the Reds" called at the venta—took the old man out—he was eighty-three, and shot him on a rubbish heap.

In telling this story of the Venta des Aires the old lady has been allowed to speak of "the Reds." Throughout this book the word has been avoided, simply because in some circles it might be thought to carry a derogatory sense. Actually "the Reds" was the only name by which the Government forces were ever spoken of, either by the people of Toledo or by the garrison of the Alcazar. Nor would this have been resented by them. For they daubed their sickles and their hammers on all the buildings they occupied; they fought under red flags; they wore red shirts or sashes when they could find them; they scrawled "Up the Reds!" beside the loopholes they defended.

The Internationalism of the Government in Madrid led to an old and incongruous situation. For, as "Rebels" went into battle with the cry "Viva España!", it became treason to use the phrase among the Government forces. But, as to scrawl up catch-phrases seems a human need, "Viva Rusia!" took its place. For example, it was painted in blood by Government troops upon an outbuilding of the Alcazar, as elsewhere. The photograph I took of it is given on Plate 29.

This leads directly to a matter which must soon be decided. In civil wars names must be found for the opposing sides. By all means let the Government remain "the Government." Indeed within the Alcazar, in orders and official use, the besiegers were properly and punctiliously referred to as "the forces of the Government." But, as the supporters of General Franco's cause disliked the name of "Rebels" or "Insurgents"; and as the Government in Madrid had preferred "internationalism" to "nationalism," the forces of General Franco will be called, in chapters that follow this, "The Nationalists."

Two things I must repeat; that this book sets out to tell nothing more than the defence of the Alcazar and such other events as directly concern it; and that, though the Government in Madrid must be held responsible for faults in its general policy, it would be unfair to blame it for such excesses as its supporters committed in Toledo.

THE TWENTY-SIXTH OF AUGUST

The day was quiet until towards noon. Then three planes approached from the west. They had no distinguishing marks but it was soon clear that they belonged to the Nationalist columns. For they began bombing the positions of the besiegers, flying low and choosing their targets with care. Some bombs were dropped over the gun positions, both those on the Dehesa de Pinedo and on the Campimento; some along the lines in San Servando, across the river; some on the detachments resting in the olive groves; and lastly on the Arms Factory.

Having dropped all their bombs the planes flew away. But

their visit must have at once been reported to Madrid. For in less than an hour two Government planes appeared, made a reconnaissance over all the ground which the Nationalist planes had bombed, were cheered, and flew away northwards.

Just before sundown, when the light was still good and the air so clear that the most distant mountains fifty or sixty miles away could be seen, some groups of men were observed very far away, on the high ground beside the road to Avile. These were taken to be observation posts of the Government forces, on the lookout for the vanguard of the Nationalist columns which might by now have progressed almost to that point. Their whereabouts were not exactly known by the garrison of the Alcazar, as the extemporized wireless receiving-set had not been so satisfactory for the last night or two.

At dusk a sortie was made by some officers and men from the Capuchinos to houses on the farther side of the Corralillo. This had been carefully planned and the moment chosen was one when the garrisons of these houses had been seen leaving them and strolling past the corner of an alley near by. The raiders by keeping close to the sides of the buildings were unseen. They scaled the garden walls of several houses and brought back a large quantity of fresh figs.

On this day there were no casualties.

THE TWENTY-SEVENTH OF AUGUST

At 7 a.m. the "155" guns again opened fire upon the north façade. Their fire was accurate and the damage was great. The upper tier of columns on that side of the courtyard had fallen. The gallery, on the edge of which they had stood, was cracked and likely to fall. In the long pauses, when the garrison waited for the arrival of the next shell, large sections of masonry, already loosened, would come crashing down. Survivors of the siege say that these unexpected falls of stone-work, tumbling as it seemed of their own volition, were far more alarming than the bursting of the shells. For they infected all with the doleful impression that the whole fabric of the Alcazar would presently collapse.

Soon after 8 a.m. the battery of "75's" joined in the bombardment and thereafter kept up an accompaniment of smaller explosions in the intervals between the rending crashes of the "155" shell-bursts.

From dusk till midnight there was neither artillery nor riflefire. Silence had descended upon the enemy. All that could be heard was the Tagus sighing in the gorge below, and from the far south-west corner of the Alcazar the muffled but ceaseless rattle of the drills.

Throughout the day there had been little rifle and machinegun fire but the need of rebuilding barricades and of keeping a constant lookout had remained, and the performance of these duties had led to there being more casualties than of late; those for the day amounting to one dead and five wounded.

THE TWENTY-EIGHTH OF AUGUST

The morning began with the usual rifle and machine-gun fire.

Soon after 11 a.m. the "155" guns began their daily bombardment. It was slow and deliberate. It was continued without any interval until 5.30 p.m.

In six and a half hours, guns of this size, working from so near a range that their fire is always accurate, and with a target on which they can see the burst of every shell, can inflict enormous damage. When the day's bombardment was over, the two corner towers were standing; and some twenty yards of the façade nearest the north-west tower. But, apart from this, all that remained of the whole north side of the Alcazar was a great shapeless rampart of dust and broken masonry, not more than a quarter of the building's original height. Seen from the interior of the courtyard the destruction seemed almost more noticeable than from the outside, because more details of the architecture had survived. For instance, at the north-west corner most of the lower arches of the gallery were still standing. These in ruin have the beauty of a Piranesi drawing. And their symmetry made the destruction elsewhere seem more sorrowful. Columns had fallen. Segments of the arches lay heaped upon each other. The gallery had crumbled to the ground. Behind all this, to about the level of where the first floor had been, rose the heap of wreckage, which still formed some defensive barrier against the enemy. From it dust and fragments had invaded all that side of the courtyard.

Meanwhile, during this bombardment, two "75's" from the old castle of San Servando had opened fire upon the House-of-the-Military-Government and upon the Esplanade. The shells were small and the damage they did to the corner of this building was not important; where in any case most of the rooms had already been wrecked. But the "grazing" fire of these guns across the Esplanade swept everything before it. The cars and lorries of the Guardia Civil were smashed and set alight. The doors of the fire-engine shed were blown in and much of its contents damaged. The Curved Passage was holed in several places. The dwarf acacias, cut down by the shells, added to the desolation; and meant the loss of leaves for cigarettes.

To deal with these two guns the same steps were taken as had been used on previous occasions. Rifle-men and the few machine-guns which could be assembled were posted in all windows on this side of the Alcazar, and in the Arab battle-mented gallery half-way up its wall. Then at a pre-arranged signal, a sudden and rapid fire was opened on San Servando. This concentration overwhelmed the enemy's gunners. They bolted for cover. They did not return to their guns till after dark. When the next day broke they had removed these to a safer place.

Throughout the afternoon there was much confused rifle-fire against the south face of the Alcazar and glimpses were caught of movement in that district. No development followed. If the enemy had intended an attack from that side, nothing came of it.

The day closed without further event. Soon after dark another sortie of the garrison from the Capuchinos brought in some much-needed salt.

THE TWENTY-NINTH OF AUGUST

The morning of these days were hot and still and frequently the observation posts high in the towers of the Alcazar reported that they heard the sound of distant battle.

The view seen from these towers was immense. Northward, westward and southward the plain stretched in long low billows, almost without variation, almost without interruption. There were no abrupt slopes, no wood, no hedge, no line of trees to check the vibrations and to arrest the travel of sound. The air upon these uplands of Castile is very clear and thin. So on such a morning a voice calling can be heard at three miles away and the sound of a rifle-shot at five. Yet, though all the observation posts reported the sound of very distant gun-fire and of explosions, and noted down the time when these were heard, the times never agreed, and no certain inference could be drawn. Nothing so far could be seen or heard of those columns which were fighting their way across this vast expanse to relieve the Alcazar. Yet the knowledge that they were there, behind those immensely distant ridges, gave hope.

At 9.15 a.m. the "155's" began their usual bombardment of

the ruins of the north façade. Then they turned their attention to the Capuchinos.

At 10.30 a.m., when the bombardment ended, it would have seemed impossible that the roofless and gutted walls of the Capuchinos could still have been of any military importance. It was a building of the 'eighties and was less able to stand such punishment than had been the great north façade which Covarrubias had planned and set up four hundred years before. The walls of the Capuchinos stood gaunt and empty, for few direct hits had been made upon them. But the roofs and floors were gone and a confusion of bricks and bedsteads, half-burnt rafters, clothing and machinery, had drained down into the bottom of the building. Indeed the main part of the Capuchinos had almost ceased to be defensible and only the wing which jutted out southward remained of military value. Here, under the gutted husk of the three storeys above, was a vaulted basement, used as the laundry of the Academy. This had windows which would enfilade any enemy advance across the Corralillo. It remained intact.

Towards five o'clock the "155's" began another bombardment of the north façade. But as there was nothing left to destroy, their fire seemed wasted.

At 6.30 this bombardment by the heavy guns ended.

Dusk was calm but soon after dark the enemy developed a new form of attack upon the House-of-the-Military Government; a form which it was so impossible for the garrison to resist that, had it been persisted in and followed up at once with strength, it would probably have resulted in the capture of the Alcazar.

The garrison in Stable No. 4 were doing no more than keeping up their lookout. In the late twilight, with a suddenness which hardly anything else can produce, a shell struck the wall just outside one of the windows, and burst. Its explosion and the report of the gun which had fired it, appeared simultaneous. Everyone in the Stable stood to arms. Then a second shell exploded against the grating of the window. Till now this part of the building had never been shelled, for it was hidden from the enemy's gun positions and was so close to the Santa Cruz that shelling it from his eastern gun position, beyond the river, would have been dangerous to his own troops in that building.

It was by now realized where the gun must be which had fired these shells. The window and portion of wall which had been struck, looked down upon the road separating the eastern end of the Santa Cruz from the now half-ruined block of houses below it and nearer the river. This road was not more than eighty yards long; at the end of it were two big arched doors leading into the Convent of La Concepcion. Behind one of these the "75" field-gun had been brought into position. This must have been done during the day. Then at dusk a single panel of the door had been knocked out, and through this narrow hole the gun had been fired.[1] At such a range the gun could blow to pieces the garrison of any of the windows it could reach. Against it no defence was possible.

The arc of fire of this gun was limited, for it could fire only down the road in front of it. Yet were its fire kept up, a twenty- or thirty-yard length of the House-of-the-Military-Government would inevitably collapse, and leave a breach in the wall of Stable No. 4.

Large numbers of men could be assembled under cover in the little square just south of La Concepcion. Passing round both sides of the block of half-ruined buildings, they could dash for the breach created by the gun. The distance to it would not have exceeded fifty yards. Some of the windows upon which the defence depended would have ceased to exist. The remaining ones could have been smothered with covering fire from machine-guns in the Santa Cruz.

Had this field-gun been supplied with a liberal stock of ammunition, it could certainly have made such a breach in two

[1] See Plate 30.

hours and left Stable No. 4 open to assault. Once the Stable had been taken, the detachments in the upper end of the House-of-the-Military-Government would have been cut off. They could then have been attacked, both from the Santa Cruz, and by bombers and rifle-men working their way through the building from Stable No. 4, its basement. Attacked from front and rear it is hardly possible that they could at the same time have held back attacks upon the Stable Approach. Presumably this would have been taken and then the way would have lain open, up the Zig-Zag, to the north terrace of the Alcazar.

There, under cover of the terrace wall, any number of men could have been massed for an assault upon the hundred-yard-wide breach, where the north façade had once stood.

None of these opportunities would have required very skilled leadership or previous training. The gun was already in action. There should have been no real difficulty in bringing together two, or even three thousand rifle-men of sorts. Had this been done the Alcazar might have been taken by storm before the sun rose.

It was not done. It may be that whoever had brought his field-gun into such an admirable position had forgotten to bring more than a dozen rounds of ammunition for it. It may be that the Government forces had not discipline enough, or their commander authority enough, to have made such an assault possible. In any case it was only something of this sort which saved the garrison of the Alcazar on that critical night.

VACANCES PAYÉES

The storming of Badajos staggered the Government in Madrid.

Wellington, with twenty-one thousand men and a siege train

of fifty-two pieces, had taken eighteen days to capture the town. Yagüe and Castajón, with just over three thousand men and four field-guns, had stormed it after less than three days; in the face of a defending force nearly three times their own number, and of approximately the same strength as the garrison which had held Wellington.[1]

The Government in Madrid had counted on the Nationalists' columns being held up for several weeks. They had not, and the Government braced itself for fresh efforts. But before it could act the Nationalist columns had pushed on again. Badajos had been stormed on the 14th. The street-fighting is reported to have lasted for thirty hours. Yet it is said that on the morning of the 16th the leading troops started back upon their tracks. Off they went, and slipped again out of the knowledge of the world.

Their force was a very small one, lost in the vastness of the rolling Spanish landscape and under the immensity of the Spanish sky. The month was August, the heat intense. The villages are very far apart. There are no trees, no shade. The column had come out of three days' fighting and the storming of a town. Away on their flank, at Caceres, a strong enemy force was said to be waiting for them. But somewhat over two hundred miles away there was Toledo, and its Alcazar.

It is said that on the 18th of August the columns slept at Merida—forty miles away from Badajos.

It is said that on the night of the 22nd, having brushed aside fugitives from Badajos and detachments sent to help them, they reached Trujillo; where their Moorish troops may have looked with wonder at the statue of Pizarro, the conquistador, native of that town.

The stage which followed must have been a difficult one. They had to pass a gap in the Sierra de San Pedro; they had to cross the Tagus, here wide and stately; they had to reckon with

[1] Their force is said to have been doubled shortly after the gates had been taken.

the flying column on their flank. Speed was essential. They chanced the dangers and rushed the difficulties.

It is said that on the evening of the 27th of August they were at Navalmoral, having fought perhaps a dozen small engagements and covered fifty miles in five days.

In any case, on the 29th of August, thirteen days after they had disappeared from the knowledge of the world, at Badajos, they reappeared at Oropesa, one hundred and fifty miles away by road.

The dates and details of the march from Andalusia to Toledo, are as yet uncertain; two things are sure; that Castajón's column was at Zafra on the 7th of August—for I know two British ex-officers who joined it at that place and on that date; and that it was at Oropesa three weeks later—for that was announced by General Franco's wireless and was eventually admitted by broadcasts from Madrid. In those three weeks the column advanced some two hundred and fifty miles; captured Badajos and fought a score of minor actions.

But at Oropesa the situation changed, for they found themselves face to face with a force greatly larger than their own, which blocked the road leading to Toledo and Madrid. Here Varela's advance came to a standstill, and it was now time to consider the general situation.

Both sides were fighting on several fronts and in the world's Press the front of Irun completely overshadowed the far more vital front where Varela's march had been checked. The reason for this is plain. There were no war correspondents within a hundred miles of Oropesa; nor would they have been welcomed by either side. The fighting at Irun, on the other hand, was within a mile of the French frontier and could be watched from French soil, and with the facilities of an uncensored telephone and cable service.

The fighting for Irun was spectacular and grim, but it had no great effect upon the war as a whole. Indeed, when Irun fell, all that the Government in Spain lost was the railway which gave them the most direct communications with their Paris supporters and sympathizers.

The front at Oropesa was a very different matter. Were it to collapse, the road would lie open for the Nationalists, not only to Toledo, but to Madrid itself. The Oropesa front was vital and troops could reach Talavera, on which the Government forces in this sector were based, by motor-coach from Madrid, in three hours. Every available man and gun was rushed there. Appeals were made for volunteers. They were given rifles, blue boiler suits. They were packed into motor-coaches and sent off to the front to the accompaniment of wild enthusiasm.

The columns which the Government massed at Talavera de la Reina were strong in numbers and equipment but they were badly staffed and badly officered. They had at least some Regular officers but these were diminishing in numbers. For their loyalty was never completely trusted; their advice was followed only when palatable; and, in case of reverse, they were apt to be held responsible and shot. As for the rank and file, it consisted of these Madrid volunteers, stiffened by a few men of the Regular Army, and by such Guardia Civil as had not wished, or had not been able, to throw in their lot with the counter-revolution. The volunteers were banded into companies; some according to their trades, some according to their district of Madrid, some according to their political views; Marxists, Syndicalists, Anarchists. They were brave, enthusiastic, in holiday mood, ready for anything.

Now in France the Front Populaire Government had just decreed the vacances payées for workers—holidays for all, to be paid by the employers. In Spain, too, it was the season of holidays. Madrid was intolerably hot. Pavements burned the feet. No shade! What could be more pleasant than a country holiday? Here was the Government offering holidays for any who cared to take them; all found; with a nice new suit of blue overalls, a cap with an embroidered badge, five pesetas a day, and a spice of excitement. And would they not be helping a noble cause—the defence of freedom and democracy? The thing was too good to be missed. The volunteers flocked to join up.

There was no tedious drilling, no irksome discipline. The volunteers were given their rifles and ammunition; they climbed into the waiting coaches. Off they went, singing, shouting, waving to passers-by. Piled inside the guard-rails on the roof was an incoherent mass of their possessions; mattresses they had brought with them, or looted for the occasion; suitcases daubed with their names and the initials of their political party; travelling-trunk; fruit and vegetables, picked up on the way; baskets of bread, cases of canned provisions; skins of wine.

Off they went, with red flags fluttering from wings and radiators. Inside, upon their knees, gramophones or "portables" made music for them.

The road to Talavera is superb; wide, straight, flowing on over the naked billows of the Castilian plain. It runs through dusty villages, past groves of twisted pale-leaved olive trees, under the walls of crumbling amber-coloured castles. New country! And few of them can have seen any before.

There was bread and raw ham, wine, prawns and barnacles, fruit cheeses, marzipan, free cigarettes. Time of their lives! Viva Communism! Syndicalism! Anarchy! Viva freedom and democracy!

Nearly all were young. They were inspired by words. They were fighting, as they well knew, for truth, progress and a new world.

But they were townsmen, never at home when out of sight of pavements. Once they left their coaches the bareness of Castile seemed desolation to them. They clung to villages. To hold a trench outside one seemed banishment. Even in flight, with all the empty hills and olive-groves to hide in, they ran along the roads; they ran along the roads and aeroplanes swooped down and slaughtered them.

Such troops are not easy to control. They are impossible to manœuvre. To get a company of them onto their feet is hard, at least when there is straw to lie on and cigarettes to smoke. A few get up. The rest sigh and look away. Then, as some more get up, those who were on their feet have looked round, and have sat down again. Yet, place such men behind a wall or barricade, put rifles and ammunition in their hands, and they will fight Satan and all his fiends.

The Government commanders used these troops in what was probably the only way. For the Nationalists speed was essential; or the Alcazar would fall. Therefore, to delay their advance, every village on the road must be held; walls loopholed, trenches dug, guns brought into position.

To take these villages, with the little artillery and few shells, must entail loss of time and life. The Nationalists had training, but they were few.

General Varela's columns, brought to a halt at Oropesa, probably had not more than eight or nine thousand men, all told. They were "in the air," with no certain line of communications, and no reserve of arms or stores. But they were fresh from dazzling achievements and they had victory in their eyes.

I have seen such a column on the march and it is right that such a one should be described.

Ahead comes as scout, an improvised armoured car, captured from the enemy: a space: three or four touring cars with legionaries and machine-guns: another space: then the main body, a main body carried in the strangest fleet of motor-coaches that it is possible to imagine. They have been impressed where found and are gaily coloured, in peasant and small-town taste; scarlet, white, bright blue, orange, apple green, purple, pink. They are packed with armed men. Forty coaches of legionaries: forty coaches of Moors: eight lorries of ammunition, perhaps with two field-guns in them: another forty coaches of legion-

PLATE 19

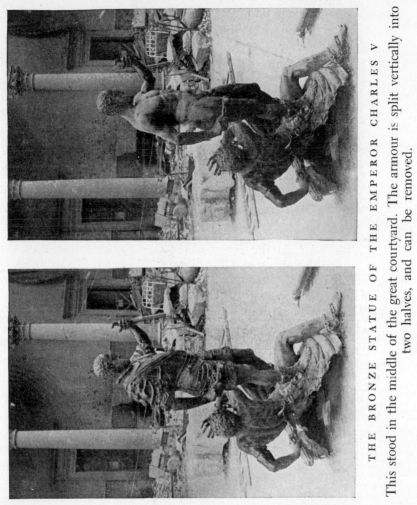

THE BRONZE STATUE OF THE EMPEROR CHARLES V

This stood in the middle of the great courtyard. The armour is split vertically into two halves, and can be removed.

PLATE 20

THE RAMP

This led from the House-of-the-Military-Government to the
Esplanade terrace and the Alcazar. High left is the wrecked
dining-hall. In the middle of the photograph is a niche, an
enlargement of which is seen below.

AN ENLARGEMENT OF THE NICHE

The plaque represents the Blessed Virgin of the Alcazar and
its preservation was regarded as a miracle.

aries: a wireless signal wagon, hastily contrived; an ambulance or two: a tank-wagon for motor spirit: a touring car with machine-guns trained to the rear.

Upon the roofs of all the coaches is the baggage; mattresses of every colour—for the Spaniard who will fight starving and unpaid, hates to lie hard; bundles in counterpanes, in women's shawls, in gay striped blankets; valises, items of loot—for of all the world's looters the Moor is king;[1] a coop of hens; a parrot in a cage; a nanny-goat in milk; a net of melons; then, perhaps on every twentieth roof-top, three men lounging beside an anti-aircraft gun, cocked skyward, ready to fire.

Fastened to the radiators are religious mascots; a crucifix found in a wrecked church; a Blessed Virgin with crown of cracker jewels—and perhaps beside her, placed there without a thought of irreverence or incongruity, a Mickey Mouse.

The legionaries are in khaki shirts, short-sleeved, with gilt-embroidered badges on black tabs, with bandoliers, slung rifles, tasselled glengarry caps of khaki drill. They have taut faces, burnt with the sun, plastered with white dust. They are fit, alert, confident, conscious of being masters of their trade, certain of victory; and, knowing that, cheerful and gay.

The Moors are solemn and patient. Sometimes at this or that unusual sight they may be momentarily curious. They are as a rule not much darker than the Spaniards, but there is a certain grey or yellow tinge under the dry walnut pigment of their skin. They are shanky, hollow-cheeked, sinewy. They are polite. They seldom smile. They walk softly, and with the forward thrust of animals that live dangerously. They wear the baggy trousers of their corps, turbans, and open tunic-shirts.

In battle the legionaries advance in those short baffling rushes which only the finest infantry, once down, will rise to, when under fire. The Moors in battle work upon their stomachs and wriggle forward at a reptilian speed. "In-bussed," upon the line of route, they sit huddled in their blanket-like burnouses; for,

[1] Looter, that is, of abandoned villages.

when not active, they seem always cold.

The tactics of such a column had been devised to suit the
conditions of this campaign. The enemy had always the advantage of numbers; but no knowledge, little skill, no final
steadiness. For the Nationalists, therefore, the game was bluff;
audacity, manœuvre; speed. And the battle was every time the
same.

The leading armoured car breasts a rise. The road stretches
on, grey asphalt powdered with dust, and on each side emptiness. A mile ahead there is a village; one-storeyed, mud-walled,
clustering around a lofty dusty Baroque church. The armoured
car slows and sends back a signal. There are two flashes from
the village, bright even in the sunlight. Guns! The village
held! Ah!

Two shells sing. They burst high overhead. The armoured
car stops. Its driver finds reverse. The car drones slowly back
behind the skyline. The plain is empty once again; stubble,
dry maize, scorched prairie, rolling land the colour of a lion's
mane, stupendous distances, a range of hills, coral pink and
far away; horizon; blue sky; silence.

Behind the slope the coaches close up and stop. The legionaries are out. The Moors are out. The plan is ready; "Sealed
Pattern Order of Attack"—to meet—"Sealed Pattern Village
with Sealed Pattern Order of Defence." A little party with machine-guns doubles out, clears the road, and makes ready to
advance, astride it. A battalion with its machine-guns is doubling out into the empty land that stretches for ever to the
left. Another battalion is doubling out upon the other side,
into the emptiness that stretches to the right. The battalion in
reserve—"less the party with machine-guns on the road"—takes
position, scattered in little groups. The wireless in a lorry has
reported and is calling for planes.

Now the empty coaches are all in reverse, creeping back cautiously, clear of the fight. The anti-aircraft guns are ready, wait-

ing. The commander of the force draws near behind the hill-crest, and with him goes a little group of men with field-glasses.

The word is given. The centre party with its machine-guns breaks cover over the ridge and, well extended, goes forward on each side of the road; cautious but never checking. For some time they continue on their way. The field-guns on the village fringe bark at them. Two shells burst overhead. Then all at once the mud walls of the village blaze with rifle and machine-gun fire; and from the trenches, scraped in the fields on left and right, and up till now unseen, a furious fusillade begins. The men of the centre party throw themselves down. Their machine-guns come into action.

For half-an-hour the air whistles with bullets. Once or twice the commander of the columns crawls to the crest line of the ridge, to see that everything is progressing according to plan. To left and right the flanking battalions have trotted out. Now they are a mile, or more, outside the farthest trenches of the enemy. They face "front" again, and order their advance, so as to pass a mile wide on each side of the village. The town-bred volunteers catch sight of them and, after shouting and pointing, bring their rifles round. The range is fifteen hundred yards. At this distance such rifle-men are hardly dangerous. The bullets sing overhead. Now and then one falls short, flicks up the dust and goes by, humming.

The advance goes on round either flank. Now the machine-guns in the village cannot fire at the advancing troops, who are already too far round for them. The volunteers within the village look about them, wondering what will happen next. Planes have been called for by their commander, also. But in an army of eager amateurs messages arrive, or not, according to their luck. The gunners on the village fringe grow restless. Guns are not rifles; they are valuable! They clank the drop-fronts of their ammunition limbers shut. Presently they begin man-handling the guns out of position. The rifle-men hear that sound. So the guns are off? Some fire faster. Some look about them. A few slink back.

Now the flanking battalions of the Nationalists can see clear behind the village. They halt, lie down, make ready their machine-guns.

In the village all is confusion. The Marxists have gone into committee. Syndicalists are keeping up their fire. Anarchists favour a forward movement and a charge, at any cost. But soon the less courageous of the militia-men are slinking back. Someone tries to stop them. An argument ensues, bitter, wordy. Others come up and take part in it. Someone in comparative authority forms up a party and starts it off towards the rear. But at such times a formed body moving rearward is like a magnet. Stragglers dribble out after it. Presently the exit of the village is like the exit of a cinema, after the show is done. The militia-men trot away. Some motors in the village are sounding horns, perhaps to rally the troops, perhaps to get the road clear for themselves. Presently the retreat is general; and in no order at all. Three, four, five thousand men; all keeping to the asphalt road which runs ahead of them, over the naked countryside.

Out on the flanks are the Nationalist machine-gunners. They have been waiting long for this. They open fire. Their bullets intersect upon the road, at a spot perhaps half-a-mile behind the village. The volunteers' retreat becomes a rout, and all press on, but no man can pass the zone beaten by the machine-guns' fire. Those near the front of the retreating crowd halt and recoil from the corpses of their comrades, lying in the road; those behind press forward, clamouring. There comes a moment when the surging mass bursts forward like a flood. It forms the perfect target. Two of the guns keep up their cross-fire. The others traverse. The militia-men go down like dry thistles before a scythe. At last they realize the road is death. They scatter from it, out into the fields. There they are lost indeed; no pavements!

Four planes come droning up from the south. They part

and swing wide from the village, two on each side of it. Flying
low, they drop some little bombs, well on the flanks of the
scattered militia-men. They circle round, closing in, dropping
their bombs, shepherding these townsmen back to the road
again. The leaders of the rout take to the asphalt. The going
is easier. They have dropped their rifles; they struggle out of
bandoliers and toss them aside. They are out of breath. They
jostle each other as they run. They keep to the road. When
they are thick enough, the planes wheel round and swoop low,
machine-gunning them. The pursuit goes on till there seems
nothing left worth chasing. For two, three, perhaps four miles
the road is dotted with dead and dying.

Behind the village the centre detachment of the Nationalists
has closed, and packed its machine-guns. Already it is in its
coaches. The flanking battalions are legging it, back across the
open land to where their transport waits for them. The legionaries come to their coaches. Sometimes, passing a saint or
Blessed Virgin on a radiator, they will touch the medallions
dangling outside their shirts, or cross themselves. They climb
back into the coaches and they settle down. Ready!

Two hours and twenty minutes' delay! A dozen casualties
among the legionaries and Moors. Another set-piece engage-
ment. Another six hundred militia-men less to fight. Always
the same!

Not quite always, for sometimes the Government commander, farther back, will rush up another motorized column
to retrieve the day. The men will "de-buss" and come forward
with a ragged valour, in a counter attack which would daunt
Regular troops. The legionaries will extend again, a little
wearily, lie flat and mow them down with fire. The delay will
be longer. There will be another half-dozen casualties among
the Nationalists. A coach will somehow be set on fire. And in
the end, when the counter-attack is broken, there will be another five hundred militia-men who will not fight again.

The column forms up. The coaches are ready now; scarlet, white, bright blue, orange, apple green, purple, pink; like a variegated paper streamer stretched incongruously across this tawny field of war.

The armoured cars move on, stopping sometimes to clear the road of dead and dying militia-men. They pull the bodies to the side and leave them. There they will lie for weeks, horrible, worried by dogs at night, stinking in the sunlight. The column moves on and leaves them. Toledo and the Alcazar are still a hundred miles away, and the little Army of Africa has neither men nor time enough to bury dead.

THE THIRTIETH OF AUGUST

In spite of opportunities which the field-gun in La Concepcion had offered, no enemy attack was made during the night. But the commander of the defence had another matter which troubled him. So great was the damage done by recent bombardments that he felt it necessary in some way to reassure the garrison.

The north façade no longer existed and shells passing over the ruins of it had been bursting within the three remaining sides of the building. The destruction caused by these had been enormous. The galleries were crumbling and columns had fallen like ninepins. Pieces of balustrade and broken cornice, tiles and segments of fallen arches lay everywhere heaped in confusion, stained yellow by high explosives, and here and there blackened by incendiary bombs. The sight of all this could not fail to have its effect upon the morale of the garrison. Hour by hour, day by day, they had watched one side of the Alcazar being knocked to pieces. In a fortnight's time how much of the building would be left? Officers have said that this impression of the coming dissolution of the whole building was so strong that it was hard to put it out of mind.[1]

A reasoned statement was therefore drawn up and issued, pointing out to the garrison:—that though the damage was certainly spectacular, it was in truth more apparent than real; that the enemy would find it more difficult to assault the slippery glacis of dust and rubble which he had made, than he would have to storm the gateway which now lay buried beneath it; that in any case he had no means of trying this, for he had been completely unable to break through the outer line of defence; that though stone ornaments and fine rooms had been demolished, this had been but a waste of time and ammunition; that the defence depended, not upon such things, but upon the strength and spirit of the garrison; that in spite of hours of bombardment and endless rifle-fire, the casualties of the previous day had been only two wounded; that the relief columns were drawing nearer day by day; that if all were of good courage, there was no doubt that they could hold out till these columns arrived.

This statement, prepared during the night, seems to have been circulated early in the following day, and was explained by the officers to all members of the garrison.

During the early morning enemy planes were sighted in the distance but these were bound southward and did not come towards Toledo. Later more were seen, this time in the southwest and flying in the direction of Talavera de la Reina.

Soon after 10 a.m. the enemy guns on the hills across the river opened fire upon the various buildings of the riding-school terrace, and continued until noon.

At 1 p.m., an hour when there was normally little activity, the enemy in the Santa Cruz delivered a surprise attack upon the Stable Approach. The posts defending the Approach were

[1] See Plates 10 and 22.

on the alert and opened fire at once, but the enemy succeeded in dousing with petrol the walls and doorways, and also the barricades and the iron gates which were some way inside the Stable Approach, and which till then he had never been able to reach.

The enemy then set light to the petrol by throwing bombs. The fire spread and became dangerous. Reserves were rushed down from the Alcazar and with them parties carrying extinguishers and water; the latter having been taken from supplies too foul to drink, and having been kept in readiness.

The enemy attempted with hand-bombs and rifle-fire to drive away the parties trying to extinguish the blaze, and increased it by throwing more petrol. Meanwhile from the Alcazar itself some machine-gun fire was brought to bear. The reserves who had come down to the Stable Approach engaged the enemy with sub-machine-guns. For some time the fusillade continued. The enemy had the advantage of a large supply of bombs. Keeping close to the walls and out of sight behind corners, his men were able to throw their bombs and canisters of petrol. The men of the garrison, equally, had orders not to show themselves, and so the contest round the entrance to the Stable Approach was conducted with much noise of bursting bombs and rattle of sub-machine-guns, but with few casualties.

Eventually the fire of the garrison reserves made it too dangerous for the enemy to appear even for an instant at a corner. Realizing this, his men withdrew to the Santa Cruz, covered by fire from its upper windows.

A lull followed.

Soon after 3 p.m. the enemy's "155's" opened fire upon the north-east tower. There seems to have been little military gain in shelling the towers but he persisted in this until the very end of the siege. By intensive bombardment three of the towers were ultimately brought down, while the fourth was blown to fragments by the explosion of the mines.

The evening was quiet and the garrison did everything possible to repair the damage done to the defences of the Stable Approach.

The casualties on this day amounted to four wounded.

THE JOY-RIDERS

There is one incident of the siege—bizarre, absurd, tragic, un-related in any way to the rest of the story. I do not know at what exact period it took place but I will set it down here.

The Quarters-of-the-Soldiers, it will be remembered, stood sheer out of the slopes above the Tagus. Below this building, along the slopes, was a rough track which ran diagonally and which slowly mounted from the river to the farther corner of the Corralillo.[1] There, just below the end of this wide-open space, is an ancient, dusty cottage round which are sheds with tanks and such-like in them; and which notices announce to be the Municipal disinfecting station.

The slopes out of which the Quarters-of-the-Soldiers rises are so steep that this track, passing half-way down them, is hidden even from the upper windows. But a few yards farther on, the track rounds a little bluff and comes suddenly into full view of the building.

It is a rough road, but a motor-car, bouncing somewhat, can mount and remain unseen, from the river to the point where it passes this bluff. There, just where the car comes into view from the windows above, the gradient eases, and the car can gain speed and in thirty seconds reach the disinfecting station and disappear from view.

On the day in question a friend of mine, a man in the early thirties, a Toledan and one of the Falangistas of the garrison, was on duty in the Quarters-of-the-Soldiers. With five or six others he was responsible for those corner windows which

[1] This track can be made out on Plate 39.

overlooked the Corralillo and dominated the slopes below it to
the river. These windows, though never a possible target for
enemy artillery, were almost constantly assailed by bursts of
machine-gun and rifle-fire.[1] They were occupied, therefore,
only in time of emergency; though a ceaseless look-out was kept
and there were always defenders at hand ready to man them in
case of the slightest sign of enemy activity.

On this morning my friend was near one of these windows,
but was not on sentry duty. Suddenly from round the corner of
the bluff below there appeared a small black saloon car, the distance to it being not more than sixty yards. It was bouncing
along the track towards the disinfecting station and out of its
window a large red flag was being waved. It might have been
the vanguard of an enemy attack, massed in the dead ground
on the slopes. In any case no motor-car could be there, unless
an enemy, for the ground it was now accelerating across had
been a no-man's-land for weeks.

The sentry shouted the alarm: the windows were manned: a
rapid rifle-fire was brought to bear. The car stopped with a
jerk: the door on the farther side flew open: the driver sprang
out and without looking round leaped down over the edge of
the slopes at his side and disappeared. These slopes are steep
but anyone jumping on to them could stop himself before he
had rolled ten or fifteen yards.

There was an instant's pause. Then the door on the side of
the Quarters-of-the-Soldiers opened. A girl slid out, staggered
a few steps and fell. The men at the windows had ceased fire.
They waited. For a few moments the girl's arms twitched.
Then she lay still.

Nothing further happened. The man had got away, the girl
was dead. The day passed. The sun beat down upon the body
lying beside the track. It never moved. The day ended. Twilight crept up the valley. The body lay there, still beside the

[1] A glance at Plate 17 will show how the brickwork round the windows
has been eaten into by the constant impact of bullets.

car. There was no chance of rescue, for it was in full view of the enemy's line. Colours faded. Beyond the splutter of enemy's machine-guns was the evening quiet of the plain.

The moon rose. The body lay there, like a dark stain on the track. The rats came out to sniff around. Presently they began to nibble at the hands. My friend has told me with what disgust he and his companions watched. They opened fire. The rats scattered. After a time they came back, threading their way through the shadows. The men at the windows fired again. They killed one rat, the others scattered; only to return.

The moon was near full. Night after night the rats came back to feed upon their own dead and upon the body. To the garrison of the corner windows the sight grew intolerable. They made a sortie and with a tin of petrol tried to burn the body. They failed but the flames spread, the car caught fire and burned fiercely. The blaze drew down a fusillade of rifle-fire upon the windows of the Quarters-of-the-Soldiers. The blaze died out. For a time the reek of burnt rubber hung on the stillness of the night. Presently that lessened and they could smell the corpse again.

The moon waned. But even then, while the sky is clear, star-light reflected from the Tagus prevents the darkness in the gorge from being absolute. Then there was a cloudy night. For hours the track and the burnt-out car were visible. At dawn the body which had lain beside it was gone.

There is no explanation of this incident. There could have been no military purpose in driving the car along this track. Presumably the thing was done out of pure bravado. The young man at the wheel had wanted to show his girl friend what sort he was. He judged badly. The garrison was alert.

Was it he who came back for her body?

The burnt-out car was there for months. It was a Peugot. Its Spanish registration number was M.54269; maker's chassis number 377006—type 301 D. There are the data for any who may wish to solve the riddle that the story sets.

THE THIRTY-FIRST OF AUGUST

The early part of the day was quiet, though it could be seen that preparations were being made in the enemy batteries and that large supplies of ammunition were being brought up.

At 4 p.m. a fresh sally was made from the Santa Cruz against the Stable Approach. This time the enemy adopted another form of attack; instead of trying to set fire to the buildings and the barricades at the gates, he attempted to blow them up with T.N.T.[1]

The lessons of the previous day had been learned by the garrison. Other arrangements had been made. The posts on the corner of the House-of-the-Military-Government withdrew somewhat and the enemy was met by rifle and machine-gun fire from the Alcazar itself and from concealed posts on the corner of the terrace which looked down upon the Stable Approach. In this way the garrison was less exposed to view and the fire brought to bear was sufficient. The enemy was forced to retreat, having caused explosions which blew down the corner walls of the House-of-the-Military-Government.

At 5 p.m. a second such attack was made from the Santa Cruz. This time with both more men and more determination. T.N.T. was placed and exploded. Some wreckage was caused. The posts by the mouth of the Stable Approach having been withdrawn, so as to avoid casualties, the enemy was able to establish himself inside it. There, keeping close to the walls, he could not be seen from the Alcazar. Reinforcements were dribbled across from the Santa Cruz, till there was a large number of the enemy within the Approach.

Reserves from the garrison were brought out and rushed to the spot. But the position appeared so serious that it was de-

[1] The explosive known to the Spaniards as Trilite is, I believe, the same as T.N.T.

cided that the mortar, for which there was so little ammunition, must be brought into action. This was done. Bombs were thrown by it into the mouth of the Stable Approach and, exploding with great force in this confined space, compelled the enemy to retire.

The reserves were brought back into the Alcazar and conditions became normal again.

On the afternoon before, one of the half-ruined houses which formed a block between Stable No. 4 and La Concepcion had been set alight; either by parties of the enemy or by shell-fire. The garrison of Stable No. 4 had believed that the enemy wished to burn these houses and had kept up a heavy rifle-fire to prevent this being done. The houses in question were still smouldering and the enemy were now seen extinguishing the fire with streams of water from a hose. As the garrison, also, were anxious that the houses should not be destroyed, they offered no opposition. The enemy's detachments, realizing this, exposed themselves when necessary, but no shots were fired at them.

At dusk all was quiet. It was a night of the full moon and by the light of it, which seemed as bright as day, the normal night fatigue and other activities began. But so much damage had been done to the defences of the Stable Approach that these had been seriously and permanently weakened. Some corner walls of the House-of-the-Military-Government had fallen out and others had been cracked and would easily collapse. The rooms had all been revealed, the barricades blown in. Indeed the whole end of the building was crumbling.

At 9 p.m. yet another attack was made upon this spot. A soldier of the garrison, recalling that evening, remembered that the moonlight was so bright that every pebble, of which the road separating the Stable Approach from the Santa Cruz was formed, was distinct; and that the road was littered with caps, empty canisters and two rifles which the enemy had abandoned that afternoon. Nevertheless, despite the brightness of the moonlight and his two failures a few hours before, the enemy, covered by a sudden and heavy machine-gun fire from the upper windows, sallied out of the Santa Cruz and rushed across the road.

This time the attackers followed their old practice. They threw petrol canisters into the now half-ruined corner of the House-of-the-Military-Government. This was easy as in many places the walls were gaping and the defenders had withdrawn to barricades constructed in the interior doorways, which from the passages or the inside courtyard opened on to the wrecked exterior rooms. The enemy succeeded in setting the petrol alight. Both sides withdrew. And, as soon as the heat allowed them, the defenders returned to their barricades and would have prevented the enemy from entering the building, had an attempt been made. The enemy, however, retired before the flames, soused the Stable Approach with petrol and set light to it. Meanwhile rifle-fire was brought to bear from the Alcazar itself into the flames and smoke.

It was not known whether the enemy's intention was only to complete and extend the damage of that afternoon, or whether he wished to push home this thrust. In any case after a short time, having suffered severely, he retired.

By 10 p.m. all was quiet.

In the last eighteen hours the enemy had made four separate attacks upon the Stable Approach; one of which had been so serious that it had been necessary to use some of the few bombs available for the mortar. The situation was the more dangerous because the enemy could see, as well as the defenders could, that three-quarters of the north façade of the Alcazar now consisted of nothing but a long breach, inviting assault, if once the Stable Approach were forced and the Zig-Zag reached. So much was the attention of the garrison drawn to this corner of the defence that the mining, the sound of which for some reason had grown fainter, was almost forgotten.

In one way the day had been calm; for in spite of the large

quantity of ammunition which had been brought up to them the enemy's guns had not fired a single round.

So carefully had the defenders been handled that, though twice reserves had been called for from the Alcazar, the casualties for the twenty-four hours amounted to only two wounded.

THE FIRST OF SEPTEMBER

The day opened very quietly, with hardly any rifle-fire.

At 9 a.m. the enemy's "155's" on the Dehesa de Pinedo, and apparently two of his "75's" on the same ridge, opened fire upon the north-east tower. The fire was kept up steadily all morning. It was extremely accurate but the garrison on that side of the defence were kept away from their windows and loopholes.

About noon, covered by a sudden increase of shell-fire, an attack was made from the Santa Cruz upon the Stable Approach. Owing to the fact that the enemy's shells were bursting all along the north façade of the Alcazar, such windows as remained on that side could not be manned. Indeed the only fire that could be brought to bear was from Stable No. 4, the nearest windows of which were some distance down the road. And, had the enemy shown the same determination as on the previous afternoon, he might have penetrated the Stable Approach.

The attack was made with less vigour than on the day before. Parties from across the road threw petrol over the gates and barricades, set that alight, and retired to safety. The petrol burned out, no harm having been done. Shells were still bursting on this side of the Alcazar, only some eighty yards away from the Stable Approach. The enemy, therefore, finding those too close for his taste, began to dribble back to the Santa Cruz. But once back within the gates, he continued attempts at throwing petrol over the ruined corner of the House-of-the-Military-Government.

By noon the artillery bombardment ceased. The afternoon was quiet. The sound of the mining was therefore heard once more within the basements of the Alcazar.

Observers noticed further supplies of ammunition being dumped near the enemy's batteries.

At 5 p.m. the "155's" from the hills north of the town began to shell the north-east tower with more than usual vigour. Presently its window openings were so widened that the rooms within were partially exposed.

Many of the shells missing the tower, either by accident or on purpose, burst in the courtyard. On the south of the court, columns and arches on both the upper and lower storeys were brought down. These columns weighed anything from eight to twelve tons each. As they fell the whole paving of the courtyard shook, the arcades trembled. To the women and children, crowded in almost complete darkness in the vaults below, it seemed as if each column had fallen just above their heads. The women showed great courage and soothed the children as well as they could. But the screams of the children and of some of the old ladies, less controlled than the rest, resounded through the corridors in the basement, where in normal times even the sound of a falling rifle echoed loudly. The garrison at their posts, hearing the screams and not knowing whether their women and children had not been wounded, found this afternoon trying. The bombardment lasted till dusk. Then a mere heckling from the enemy's machine-guns brought the day to a close.

Two men had been wounded during the enemy attack on the Stable Approach that morning. There had been no other casualties.

PLATE 21

THE BLESSED VIRGIN OF THE ALCAZAR,
PATRON SAINT OF INFANTRY, AND SOME
OF THE YOUNG SOLDIERS

Her chapel has now been removed to the Cathedral.

PLATE 22

A SURVIVOR, DOÑA CARMEN ARA-
GONÉS, ON HER FIRST VISIT TO THE
ALCAZAR AFTER THE SIEGE

The photograph gives some idea of the shock and
noise caused by the columns when they fell on the
flagging just above the heads of the women and
children in the vaults.

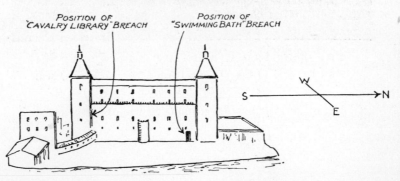

THE SECOND OF SEPTEMBER

At 5 a.m. the enemy mortar, apparently from inside the court-yard of the Santa Cruz, threw several bombs over the roof and on to the corner of the House-of-the-Military-Government, where they exploded, causing fires. These were quickly put out.

At 7 a.m. the "75's" from across the river opened fire on the north-east tower and continued it for some two hours. These shells, however, were small and after the recent bombardment by the "155's" they seemed unimportant.

Soon after noon the "155's" on the farther side of the river began another bombardment of the north-east tower, doing much damage. Shells entering windows burst inside and shook down large portions of masonry.

After these "155's" had been in action for an hour, the "155's" from the Dehesa de Pinedo joined in. The guns on the east aimed low and picked away at the footings of the tower. The guns on the north aimed high and struck the tower just below the cupola. In this way the gunners were able to distinguish between the bursts of their shells and maintain a remarkable accuracy of fire. This bombardment, with one short interval, continued till sundown. By then a large hole had been knocked through the tower, just below the cupola. This, though largely unsupported, still remained in place; for it was built of steel, wood and slates. But weeks of purposeless machine-gun fire had riddled it and in places the sky could be seen between its girders.

During the bombardment shells from the guns across the river had been aimed so low that some falling short had ex-ploded close to the chemical laboratory, which was directly in the line of fire. This laboratory was a small unsubstantial building, standing alone at the north-east corner of the Espla-nade; and so much on its extremity that, later, whole sections of it fell over the edge. Some damage was done to the building and much of its contents smashed.[1]

The fusillade, which increased as soon as the shelling was over, continued throughout the night, though slackening after dark.

The day's casualties were two wounded.

THE THIRD OF SEPTEMBER

The fusillade which had been kept up all night increased at daybreak.

At 7.30 the "155" batteries opened fire from both sides upon the north-east tower.

After a few minutes of this the enemy, repeating his tactics of the day before, made an attack from the doorway of the Santa Cruz. A shower of hand-bombs was thrown at the barricades which had been built inside the ruined rooms forming the corner of the House-of-the-Military-Government. Under cover of this bombing the enemy attempted to force his way up the Stable Approach. But barricades in it had been strengthened. Assailed by fire the enemy presently withdrew.

At 8.15 the "75" battery opened fire; their target, also being the north-east tower. This bombardment continued till nearly noon, when the enemy's gunners were seen withdrawing under the shade of the trees. After that there was no enemy activity of any kind for several hours.

At 4.30 the "155" guns again opened fire, this time upon the north-west tower. Half-an-hour later the "75's" joined in. The fire was directed chiefly against the footings on the west side of the tower, where it rose almost sheer above the Cuesta.

When this bombardment ceased it was seen that the bottom of the tower on that side was crumbling; and, as there was a

1 The laboratory is seen in Plates 35 and 39.

drop of perhaps sixty or seventy feet from the narrow terrace to the road below, it seemed likely that the tower might presently fall like a felled factory chimney. The condition of the south-east tower was by now also critical. There was some speculation as to which tower would fall the first: it was said that there were wagers.

Throughout the day the enemy's machine-guns had been spiteful. But at dusk all firing ceased and, in the hush which followed, the sound of the drilling machines seemed plainer than ever before. The engineer officer and others attempted with medical stethoscopes to estimate by cross-bearings the point which the enemy's miners had reached. But the conclusions arrived at differed widely.

The day had been discouraging; a bombardment lasting nearly eight hours; damage to the towers and steeples. These, perhaps because they had become a mark for the enemy's fire and perhaps because they stood like four standards floating at the corners of the Alcazar, had come to have a significance beyond their military value as observation posts and as machine-gun nests. The whole north end of the Alcazar was in a state of dissolution and the fact had to be faced that a quarter of the building was gone.

THE FOURTH OF SEPTEMBER

At 8 a.m. the enemy's "155" guns and his battery of "75's" opened fire on the north-east tower, aiming high and evidently with the intention of bringing down the cupola. This was now supported only on two sides, for on the previous day shells had cut a gap as large as a railway tunnel through the top of the tower. The gunners now concentrated their fire upon the east wall of the tower, near the summit. This soon began to crumble. The cupola tilted bodily towards the river. At this the enemy's gunners increased their rate of fire and a steady stream of dust and masonry poured down the side of the tower on to the Esplanade. The cupola canted to a steeper angle and began to slide. For a few moments it balanced on the brink. Then, tilting still farther, it slipped and fell down onto the Esplanade, some hundred feet below. It landed, entire, with the vane pointing eastwards, and towards the river. One observer says that it bounced and after that shivered perceptibly for several seconds. A roar of cheering broke from all sides, first from those of the enemy who had seen the actual fall, then from the rest. Regardless of exposing themselves the enemy rifle-men on flat roofs stood up and cheered.

At this, sentries on the other sides of the Alcazar opened fire. This in turn brought down a fusillade from the enemy, who continued cheering for a long time.

The gunners now turned their attention to the second tower, that at the north-west corner. From a distance this tower must have appeared little damaged; especially as, joined to it, there remained a small part of the north façade itself, curiously undamaged, and intact even to the parapet of stone pylons and balustrading which concealed the roof.

The bombardment lasted till 1.30. During the latter part of it a mortar, firing from somewhere behind the Santa Cruz, sent over bombs, so timed as to land in the intervals between the shells.

During the morning's bombardment advantage was once again taken, as often before, of the enemy's look-outs watching the shell-bursts. So while the bombardment was at its height a sortie was made onto the Corralillo, in the hope of tapping an electric cable in a house where bright lights had been seen. Keeping close under the walls the party reached the house without being observed. But to their disappointment they found that it had not even been wired for electricity, and that the lights seen in it must have been those of petrol lamps or a large quantity of candles.

In the afternoon the enemy made yet another attempt to set fire to the Stable Approach, both with petrol squirted through a hose, and with petrol thrown in canisters. These attempts had some success. The petrol soused the slopes above the Stable Approach and the flames blazing up them set fire to the chemical laboratory at the edge of the terrace. The men in the laboratory fought the flames but they had little or no water available and found the task beyond them. The heat became so great that they were forced to withdraw; retiring in good order across the Esplanade and towards the Curved Passage. There they took up a position, ready to reoccupy the ruins of their post as soon as the flames should die down. The laboratory being full of chemicals of various sorts provided some remarkable pyrotechnical effects which produced laughter and cheering among the enemy.

At 6 p.m., and before the garrison of the laboratory had been able to return to it, the enemy's "155's" and his "75" battery opened fire once more upon the north-west tower. After a while they turned their attention upon the House-of-the-Military-Government; thereby making it impossible for the garrison of the laboratory to return to its ruins. The guns kept up their fire until after 7.30 p.m.

The day had been a difficult one. The fall of the north-east cupola had seemed a definite point scored by the enemy. His morale had improved and marksmen on roof-tops and in windows hardly troubled to keep concealed.

By 8 p.m. the fire in the laboratory had died down. The garrison returned to the ruins and took stock of the damage done. Some of the walls had fallen, others were now doubtfully bullet-proof. Indeed so much of the little building had been destroyed that it could no longer be relied upon as a small but important bastion of the defence. This complicated the general situation. For the corner of the House-of-the-Military-Government was now practically in ruins and could no longer be counted on to prevent the enemy entering the

Stable Approach. Now, if he succeeded in doing this, there was nothing to stop him mounting the slopes and occupying the laboratory as well. Once that was done the House-of-the-Military-Government would be completely cut off. Thus this small and inadequate laboratory, of which the Academy had been somewhat ashamed, suddenly became of prime importance.

So serious was the situation considered, that a new plan was hastily drawn up for a second line of defence to be held, were this whole corner of the existing line to fall into the hands of the enemy. Working-parties began to throw up fresh barricades. But a bare seven hours remained before dawn; and when dawn came the work had not been half done.

After dark a large supply of wheat was brought in. For, should the enemy capture the edge of the terrace, it would be impossible any longer to reach the granary.

Though much material damage had been done, the casualties for the day were only four wounded. This speaks highly for the way in which the little garrison in the laboratory had been handled; when fighting the flames, when withdrawn across the parade-ground, and when returning after dark to the ruins of their post.

DAILY LIFE IN THE ALCAZAR

It was now six weeks since the actual siege had begun and it is time to give some picture of the daily routine within the Alcazar.

Duties. The normal routine of men of the garrison consisted of six hours of duty, six hours of rest, six hours of duty, six hours of rest. But the hours of rest were often lost because of the need of some extra work or the likelihood of an attack.

Food. During the first few days food had been normal.

During the next week it had been on a rapidly diminishing scale, but had still consisted of three meals a day. But, after the first fortnight, two meals were substituted for three, and the rations shrank rapidly.

Water. The water ration for each person was one litre per day.

It is no doubt possible for a human being living a sedentary existence to remain alive for an indefinite period on such rations, as the garrison of the Alcazar had during the siege. But the defenders were for ever building and rebuilding barricades and removing wreckage; besides carrying out all the routine duties necessary for the life of a large community living at extremely close quarters.

After the first month all fat upon their bodies had been absorbed and from about this time they began to lose strength and readiness for effort. The lifting of weights became difficult. It became easier to remain at one loophole with a shoulder against a wall, risking a bullet, than to keep moving from one loophole to another.

Washing. Already for six weeks no one in the Alcazar had had a drop of water to wash in, and very few had had a change of clothing. The men had not shaved and sparse unkempt beards increased the gauntness of their looks. Their hair had grown; few had much chance to comb it. The women wore the clothes in which they had come. They had grown thin, and their dresses hung shapeless about them. Living as they did, day after day, in darkness and underground, their skin had come to have a waxen greenish tinge.

Sleep. There were beds and mattresses, though not enough to go round. Yet even in such outworks as the wrecked Quarters of the Soldiers there were a few mattresses, and a few spring bed-frames which, used separately, provided almost half the garrison with something to sleep on. As for the other half, they must lie on straw or rags, or on the bare stone. Beyond this, it often happened that during the hours when a man was free to sleep, shells were bursting just outside the wall against which he lay.

Lights. Since the first days of the siege there had been no electricity and, at night, the only light was that of mule-fat or horse-fat dips, with a piece of string or cloth for a wick. But when, as soon happened, only one horse or mule was slaughtered a day there was little fat to be had; so it was only in vital places that there was any lighting at all.

There was always the danger of the stock of matches being exhausted, and "dips" were lit from each other, so that not more than a match or two need be used in a day.

Dress. The young soldiers were Regulars and so wore the Army's summer dress; a jacket, breeches and glengarry cap, all of khaki drill; boots or espandrils, and leather gaiters. They had no capes or overcoats, and sometimes at night they suffered from the cold. For, though these were warm months, Toledo stands at more than two thousand feet above sea level.

The Guardia Civil wore their uniform of grey-green, piped with scarlet. Their hats were of black patent leather and are surely the strangest military headdress in the world. They are the tricornes of the early eighteenth century, but with the turned-up brim existing only at the two rear sides. Their cloaks were of dark blue cloth, long and full, and with scarlet facings; and in these capes and tricornes they might have stepped straight from that little crowd of men which stands so often in the corner of Guardi's Venetian scenes. The Guardia Civil also have a roll-up pill-box forage cap, more comfortable for night work or for actual fighting.

One cannot write of life in the Alcazar without mentioning the Command which directed all. I say "command" rather than "commander," for there is no means as yet of knowing who was responsible for the successful defence; or whether it was the work of some council of officers. Control there was, and skill, and wisdom, and a most unusual intelligence.[1]

The intelligence with which the defence was conducted is seen in nothing more clearly than in its economy of human life. In certain armies, and in recent years, hundreds of thousands of lives have been thrown away in order to "keep up the offensive spirit" or "to prevent the initiative from passing into the enemy's hands." A Spanish commander may be slack in many ways and may leave much to chance, but he is not impressed, beyond their worth, by classroom phrases such as these. It was from the first clear to the command of the Alcazar that the garrison was not strong enough to indulge in that text-book favourite "the offensive-defensive," and it accepted that the only wise policy was that of a purely "passive defence." It proved astonishingly effective. For days on end not a shot would be fired by the defenders of the Alcazar. Often the enemy did not know whether this or that building were held at all. To find out it was necessary to risk a sudden burst of fire and heavy casualties. A barricade, silent for weeks, would blaze rifle-fire. And in the end the enemy came to be distrustful of every stone.

There were no lives to be wasted. No man, except by order, had the right to expose himself to any avoidable risk. Vigilance was maintained by moving sentries, who sometimes fired a round from one of a dozen loopholes—if that were the order of the day. Sniping, as such, was forbidden. Fire duels were forbidden. Indeed there was normally no rifle-fire at all, except to repel an attack. As a result of this, when reading of hours of combat, one is astonished at how small the garrison's casualties were.

One of the orders of the command is so unexpected and interesting that it must be mentioned.

On the north side of the Alcazar stood the Santa Cruz.

---

[1] Some consider the genius of the defence to have been the commander of the Guardia Civil, who was, I believe, a Colonel Martinez.

From its windows, week after week, machine-guns, rifle-fire and a flame projector harried the garrison; while from its doorway more than a score of attacks were delivered. Now the building is one of the earliest of the Spanish Renaissance and the carving round the windows and door were of particular beauty. For this reason it was impressed upon the young soldiers, who held the loopholes facing them, that these carvings were a heritage of their country and must be damaged as little as was conceivably possible. It seems hardly credible that in time of war such an order could have been carried out. Yet it was, to an extraordinary degree. The windows held by the enemy have had their iron grilles cut through by bullets, and the pillarettes which framed the windows have been here and there scarred by "wides." But the decoration above the windows remains practically undamaged, and the tympanum above the great doorway has hardly a scar on it.[1]

The Families. In their times off duty men could get permission almost every night to go and visit any relatives they had in the Alcazar. Often the men took with them their friends who had no one of their own. This helped to make life easier for the men and made all feel that they were fighting for more than a political cause or the mere walls of an ancient building. And so presently, as the life that each had lived before grew more distant and unreal, the Alcazar came to be for all their "home."

I would like to tell this of one of the young soldiers of the garrison, a boy not eighteen on the day of the relief. After the siege was over he, with other of the young soldiers, was left as

[1] See Plate No. 23.
I believe that an incident somewhat similar to the above occurred in one of Cunningham Graham's short stories or sketches, in which a Spanish officer engaged in shelling some rebels cannot bring himself to bombard one particular building, because it is a pure example of the second Mudejar style. Actually this veneration for good architecture exists in all classes in Spain and it is hard indeed to find a building disfigured with cut initials or the like.

garrison in the ruined Alcazar; partly to regain his strength; and partly, perhaps, because the High Command realized the value of young men with such a record. This boy spoke of the future. Leave the Alcazar? The question had not occurred to him. No, the Alcazar was more than his home. It had become to him what the ship he sailed in was to the seaman of the past. He and the Alcazar had been through too much together. In a way he doubtless did not understand, it had become an aspect of his own existence; and he could not bear the thought of leaving it.

These things are not fancies woven afterwards by the defenders, or worse, by others for them. They were the half-discovered motives for all the defenders thought and did during those weeks of hunger, of failing strength and of ever-present danger.

The Wounded. There was one central dressing-station, and hospital combined. To this wounded men were carried, when and how conditions allowed. There were at first three doctors, later only two. The nursing was done by the men. There were medicines and drugs enough, but no anæsthetics, and many amputations were performed without any. Work in the hospital was hard, for there were times when the wounded amounted to a fifth, or even a fourth, of the whole garrison.

Burials. The dead were buried in the riding-school, except in the last days when the garrison were driven back into the Alcazar itself and the dead were buried in the building. There was no priest. One of the officers conducted the burial services. He seems to have had some secret vision and a faith which helped the others. Everyone remembers him with gratitude.

Most of the graves are still there, in what remains of the riding-school. Some bodies have been disinterred by shell-fire; some have been taken by relatives and re-buried in cemeteries near their homes; and the sight of these empty graves gives a sense of extraordinary desolation.

The Communists and Anarchists, to their credit, respected this graveyard, when they finally obtained possession of it. All that they did was to scrawl up the unavoidable initials on the walls; "Milicias Populares"; "F.A.I."; "C.N.T."; "U.G.T."; in blue paint, in red paint, and sometimes in blood.

There is one grave the visitor remembers. For it was almost the nearest to the doorway of this big ruined roofless shed. At the head of the grave is a cross, made like the rest, from the wood of a packing-case. On it is written in indelible pencil:—

Julian Gomez

Soldado de la
Academia de
Infanteria

Murio el 20 de
Septimbre de 1936

A. los 17 Anos dedad.

THE FIFTH OF SEPTEMBER

Soon after midnight the sound of mining became so alarmingly clear that a fresh survey of the situation was undertaken. Attempts were made by cross-bearings from various windows to fix the position of the compressor. The general conclusion was that it had been moved and was now working in one of the houses near the Cuesta. At 2.30 a.m., therefore, a sortie party crept out, armed with petrol tins and bombs, for the purpose of burning the house. The party was held up almost at once by a blaze of enemy rifle-fire and by obstacles which had been newly erected. For some time a rifle duel was kept up, in hopes that the enemy's fire might be mastered and that the party might be able to complete this task. After some ten minutes of this the sortie detachment were forced to withdraw, having accomplished nothing.

At 7 a.m. the "155's" and the "75" battery opened fire upon that small part of the north façade which still remained, joined to the north-west tower. Most of this was brought down in less than an hour. Many of the shells, passing through walls or windows, crossed the courtyard and burst on the farther side of it. All the arcading of the south-east corner was wrecked and the ruins of it covered the giant stairway; so that, where there had been a wide flight of steps leading up to the gallery, there was now a mass of débris, as steep and difficult to climb as a mountain side.

After two hours of this the enemy turned his guns upon the Quarters-of-the-Soldiers. To this building, already little more than an empty husk, further damage was done. The floors of the upper storeys fell and thereafter most of the upper windows could not be manned.

At noon all guns ceased fire.

The early afternoon was quiet but the garrison could not go on with the construction of the new second line of defence. For in broad daylight and in full view of the enemy's artillery it would have been impossible for work to be carried out, either upon the Esplanade or the terrace of the riding-school.

At 4.30 the "155's" opened fire again, this time upon the north-west tower.

At 5.15 the gunners switched onto the House-of-the-Military-Government and kept up a rapid rate of fire for some fifteen minutes. They then returned to their original target.

Almost immediately after the barrage had been lifted from tho House-of-the-Military-Government, several posts sent in urgent messages, making it clear that the artillery fire had been lifted, only for an attack to be made. Enemy troops were said to be massing in the upper end of the calle del Carmen, close to the now ruined inn of Cervantes. Here several houses, standing more or less intact, offered cover, not more than forty or fifty yards up the street from the doorway of the Santa Cruz and the entrance of the Stable Approach. By keeping close under the walls of the houses these men would be able to reach the entrance to the Stable Approach without being seen. Then, doubling round, they could rush the narrow passage, being for only a few seconds under fire from the barricades inside the ruined corner rooms of the House-of-the-Military-Government.

The danger was immediate. Barricades were manned: reserves were distributed: several barricades were thrown up across paths normally left open for communication: all prepared to face a general assault.

As no attack had been made since the laboratory had been wrecked the afternoon before, it was not known whether what remained of the defences on this side would be sufficient to prevent the enemy gaining control of the Stable Approach. Nor had there been time enough to construct the second line of defence, decided upon the night before.

It is difficult for even disciplined troops to change direction during an attack. It seemed likely, therefore, that even if the enemy's objective were the Zig-Zag or the corner of the Esplanade, many of his men, when charging down the Stable Approach, would continue their way straight on and thus pass between the Alcazar and the House-of-the-Military-Government, cutting it off.

During the next half-hour or even the next hour, the sequence of events is not clear; nor, indeed, is anything, until the garrison by a magnificent counter-attack recaptured the Stable Approach and Stable No. 4. Thus what follows here is but an attempted reconstruction, made from the accounts of several of the garrison of this corner.

The enemy's attack upon the Stable Approach was successful. It has not been possible to discover whether the men holding the barricades inside the corner rooms of the House-of-the-Military-Government withdrew, or whether they were bombed from their posts. In any case large numbers of the enemy rushed this corner and occupied almost the whole length of the Stable Approach. Near the downhill end of it they were stopped by a barricade held, either by those men who had retired from the corner rooms, or by some of the young soldiers from Stable No. 4, or by some local reserves rushed to the spot to meet this danger. Nor has it been possible to discover how the enemy's troops obtained possession of Stable No. 4. They may have forced the barricades in those ruined corner rooms and so have worked their way through the building and taken the Stable by surprise. It may be that the garrison of it was hastily withdrawn, as soon as it was realized that their line of retreat was in danger.

In any case Stable No. 4, the Stable Approach, and presumably the whole of the House-of-the-Military-Government, fell into the hands of the enemy.

To meet this emergency, some reserves were rushed from the Alcazar to the south end of the Esplanade. There, in full view of the enemy's gunners and rifle-men on the other side of the river, they set to work upon a barricade which had been commenced during the previous night but which for lack of time had not been finished. This barricade was to give cover from the doors of the dining-hall to a communication trench cut in the roadway which can be seen running along the face of the terrace wall.[1]

There is no certain means of knowing how the retirement from the House-of-the-Military-Government was carried out. But presumably it must have been done in good order, for the casualties of the day do not suggest that there was hand-to-hand fighting.

The enemy wasted their time; for they did not follow up their success.

For the garrison of the Alcazar the situation was extremely serious. All available reserves were massed and, after careful

[1] See Plates 20 and 39.

planning, a counter-attack was made.

The enemy troops do not seem even to have taken up a defensive line and, when the counter-attack swept down upon them, they were found in the act of carrying off mattresses and clothing which they had captured in Stable No. 4. Farther up the Stable Approach two or three of them were caught in a garage, going through the tool-box of a motor-car. Taken by surprise the enemy retired in disorder. The Stable Approach was regained, and the posts on it were occupied once more.

Stable No. 4 was entered cautiously and was found to be empty.

The astonishing thing about the afternoon's fighting is that the garrison's casualties amounted to only eleven wounded.

Attacks upon the House-of-the-Military-Government were made on so many days that it is hard for members of the garrison to separate them in their minds. Thus one of the young soldiers who was promoted to corporal "for his gallantry in defending his post while the House-of-the-Military-Government was burning" is not clear as to the day on which this happened. But it appears likely that it was on this afternoon, the 5th of September. And, if that be so, then the sequence of events in this corner can be deduced.

When the enemy's men rushed past the corner of the Stable Approach they followed their usual practice of throwing petrol and bombs at the barricades erected well inside the ruins. The fire thus started prevented them from penetrating into the building, and finding Stable No. 4 as quickly as they otherwise would have done. Realizing this the boy with two or three companions entered the part of the building which was in flames, and by their rifle-fire round corners and across the ruined courtyards, hindered the enemy's advance and gave time for the remainder of the garrison of Stable No. 4 to be withdrawn.

This young soldier's name was José Outesa. His age was seventeen. He was promoted for gallantry in the circumstances

PLATE 23

THE
DOORWAY
OF THE
SANTA CRUZ

From this endless attacks were launched. But the garrison of
the Alcazar were told to spare its carving, and it remains almost
undamaged.

AN ATTACK FROM THE DOORWAY SEEN ABOVE

The Stable Approach is seen through the arch. The House-of-
the-Military-Government is 40 yards away on the left front.

PANORAMA ILLUSTRATING THE MANY ATTACKS FROM THE SANTA CRUZ
UPON THE STABLE APPROACH. (The doorway of the Santa Cruz is just out of sight on the left.)

PLATE 24

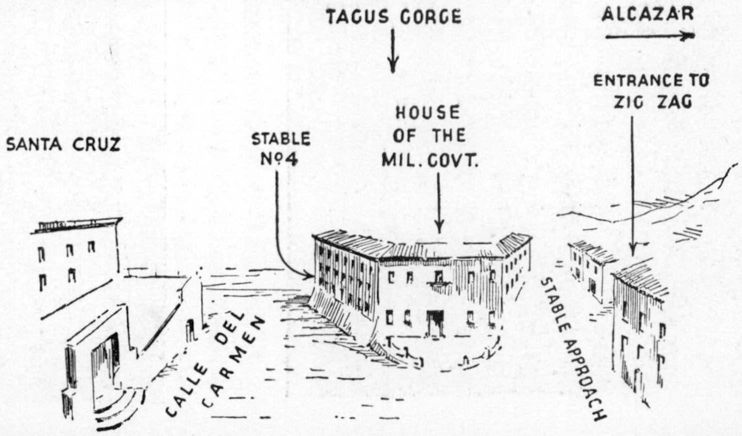

SANTA CRUZ

TAGUS GORGE

ALCAZAR

STABLE No. 4

HOUSE OF THE MIL. GOVT.

ENTRANCE TO ZIG ZAG

STABLE APPROACH

CALLE DEL CARMEN

recorded. But whether it was on the 5th September or not he is uncertain.

These events lasted until after dark. Then enemy activity ceased and all was quiet.

During the night detachments were sent out and many bags of wheat were brought in.

Later, too, the captain of engineers, accompanied by others who had interested themselves in the matter, crept out to the Cuesta with medical stethoscopes and by other means attempted to locate the position of the enemy's compressor. They returned after a lengthy investigation. Their report was that there were two compressors; that they believed one of these to be in the Plaza de la Magdalena (one hundred and fifty yards west of the Alcazar); and the other in the Rojas Theatre (some two hundred yards to south-south-west and on considerably lower ground). However, none of the information was sure.

The casualties of the day consisted of eleven wounded; and one lady of seventy-two who had died from natural causes.

In view of the enemy having been able to break through the defences and for some time occupying part of them, a special order was issued to reassure the garrison. In this it was pointed out that the wrecking of towers did not reduce the real strength of the Alcazar; that the increase in the enemy's offensive efforts was certainly due to the pressure of the relieving columns which could not be more than one hundred miles away; that the very fact that his broadcasts were so untrue proved his necessity for keeping up his spirits by lies; that the garrison had food enough, and small-arm ammunition enough, to hold out until the relief forces could arrive.

THE SIXTH OF SEPTEMBER

At 7 a.m. the enemy's "155" guns opened fire upon the north-west tower. Half-an-hour later his "75's" joined in. The small shells from these guns did more damage than would have been expected. For often they would pass through windows, or holes already blown in the walls, and burst inside the tower.

About 10 o'clock the gunners changed their target and began shelling the Moorish bastion and the battlemented gallery, on the east façade of the Alcazar. This gallery had been manned on occasions when it had been desired to develop maximum fire power on this side. It was of ancient but very solid construction, and the damage done to it was at first extraordinarily slight.

Shortly before 1 p.m. the guns ceased fire and for four hours there was no activity of any kind.

A little after 4.30 p.m. all the enemy's guns opened fire once again upon the north-west tower. Their fire was maintained till dusk.

During the afternoon observation posts had reported many motor-coaches leaving the outskirts of Toledo and taking the Avila road. It appeared that these coaches contained men, women and children, whom they deposited somewhere out of sight beyond the hills; for shortly after they disappeared, they reappeared, this time empty.

The night was quiet. A large detachment was sent out and more wheat was brought up into the Alcazar.

Towards midnight the captain of engineers and other technical experts crept out of the Alcazar, protected by an escort. Once again they spent much time over their investigations. They worked silently and managed to avoid being seen. According to the report they made it was now certain that two compressors were at work; that two mine-shafts were being driven towards the Alcazar; that the rock was so hard that explosive charges were being used to split it; that large charges were exploded at long intervals, whereas the normal method was to use small charges at short intervals; that thus it was clear the work was not being carried out by experts; that there was, therefore, a good chance that those who were driving the shaft would lose their direction; that in any case they could not reach the walls of the Alcazar within eight days.

All considered, this was encouraging. There had been far less fusillade than usual and the casualties for the day amounted to only one wounded.

THE SEVENTH OF SEPTEMBER

At 7.45 a.m. the "155" guns opened fire; and, as usual, the "75's" joined in soon afterwards. At first their target was the north-west tower, the footings of which had been already so cut away that the tower seemed likely to fall soon.

At about 11 o'clock the gunners changed their target and began to shell the Quarters-of-the-Soldiers, the riding-school and buildings near it. The fire was kept up later than usual; indeed until after 1 p.m.

At 11.30 a.m., following the practice usual during a bombardment, a sortie was made by Falangistas from the south side of the Alcazar; where there was the diminutive plaza of the Capuchinos, little wider than an ordinary road. The houses on the other side of it were very close to the windows of the Alcazar and therefore were not normally occupied by the enemy. It was hoped that the sortie party would be able to cross the plaza, reach an alley that ran downhill towards the market, and so enter houses and obtain supplies of food.

However, as soon as the men of the sortie party had reached the middle of the plaza heavy fire was opened on them from these houses, barely fifteen yards away. They retreated. Only when they were under cover was it discovered that one of their number, Maximiliano Flink, was missing. His dead body was then seen, lying in the middle of the plaza. Upon this another of the party, Godopedo Bravo, rushed out and attempted to drag it back into safety. A rain of bullets was poured upon him and he, too, fell dead. A third, José Canosa, ran out with a rope to the body of the first man and, throwing himself down beside it, succeeded in tying the rope round it. But running back he tripped and lost the rope. The fire was now so heavy that he had to abandon it and run for safety. While he was doing this another of the party, José Berzosa, ran out, seized the body of the second man and in spite of heavy fire succeeded in dragging it into the precincts of the Alcazar. A senior officer now arrived on the scene and forbade further attempts to rescue the body of the first man. There it lay in the middle of the plaza, target for the enemy's senseless rifle-fire for the rest of that day.

The fusillade, thus produced, spread to other fronts and was continued with intense violence until dusk. Then it subsided.

At 4.45 p.m., that is at the same hour as on the previous day, all the enemy's guns opened fire upon the north-west tower. This was kept up till dark. But, although the tower had long seemed about to fall, it was still standing when the firing ceased.

At 6 p.m., while this bombardment was going on, a large three-engined bomber was seen approaching from Madrid. It flew over the Alcazar for three-quarters of an hour. The bombs it dropped were heavy and its aim extremely accurate. A few fell in the courtyard and blew in all the doors facing onto it.

After this plane had flown away, rifle-fire slackened. Presently all was quiet, except that within the basements of the Alcazar the sound of subterranean mining was louder than on any previous evening.

The moon did not rise till late. So, as soon as darkness made it possible, the body of Maximiliano Flink was brought in. Although this was carried out with as little noise as possible it led to a renewal of rifle-fire, both from the houses across the little plaza of the Capuchinos and from other sides of the Alcazar.

THE CIGARETTE TRAP

As time went on the lack of anything to smoke troubled the garrison of the Alcazar more and more. It led to the following chain of incidents. Not knowing to what days these belong, I give them here.

The reader will remember the "Simplon," that long dark tunnel inside the terrace wall which frowned down upon the Cuesta.[1] In the thickness of that wall, and below the "Simplon," there were workshops, the doors of which are seen in the photograph. Above these workshops were store-rooms. These had wooden floors. The uppermost rooms, however, were roofed with brick vaults which formed, in fact, the floor of the "Simplon" passage, just above.

During the early days of the siege the doors of these workshops had been blown in and the enemy sometimes entered. For these workshops were out of sight of the defenders overhead; and were shady and cool for a midday rest. But the fact that the garrison were known to be above, led to most of these workshops being set on fire and gutted; so that the floors of the upper storeys had collapsed into the cellars. In one place a bomb blew a hole through the vaulted roofing, far overhead. Thus a gap, the size of a trap-door, was created in the floor of the "Simplon." For convenience and safety this had at once been covered over by the garrison. No light showing through

[1] Its windows are the higher ones seen in the terrace walls on the left of Plate No. 5.

this, it remained unnoticed by those of the enemy who happened to enter the workshop below.

One day a Government militia-man chanced to want shelter from the heat and came in here. He made himself comfortable among the wreckage. He lit a cigarette. Presently the tobacco smoke drifted to the roof and penetrated through the boarding of the hole. A passing sentry sniffed at it; he called his comrades. Peering down between the planks they could see the militia-man lying at his ease. They fetched their rifles, took careful aim and shot him dead. If any of his comrades in the houses opposite saw him, they must have fancied him asleep.

The man was dead but the cigarette went on burning. The smell of it gave an idea to the men in the "Simplon." They fetched a rope and hook, lowered them through the hole and drew up the body. In the pockets were packets of cigarettes. They took these and let the dead man down again.

Next morning the body had disappeared, but his comrades must have thought that he had been wounded in the street and had crawled in there to die; for during the next days several of them entered the workshop.

For a long time no opportunity for another shot occurred. A trap was therefore set. At a moment when it was certain that the loopholes across the street were occupied, a package was dropped through the hole and down into the workshop below. The rope and hook were then lowered and dangled, as though attempts were being made to retrieve it. The trick succeeded. Two militia-men came dashing across the road, into the workshop, and tried to seize the rope. Rapid fire was opened from above. One man was shot dead and fell near the package. His body was grappled with the hook and drawn up into the "Simplon." On this occasion, also, the garrison obtained a good supply of cigarettes.

For a long time the enemy did not take the bait again. But later, no doubt when another company of militia-men had come to garrison the houses across the road, it was tried again, and with success.

It is said that in all, three, if not four, of the enemy lost their lives in this way and their supplies of cigarettes were obtained by the garrison. In the pocket of one of the dead men was a considerable sum of money. This was handed to the Command, to be put in trust for the two babies who during the siege had been born within the Alcazar.

THE EIGHTH OF SEPTEMBER

All night the fusillade produced by the rescue of the Falangista's body remained severe on all sides.

At 8.45 a.m. the enemy's "155" guns opened fire upon the north-west tower, which seemed ready to fall. This tower, with its cupola and weathervane, rose some hundred feet above the terrace. But the terrace at this side was narrow and at the edge of it there was a fall of some fifty feet to the road below. Moreover this terrace was of "made earth" and of no great solidity. So it may be said that the tower which rose to this dizzy height had its real footings on the level of the street.[1]

With the first shells the loosened masonry on the west side of the tower began to flake off and soon fallen blocks of stone had spread across the terrace and were toppling down to the road below. The bombardment continued. After an hour or so the tower began to crack vertically. Presently it seemed to subside slightly towards the west and then with a rumbling crash fell clean across the Cuesta.

The drop, as has been said, was anything from eighty to a hundred and twenty feet, and the noise produced was enormous. For the tower, which was in parts almost solid, may

[1] See Plate 5.

have weighed as much as a thousand tons. It blocked the whole road: it crushed to atoms the houses on the other side. A Falangista who was on duty in the Simplon says that as the tower fell he remembered suddenly an account he had read of an earthquake in some volcanic island.

For a time little could be seen on account of the cloud of dust and mortar. When this subsided it was seen that the whole wide Cuesta had been blocked from side to side, as by a cliff fall. This main approach to the Alcazar was now choked against any attack by tanks or armoured cars; and even infantry would find it difficult to scramble over the forty feet bank of loose and crumbling debris. Thus the enemy had gained nothing by the destruction of the tower.

However, its collapse produced salvos of cheering. In all parts of the town rifles were let off in a wild feu-de-joie and motor horns were sounded. This was kept up for at least ten minutes, while the enemy's gunners poured a rain of shells upon the dust and chaos.

Soon after 11 a.m. the artillery ceased fire and the machine-gun and rifle fusillade increased in violence.

All the afternoon the enemy showed his delight and in various ways taunted the garrison. Red flags were waved on rooftops. Trumpets were blown, and bombs thrown from their windows against the walls of the Alcazar, on which they exploded, doing no harm.

With the fading light the fire of rifles and machine-guns faded also. After that only an occasional shot broke the silence. In the basements of the Alcazar, however, the rapping of the miners seemed a more hollow sound and to be much nearer than before. According to the experts' estimate, they could not reach the Alcazar for another six days. But there were probably few in the garrison who did not fancy that this might be an optimistic view and that in truth only four or five days remained to them.

At 10.30 p.m. a look-out on the south façade heard a voice

calling from a window across the little plaza; one of those from which the rifle-fire on the day before had been poured upon the bodies of the two Falangistas and upon their rescuers. The voice asked if an officer would come to one of the windows, to hear something of importance. One did so. After a pause another voice from across the plaza, one which he knew, called out that a Major Rojo wished to make certain proposals to Colonel Moscardó. This was reported to the Colonel. The proposal was agreed to and the hour was fixed for 9 o'clock on the following morning.

After that there was no more firing of any sort.

The casualties of the day had been three wounded.

THE NINTH OF SEPTEMBER

Since the parley of the night before not a shot had been fired.

At 9 a.m. Major Rojo, with a white flag, was seen coming from one of the houses opposite. He approached the south door of the Alcazar and was instructed to go round to the Waggon Entrance, in the west façade.

Outside the doorway he was met and blindfolded, in the manner laid down in the field service regulations of the Spanish army.

The rôle which this officer had chosen must have been a hard one to sustain. He had been a cadet in the Alcazar and the building itself was linked with at least three years of his own youth, as well as with the history of his country. He had been, also, for several years one of the officer instructors of the Academy and must have been known to practically all the officers in the garrison and to many of the men. It is impossible to know whether he acted in accordance with political beliefs which were opposed to theirs, or whether considerations of personal gain swayed him. But he must have realized that to them he appeared, not as an enemy, but as a traitor to themselves and to the very stones they were defending.

He was led to the office of Colonel Moscardó and was then asked the object of his visit. He stated that he came as an envoy from the Government forces and that he was empowered to promise the garrison their lives if they would surrender at once. In case of refusal the Government intended to "tighten their grip" upon the Alcazar and to use every means of attack available.

No discussion took place. Colonel Moscardó and this officer had known each other for many years. Colonel Moscardó had always a shy and retiring manner but he had a high sense of what he felt to be his duty. He had suffered, moreover, a grievous personal loss at the hands of the besiegers. The threats which had been conveyed to him cannot have eased the situation. He now repeated, in terms which must have been familiar to the other, that nothing would ever induce him to surrender the Alcazar which circumstances entirely unforeseen had placed in his charge.

As he was about to leave, Major Rojo asked if there was any request he could convey to those who had sent him. Colonel Moscardó stated that the garrison would be grateful if a priest might be sent, both to say Mass and to baptise two children who had been born during the siege.

Major Rojo was then blindfolded again and marched out into the open air once more. He returned to the place from which he had come.

After ten minutes' delay a storm of machine-gun and rifle-fire broke out from all sides, and within a few minutes the "155's" opened a bombardment which continued till midnight.

Shortly after 4 p.m. three big aeroplanes appeared and dropped bombs on the hill known as Los Palos, on the Cuesta, and on what remained standing of the north-west tower. (The bomb penetrated through two storeys, sliding down the stairs without exploding.) The question then arose as to whether the planes had been those of the enemy or of the columns marching to the relief of the Alcazar. The general opinion was that the planes, being of a new type, must belong to the relief force.

Presumably the Government, informed of Colonel Moscardó's refusal of the terms offered, determined upon even greater efforts. For towards dusk several large searchlights mounted in lorries were seen approaching Toledo. Soon after dark these were turned upon the Alcazar, flood-lighting it far more effectively than the small lamps installed in the Zocodover had. This enabled the enemy's artillery fire to be henceforward as accurate by night as by day.

At midnight all the enemy's guns, except one "155," ceased fire. His machine-guns and rifle-men, also, closed down for the night. Thereafter the sound of compressors and of blasting continued alternately throughout the night. At long intervals the "155" gun sent over shells, all of which landed in the courtyard. The noise made sleep impossible.

The garrison waited until an hour before dawn; then two sorties were made, one to find the entrance to the mines and to destroy them, the other to seize food. The enemy was on the alert and opened such a heavy fire that neither party made much progress. But the one sent out to find the mines brought back news which somewhat changed the view of the situation. The opinion of the experts now was that there were two mines; that both were being worked from the same entrance and were being driven towards the south-west tower; that one had advanced considerably farther than the other and would soon reach the foundations of the Alcazar.

The day's casualties amounted to one dead and three wounded.

THE TENTH OF SEPTEMBER

Sleep had been impossible. And, after the sorties had been attempted, the rifle fusillade became as heavy as during the previous day.

At 6 a.m. the rest of the "155's" joined in. Much structural damage was done. Some rooms especially dear to all who had been connected with the Academy, were wrecked. This fire was kept up till 11 a.m. Then it ceased, the bombardment having lasted eighteen hours.

No sooner were the guns silent than the enemy again increased his rate of machine-gun and rifle-fire. At 5 o'clock the enemy's guns again opened fire, the heavier guns taking the courtyard of the Alcazar for their target, and the "75's" distributed their fire along the terraces.

At 10 p.m., during a lull in the firing, a voice was heard calling from one of the little houses on the plaza of the Capuchinos. An officer replied. The voice then stated that the Government had agreed to the request made and that a priest, Canon Vasquez Camarassa, would visit the Alcazar at 9 o'clock next morning.

The parley ended, the bombardment began again and was continued until the hour of the priest's arrival. As a result sleep became impossible for the second night in succession.

Added to this the sound of the drilling machines had become so insistent that it echoed through all the subterranean passages and vaults of the Alcazar. Indeed, even as far away as the House-of-the-Military-Government, anyone who in a reclining position pressed the palm of his hand against his ear, and leaned the elbow of that arm upon the ground, could sense the vibration of the drills.

Thus the garrison were kept in a constant state of anxiety. The women especially felt the strain. The children, however, seem to have been little worried, except by the fall of masonry on the paving just above their heads.

THE ELEVENTH OF SEPTEMBER

That night the garrison of the Alcazar was afraid. Two steady men of the Guardia Civil volunteered that: an officer with much active service in Morocco said it: one of the women said it, also. For the enemy who had shut the churches and forbidden services throughout Spain, was sending a priest into the Alcazar. And that, all agreed, could only be because they were now all going to die. And, beyond the natural fear of death, there was the sense that they had failed and that all they had endured had been but a waste of time. That last, the officer said, seemed the worst part of all.

An hour before dawn a strong party was sent out as a forlorn hope, to find and destroy the mine-shaft. But all the alleys leading into the town had been blocked. Several attempts were made by different routes to enter the barricaded area, but without success. And such a heavy fire was opened that this sortie party had to withdraw.

At 6 a.m. the "155" guns opened fire on the group of buildings on the south end of the terraces, which the older officers still called the Santiago, after a long-vanished hostel of the Knights. This so-called Santiago included the Quarters-of-the-Soldiers; and these were further wrecked. It also included the dining-hall and riding-school; these were both already roofless, but now once again they were set on fire.

At 9 a.m. all firing ceased abruptly and after a few moments Canon Camarassa,[1] in lay clothing but with a crucifix in his

---

[1] Canon Vasquez Camarassa was a well-known Madrid preacher and a Canon of the Madrid Cathedral. He had always been known to hold the

hand, was seen coming out of one of the houses on the far side of the plaza of the Capuchinos. Watched in silence from the windows of the Alcazar, he took the way arranged for him and went round to the Waggon Entrance. He was admitted and escorted to the chapel. The two babies, one a boy, the other a girl, were baptised. Mass was celebrated. And, the whole garrison having fasted, the Holy Communion was administered. The Canon now preached with great eloquence a sermon which filled the hearts of all who heard it with dread. For he spoke of the unescapable doom which hung over them and over the very walls which sheltered them. He spoke of the wickedness of human pride and of stubbornness of heart. After a small silence he pronounced the General Absolution, and all considered themselves shriven for their coming death.

The service over, the Canon visited the wounded in hospital and gave them, also, Absolution. At twelve noon he left the Alcazar, due formalities having been performed.

Thereafter there was no artillery fire until 9 o'clock on the following morning—except that in the middle of the afternoon the guns of the "75" battery fired one round each.

At 7 p.m. Major Rojo again called from a window on the other side of the Capuchinos and asked for a parley with the commander of the garrison. It is understood that he was allowed to proceed to the Waggon Entrance, was blindfolded and brought in as on the previous occasion. He was shown into the office of Colonel Moscardó which was lit, as always, only by a single mule-fat dip and was deep in shadows. He said that he had come to beg for the evacuation of the women and children. He said, also, that Canon Camarassa and himself would personally guarantee their safety and good treatment. Three representatives of the women were then sent for.

political views of the extreme Left. It is probable that when the service he had rendered the Government in this matter became known, his position among such other priests as remained alive in the capital would have become difficult. It is said that he, alone of all the priests in Spain, was allowed to leave the country and that he at once retired to France.

They were told, in his presence, to go and consult with the others and to bring back their answer. The women then went out.[1]

After a few minutes they returned and, on being asked for their answer, said that the unanimous reply of the women was this: that they would never desert their men; that, even if the men wished it, they would always oppose the surrender of the Alcazar; that, if the time should come when there would not be enough soldiers left to man the defences, then they would take up arms and do so themselves—as had the women of Saragossa.[2]

After this Major Rojo was escorted out of the Waggon Entrance and returned to the house from which he had come. There followed some minutes of complete silence. Then a furious fusillade broke out, at first from the side on which Major Rojo had disappeared, and afterwards from the others.

At 10.30 p.m. two violent bombing attacks were made; one from the Stable Approach and up the Zig-Zag, the other against the Waggon Entrance (in the west façade). To these attacks no reply was made for some time. Then a burst of concentrated rifle-fire, poured suddenly upon the militia-men, drove them back.

It seems that the enemy, believing that the defenders of the Alcazar now realized the hopelessness of their position, expected a sortie en masse by the whole garrison. During several hours voices kept calling, "Come on then!" "We are ready for you!" "When are you coming?"

---

[1] The calling of the three women, the questions put to them, and their answer, are especially interesting. But, whereas most of the garrison say that Major Rojo entered the Alcazar on that night, others say that the women were called to the office but that the answer was shouted to him across the plaza or given over the telephone—this being still serviceable.

[2] The siege of Saragossa referred to by the women was the second of the two in the year 1808. There being no regular garrison, the men and women of the town manned the ramparts and defended the place for two months against a French army of eighteen thousand, equipped with siege artillery. And, even when the French stormed the ramparts, the inhabitants continued to defend, street by street for another three weeks. One girl, known

The sound of mining, which had been low and even, became louder at about 3 a.m. and there were small explosions at regular intervals.

The casualties of the day were one dead and six wounded.

THE TWELFTH OF SEPTEMBER

The next six days proved a greater strain to the garrison than any up till this time. Now the sound of mining was always to be heard, and no one warned for duty on the threatened side of the Alcazar can have failed to wonder what the chances were of the mines being exploded before his term of duty was over. Only officers and a few selected volunteers were employed on those posts which it was believed must inevitably be destroyed; and their tour of duty was only two hours. But the strain seems to have been felt by the garrison at large. There were several suicides, but none among the women. Those who blew out their brains when at their posts, or more commonly when waiting to go on duty, were neither all of one class or age. It is said that they included an officer, who was thought to be particularly level-headed and phlegmatic; a rather stubborn sergeant of the Guardia Civil; and at least one young soldier.

At 6 a.m. the "155's" and the "75" battery opened fire and continued it throughout the day. The shells were at first directed into the courtyard; especially against the inner side of the south façade. After some hours of this the gunners turned their attention to the inner side of the west façade. The Quarters-of-the-Soldiers were also bombarded but, short of levelling their ruined walls to the ground, no further harm could be done to them.

---

afterwards as the Maid of Saragossa, especially distinguished herself, directing for weeks the cannon, of which her dead lover had been in command.

PLATE 25

THE MINES

The explosion of the two mines on September 18th, seen from the point where the "movie-men" stood in the Chapter "News Reel."

THE RESULT

The whole south-west corner of the Alcazar has been blown away. Across the foreground sprawls the framework of the cupola which topped the tower. On the extreme left is seen the "Arms Museum Breach." Between the two breaches a fang of wall remains. This is seen also on Plate No. 9, to the right of the church tower.

PLATE 26

ALCAZAR CAPUCHINOS DINING-HALL

(behind the low wrecked walls is the
famous wash-house basement).

THE ALCAZAR AND ITS DEFENCES ON THE SOUTH SEEN FROM ACROSS THE CORRALILLO

In Toledo the event of the day was the arrival of the Chilean Ambassador. The defence of the Alcazar by, as it was then generally believed, the cadets of the Academy had stirred the admiration of the world. So after the failure of Canon Camarassa's visit, the Chilean Ambassador, as doyen of the Diplomatic Corps in Madrid, had approached the Government. He wished to assure these young men that in the eyes of all the world their honour had been more than vindicated, and that they should rightly take the chance offered of saving their lives. Permission had been given him and he came to Toledo. For reasons not stated, he wished to make the appeal himself, and by telephone. Possibly it was felt that an ambassador could hardly allow himself to be blindfolded, even in order to penetrate into a besieged fortress. Till the night before the telephone wires had, by strange chance, never been cut. However, after Major Rojo's last parley some militia-men had smashed the wires by throwing bombs at them. The Ambassador was therefore unable to get in touch with the Alcazar, and as the besieging force seems to have made no further attempt to help him get in touch with the garrison in any other way, the defenders of the Alcazar never heard of this diplomat's kindly intention.

On this day the expert captain who had been charged with constant observation of the mining operations, made a confidential report to the commander of the garrison. From the sounds heard and from the regularity of the blasting charges, he was convinced that the mining was now being done by experts and that they were making rapid progress towards the south-west tower. As a result of this information it was decided that the final preparations could no longer be delayed. The women and children, therefore, were moved; some into the sub-basement on the east, in which the swimming bath was situated; others into the part of the "catacomb road" which ran under the north side of the Alcazar.

In the swimming-bath there was some ventilation, but the smell from some drains of stagnant water, too foul to be used for any other purpose, was by now atrocious. As for the vaults on the north side, they had no light and no ventilation except the door onto the dark corridor out of which they led. After a few days the smell was terrible. Movable sanitary arrangements had to be improvised but there was no means of scouring out these receptacles and, as time went on, they became unspeakably foul. Burning them out was tried, but resulted in a still more sickening stench. But these quarters were thought less dangerous than any others and in them the women and children remained until the Alcazar was relieved.

The guns ceased fire when the light failed. The night was comparatively calm.

The casualties as reported, were:—one died of shock, two wounded.

THE THIRTEENTH OF SEPTEMBER

Throughout the night the compressors had been at work and the drills busy in the mines.

At 7 a.m. the "155's" all opened fire and continued their bombardment throughout the day. The damage was done chiefly to the interior of the courtyard, where further portions of the galleries were knocked down. These crashing to the ground caused the whole basement to vibrate, to the terror of the children. The bombardment was continuous and gave no breathing space all day. There was difficulty in distributing meals. Men in some of the outworks did not get their food till the day was done.

At dusk the gunners ceased fire and after that the rifle fusillade was no more than spasmodic.

Some time before midnight a call for a parley was made

from a house on the south. All firing ceased and the parley was held, from window to window, across the little plaza of the Capuchinos. Once more the question of evacuating the women and children was raised. The speaker on the farther side of the plaza asserted that all newspapers published in Seville and Salamanca (and therefore under control of the Nationalists) urged that the women and children should be allowed to leave the Alcazar; and that it was reasonable to assume that this represented the views of General Franco and of General Mola.

To this, answer was made that the women and children would be evacuated if a letter ordering this were received, duly signed and rubricated by these Generals or by responsible members of the Burgos Government. The words "Burgos Government" were drowned by shouts and oaths, and heavy fire was poured upon the window at which the spokesman of the Alcazar had been standing. The fusillade spread to the other sides. Bombs were thrown, with no military object, against the walls. For a long time this hubbub continued.

Even had the commander of the garrison felt disposed to send out the women and children, he could hardly have been encouraged to do so by the newspapers published in Madrid. Many of these had lately been tossed into the Stable Approach and other places where they were sure to be picked up by the garrison. In several of these, including comparatively moderate Socialist papers, the view was expressed that the Government had no authority to guarantee the defenders of the Alcazar their lives, nor the lives of their families; that the garrison of the Alcazar had defied the people, and whatever the Government might say, the militia-men would see to it that not one in the Alcazar escaped death.[1]

When the noise which had ended this parley ceased the compressors could no longer be heard, and it was thought by many that the moment for the explosion of the mines had

---

[1] The Socialist "Claridad" is one of the papers quoted, and was the organ of the Prime Minister, Largo Caballero.

come. Many of the women spent much of the night upon their knees, praying.

Owing to this alarm, the wounded had been taken down to the sub-basement on the south, previously occupied by the women and children. Later, however, hand-work was begun again by the miners.

The casualties of the day had been two wounded.

THE FOURTEENTH OF SEPTEMBER

Before dawn the compressors had resumed work and the chattering of the drills could be heard throughout the basement. Soon after it was light the miners must have encountered other difficulties, for they took to hand-work again. Then after another hour or two the drills started. In the lowest chamber of the north-west tower the sound seemed so close that someone might have been hammering furiously on a wall in the next room. The engineer captain, and those whom he had instructed, after further prolonged soundings expressed the view that one mine was already level with the tower; that, if it was continued, it would pass under the tower; but that it would not be below the level of the sub-basement. In spite of this it was decided to remove the wounded once more, and they were taken to the old-time chapel under the tower on the north-west corner. Thus the west and south sides of the basement had been cleared. No more could be done.

At 8.15 a.m. the "155" guns and the "75" battery opened fire and kept up this fire all day. The rifle fusillade, too, was intense. But, as often, no reply at all was made to it.

At dusk the enemy commenced one of his usual bombing attacks from the Santa Cruz against the Stable Approach. On this occasion there was no real attempt to penetrate the defences. The militia-men contented themselves by advancing in small numbers to behind the gate of the Santa Cruz terrace, which made for them a sort of half-way house. From there they lobbed bombs across the road into the ruined corner of the House-of-the-Military-Government. All these efforts were completely disregarded by the defence.

At nightfall it appeared that the enemy had made new dispositions in order to keep up the fusillade throughout the hours of darkness. At dusk several freshly placed machine-guns opened fire and remained in action, at short intervals, throughout the night.

At about 10 p.m. much shouting was heard from San Servando and all the enemy's positions across the river. At first the words could not be understood but at length some parties of the enemy settled down to singing, to a tune well known at the time, "Send out the women! It will soon be too late!" The last sentence was repeated at intervals for a long time.

THE FIFTEENTH OF SEPTEMBER

The fusillade had hardly slackened all night and with that and the chatter of the miners' drills, sleep had been hard to come by.

Before 7 a.m. the "155's" on the Dehesa de Pinedo (north of the town) opened fire, dropping their shells into the courtyard and especially against the north side of it. The galleries on the south side had all collapsed. That side of the "Hall-of-the-Great-Stairs" [1] had now been broken down and the state stairway was all exposed. Thus the shells crossing the Hall began to wreck, from their rearward side, the rooms which faced south.

Throughout the morning the miners alternatively blasted and worked with their drills. It was estimated that one of the two

[1] This state stairway and the remains of the Hall can be seen in Plate 10.

mines was now complete and work in it had ceased; but that the other had not yet reached the point at which the enemy proposed to place the explosives.

During the morning the observation posts, high in the Alcazar, reported a big gun being brought towards Toledo in a lorry. This disappeared for some time, but finally the gun was seen being brought into position on the Campimento (across the river). Shortly afterwards it opened fire upon the east flank of the Alcazar and began pounding at the foot of this façade. The gunners got the range quickly, their fire was accurate and most of the shells did much damage to the walls, which rose like a cliff above the Esplanade.[1] Several shells, landing at exactly the same spot beside one of the lofty windows near the south-east corner, split the wall; though it was here some ten feet thick. Subsequent shells detached this portion and it crashed down onto the Esplanade; leaving a gap through which the interior of the room—the ante-room of the Cavalry Library—could be seen.

In the late afternoon the gunners switched their fire more to the south and dropped some shells upon the Curved Passage, wrecking it still further. Then, just before dusk, they sent a few through the narrow gap between the Capuchinos and the Alcazar itself. These burst by the steps of the south façade. Soon after 6 p.m. the light became bad, and as this side of the Alcazar was not floodlit the gunners ceased fire.

No gun which had shelled the Alcazar had been so well handled as this new "155"; and as soon as it opened fire the other guns were silent and did not fire again that afternoon.

The evening fusillade was particularly fierce.

Later, another bombing attack was made from the Santa Cruz against the Stable Approach. This was again disregarded.

All through the night blasting at frequent intervals in the mine kept those in the Alcazar on edge and made sleep difficult.

[1] See Plates 32 and 39.

The bombardment of the east façade had caused losses to the garrison. For several shells passing through the windows had wrecked some of the classrooms on this side. The observation posts, and such sentries as were essential, had also suffered. The casualties for the day were:—four dead; four wounded.

THE SIXTEENTH OF SEPTEMBER

At dawn it was observed that another "155" gun had joined the one which had been brought into position the day before, in the olive yards of a slope two miles away, across the river. There had been two "155's" for several weeks in the Campimento de Alijares, which were also on the other side of the river. Thus there were now four of these guns on that side and facing the east flank of the Alcazar.

At 7.45 all four began a bombardment of the east façade. This façade being two storeys higher than the north one, not only provided a better target but also was more vulnerable. Hammered by these heavy shells, many of the facing stones were broken and shaken down. The breach made in the anteroom of the cavalry library the day before was widened, till the hole was large enough for a motor-car to have been driven through it; though it was many feet above the ground. Shells entering the low windows of the basement and sub-basement began to demolish the wall from the inside. In this way some of the little classrooms were wrecked and the doors which led from them up into the catacomb road were burst in. This necessitated building barricades behind these blown-in doors, to prevent shell splinters entering the catacomb road, which was now the chief means of communication from one part of the Alcazar to another, and one of the few fairly safe places in the whole building. Soon the lower part of this cliff-like façade looked as if it had been attacked with a giant's pneumatic road drill.[1]

The bombardment continued with intervals throughout the day.

But in spite of the damage that was being done to this side of the Alcazar and of the growing possibility of a breach being made in this side, also, the chief interest centred always upon the mines. One was now always silent. In the other a series of explosions was heard, much louder than those of ordinary blasting. Now only such of the sentries as were absolutely essential, were employed upon that threatened side of the building; and the garrisons who would have to defend the rooms and windows in case of attack were kept as far back as possible. The expert squad was for ever on the alert and reported that the nearest mine was now just below the outer corner of the south-west tower.

During the morning three large Nationalist planes appeared and bombed the enemy who had turned out in great numbers on the Zocodover to watch them. Screens were spread in the courtyard of the Alcazar to signal to the planes which, after circling overhead, flew off towards Marqueda and Talavera.

Only a few minutes after they had disappeared, enemy planes hove into sight. They reconnoitred for some time. Then they flew back towards Madrid.

In the late afternoon the enemy's "75" battery joined in the bombardment.

As the light failed all guns ceased fire. The evening was calm.

After nightfall, there being no moon, a detachment was sent out and brought in more wheat. It seems that wheat was now being stored, also, in the House-of-the-Military-Government; this being done so that, if the Alcazar itself were entirely

[1] This façade, with the windows of its basement and sub-basement, are seen in Plate 32; and a barricade such as has been described is seen in the photograph of the catacomb road on Plate 7.

destroyed by the explosion of the mines, there would still be some of the defenders left to carry on the tradition and the defence.

Many of the garrison had for some time been expecting the explosion of the mines at any moment. Sentry duty in the rooms on the threatened side had become a great strain. Presumably as one result of this, an officer disappeared during the late evening and was never seen again, though how he made his way out of the Alcazar remained a mystery.

The casualties of the day were one killed and six wounded.

THE SEVENTEENTH OF SEPTEMBER

The night passed uneventfully, though there were bursts of machine-gun and rifle-fire at times. To these, as usual, no reply was made.

At 8.30 a.m. all the six "155" guns opened fire; the two on the north side sending their shells into the courtyard, and the four across the river hammering at the east façade.

The mines were silent and everyone at that corner of the Alcazar expected the explosion from minute to minute. Most of the women and children were transferred to the sub-basement on the east side, the rest of them to a vault on the north side. The hospital, the furniture of the chapel, and the Blessed Virgin of the Alcazar, were also taken to the north basement; it being thought that these places stood some chance of not being destroyed by the coming explosions.

During the afternoon the guns were quiet and in the silence the strain of waiting seems to have been greater. It is said that on that afternoon there was another suicide.

At 5 p.m., so shortly after the "Take Cover" that the garrison had hardly had time to do so, all the "155's" opened fire simultaneously from both fronts.

A little later the observation posts reported another two "155's" being brought into position on the Campimento de Alijares. These shortly joined in the bombardment of the east façade. The gunners of this section seemed skilful and got the range almost at once.

At dusk a violent fusillade broke out on all sides. The compressors started again. This came as a relief to everyone, as it was believed that, as long as they were running, the explosion could not take place.

With the coming of night the guns ceased fire. The fusillade, however, was kept up with great vigour for several hours.

The reported casualties of the day were two wounded.

A man I knew, one of the Falangistas who were in the Alcazar, told me how calm and dark this night was; how being off duty he went out onto the Esplanade and strolled to and fro in the darkness. The ground near the Alcazar was too full of shell-holes, but over by the edge of the terrace it was better walking. He strolled about for a long time, listening to the sound of the river flowing over the weirs below. Sometimes he could hear the enemy talking in their positions across the gorge. He told me how he noted, as he came to each dwarf acacia tree, which of his feet was leading; how the left foot meant that it would be "to-night," and the right foot meant that it would be "to-morrow" that the mines would be set off and end him and his universe; how sometimes he cheated and hung back; "to-night . . . to-morrow . . . to-morrow . . . tomorrow!"

THE EIGHTEENTH OF SEPTEMBER

With the first light there began from all sides the most furious fusillade which had yet been experienced. Meanwhile the sound of the drills had become so close that it seemed they might at any moment break through into the south-west tower. At 6 a.m. the fusillade all at once ceased.

Five minutes later all the "155" guns began an intense bombardment of the east façade. In the swimming-bath, which formed the sub-basement on that side, were many of the women and children. The few windows, high up and slanting, had been barricaded with bricks and masonry, and the place was in almost complete darkness. At ordinary times this great empty chamber was full of echoes. Now with these heavy high-explosive shells bursting against its outer wall, and on the terrace just beyond, the din was stupendous and terrifying. Here, nevertheless, the women and children were kept; for it was believed that this intensity of artillery fire was designed to drive the defenders to the other side of the Alcazar, where they would then be destroyed by the explosion of the mines.

The fact that rifle-fire had ceased convinced the Command that the time had now come. It is said that across the official log-book of the Alcazar a line was drawn and under it was written:—

"All possible having been done, we commend ourselves to God."

NEWS REEL

All indeed was ready. The explosive charges had been carried to the mines more than thirty hours before. The electric wires had been laid. The population had been warned.

Orders had been given that everyone should be clear of the town by five in the morning and should be at certain assigned points, a mile or so away, by six. But the order was largely disregarded; as orders are in Spain. The houses near the Alcazar had for a long time now been occupied by the militia-men and there were no inhabitants left in that quarter. In other parts of the town most of the occupants had shrugged their shoulders and remained. An old man and his daughter, questioned later, gave me these as their reasons for staying where they were; firstly, they feared that, if their house was left empty for a few hours, the militia-men would pillage it; secondly, so many awful things had happened during the past weeks that the odd chance of a stone, hurled aloft by the explosion, falling and crushing them did not seem worth worrying about; thirdly—and this perhaps proved decisive—they "did not like the country," and as likely as not, neither of them had been outside the city walls twice in the past twenty years. Some preparations they did make. They hung up again the religious pictures which they had hidden, and they put a crucifix in each room.

Some five or six thousand persons, however, did leave the town and assembled not far from the Arms Factory.

The Government forces in Toledo had resorted to mining, only when other means of obtaining possession of the Alcazar had failed. At first they had counted on terrorizing the defenders into submission. Then they had tried starving them out. Then they had tried battering the Alcazar to pieces with shell-fire. All these had failed and now, during the past three weeks, it had been upon the mines that they had relied.

The shafts had been driven from the interior of two houses, Nos. 14 and 20 in the calle de Juan Labrada, an alley running parallel with the west side of the Alcazar, and the second street away from it. These houses were some eighty yards distant from the building and on considerably lower ground. The calle de Juan Labrada is a very narrow one and from it nothing can be seen except a strip of sky.

No. 20 was a small middle-class house, probably built in the nineteenth century but following the traditional Toledan plan. The little passage from the front door led into the usual diminutive open-air patio. This was wainscotted in glazed heraldic tiles; and out of it led the little rooms of the ground floor. The mine-shaft had been driven from a room at the back of the house, straight into the slope of the hill, and all the earth and rock from it had been piled in the patio and ground-floor rooms. No one had troubled to remove the furniture, ornaments or even the pictures on the walls. So the dust and rubble had mounted around them as waters would in a flood, till at last the debris reached more than half-way to the ceiling.

No. 14, a larger and more spacious house, with large dim lofty rooms, had doubtless once been the home of some aristocratic family. However, for a generation at least it had been used as a workshop by a small printer, and there was a good deal of machinery in various rooms on the ground floor.

In both houses there had been space enough to dispose of the excavated earth, and from the street there was nothing to show that work had been done inside. Indeed it seems probable that some of the Alcazar's sortie parties, when searching for the mine-shafts, must have penetrated into this alley and passed the doors of both houses.

The morning of the 18th of September was sunny and very clear. To east and north and west the plain rolled on to great distances. Eighty miles away, along the northern skyline, ran the Sierra de Guadarrama. The day was not yet hot. The air was deliciously fresh. On the low ridges north of the town were the camera-men and newspaper correspondents who had started from Madrid before dawn; and somewhere not very far away was the Minister for War who, it was said, was to make the contact and explode the mines. With him were other officials, and the friends he had brought with him.

The moment drew near. The camera-men and newspaper correspondents waited with their watches and their field-glasses.

"Through?"

"Yep! I'm fixed."
"Now? . . . Eh?"
"O.K. by me!"

Bending forward a little, the movie men commenced to wind the handles of their cameras, which began a dry hollow ticking, like the sound of robot beetles.

"Bet you they'll be late."
"Quite likely."
"It's a five and ten cents war, anyway."

Someone sighed. The tripods of the cameras, straddling the parched grass and pinkish dust, cast their shadows far away to the right.

The ground in front fell away steeply. The air was crystal clear. Across the open valley was Toledo, spread like a rumpled cloth over its little hills; dusty pink, dusty fawn, dusty yellow; asleep. On its skyline, to the left, dwarfing all else, stood the Alcazar, square, immense, with the two remaining spires clear cut against the paleness of the sky. The nearer end of the building was formless and curiously indistinct; as though the whole was made of wax and the nearer portions, placed too close to a fire, had melted and guttered away.

"It's the ha'f after."
"Not by my watch. How about yours?"
"Pas encore."
"What d'you suppose it'll feel like when the thing goes up?"
"Just a bang. Just a black-out . . . and then 'Good morning, Jesus.'"
"Poor silly punks."
"Y'know I just can't help feeling sorry for them. I'm that way. Always was. Poor kids!"

"Quite. . . . Quite."
"Lend me your glasses?"
"Prenez."
"Thanks a lot."
"Vous voyez bien?"
"Boy, isn't that just marvellous! I can count the stones!"

Down in the valley a man was running.

"Qu'est-ce que c'est?"

No one answered.

"And their pals can't be more than fifty miles away. They might have got here in a fortnight."
"Isn't that just too bad!"
"A bit tough."
"Fifty miles be damned! What's he got, this Varyela, or whatever he calls himself? Four boys and a truck. If these guys weren't just lousy they'd get round the arse of him and cut him off."
"Is that so?"

Their shadows stretched far along the ridge to their right, shadows of long lean giants.
In the town the first clock struck the half-hour. No one moved.

"The ha'f af-ter."

The camera-men went on turning. The silence grew more tense.
A second clock struck the half-hour.

"Fifteen seconds late."

A third clock chimed.

"Twenty seconds."
"Perhaps their bloody thing won't go off at all. It's a five and ten cents war, anyway."
"Would you mind being quiet?"

A cigarette was thrown away.

"Thirty seconds."
"Forty."
"I said it was a five and ten cents war."
"Fifty."
"One minute."
"Gee . . . . !"

Watching, they saw the great square bulk of the Alcazar shudder, heave. Then an immense volume of stones and smoke spurted straight into the sky. The fragments raced aloft; huge blocks, large lumps, stones, long things which might have been beams or girders. They tore upwards, clear above the smoke which rolled like lava over the town. The smaller stones were leading now; their lead increased. The heavy blocks paused imperceptibly and began to fall. Then they were lost in the billowing clouds of smoke which now hid all that quarter of the city. The little fragments, too, lost velocity and fell like rocket sticks. The pall of smoke rolled on, spreading outwards.

For a moment or two no one spoke.

"Alors?"
"We may as well, mayn't we?"
"The show's over. There's nothing to hang around for."
"Boy, what a noise!"
"Now that's queer, when I think of it. I never heard a sound."

The photographs are taken from the opposite ends of the same axis.

SEEN FROM OUTSIDE

One of the two breaches caused by the mines of September 18th. On Plate No. 9 it is seen behind the church tower.

SEEN FROM INSIDE

This room had a garrison of seven. During the twelve minutes which followed the explosion these built the barricade seen in the foreground and then defended it against assaults by company after company of the enemy.

PLATE 28

GOVERNMENT MILITIA-MEN ADVANCING TO
AN ATTACK ON THE ALCAZAR

The photograph was taken from under the cliff-like North
Terrace, and the Alcazar is behind the reader. The street out
of which the armoured car has pushed its snout is the Calle del
Carmen. Opposite that part of the armoured car is the arch
of La Sangre, through which steps lead up into the Plaza
Zocodover.

"No?"
"Nope. Never a sound."
"Queer."

They began drawing in the spidery metal legs of their tripods. They shouldered their cameras and set off down the hill. For a time no one spoke. A man from behind left the one he had found himself walking beside, ran on and joined the three in front.

The man behind was muttering to himself "A five and ten cents war."

The four in front walked on with their cameras on their shoulders, a little awkward in their silence.

THE DAMAGE

What happened to the Alcazar was this. The two mines exploded simultaneously, one under the south-west corner, the other under the "Waggon Entrance," exactly in the middle of the west façade.

The earth opened. From two enormous craters, as from the mouths of two volcanoes, everything was hurled into the air. The south-west tower, a hundred feet high and weighing perhaps a thousand tons, shot aloft, disintegrating as it went. Above the "Waggon Entrance" the whole façade rose and went skyward.

As for the houses on this side of the Alcazar, the street of them which was nearest to it, ceased to have any existence. There were no ruins. The houses had vanished. In the street behind this the ramshackle buildings shook and collapsed like card houses. Yet the force of the explosion was in the main vertical and, beyond these two demolished streets, not much harm was done to Toledo.

The Alcazar was hidden in a great cloud of smoke. Debris soared above it. Then, piece by piece, and the heaviest first, the fragments fell. The top of the tower, which was of stone and brick and Roman-like cement, had gone aloft in one single piece. In a single piece it landed and lay, the size of a small cottage, tilted upon the slopes of one of the craters. The spire-like cupola of this tower also went up entire, shedding its slates and woodwork as it went. It fell and lay across the wreckage like a giant pantomime crocodile, of metal girders.

After these two great pieces, the other heaviest boulders of cement and brickwork fell. Then it rained fragments over all the ground near by. It drizzled stones and bricks over all that corner of Toledo.[1]

The dust settled. The smoke cleared. The Alcazar came into sight again. The whole south-west corner was gone, and a gap, forty yards wide, could be seen in the middle of the west façade.

The spell was over. From their hiding-places where they had been sheltering the enemy's troops began to appear. They massed quickly, as had been planned. Then, led by tanks and armoured cars, they closed in upon the Alcazar for the grand assault.

THE EIGHTEENTH OF SEPTEMBER

CRISIS!

But before the undisciplined forces of the Government could be got under way, and even before the smoke had cleared, the

---

[1] A piece of cornice of the Alcazar, weighing nearly a ton, fell on a corner of the Cathedral, three hundred yards away. It fell from so great a height that its fall was almost vertical. A block, the size of an armchair, landed on the roof of a club and crashed through four storeys to the ground. Yet in the town little harm was done. The Cathedral had much of its priceless stained glass blown in, and its interior lost at once its darkness and its sense of mystery. Beyond that it suffered little.

defenders of the Alcazar were rushing to the posts they were to hold.

The explosion of the mines had come when, as often before, the garrison had been waiting for it. As the mines exploded, the whole building shivered. One officer said that the sensation was like that in a ship which, manœuvring in a dock, comes head on against the wall. The shock came first; then the sound. Then within a second or two the whole Alcazar was filled with so dense a smoke that nothing could be seen. No one knew what damage had been done, or whether he himself were not the only survivor.

The men struggled to their feet, staggered through the smoke, and felt their way up the stairs and round the corners. As the smoke thinned the greatness of the damage was seen. In place of one breach, there were now three to defend. If the courtyard of the Alcazar be considered as a lidless box, the north end had long been knocked out. Now the whole south-west corner had been torn away, and in the west side there was a gap nearly fifty yards wide.

As the men struggled to their posts they found unexpected difficulties in their way. Corridors, and the cloisters under the galleries, were encumbered by barricades which had been shaken down by the explosion. The great stairs, on which a path had always been kept clear of ruins, so that the gallery could be reached, were now choked with stones and fragments which had been shaken down from above. Some men, helped by their comrades, climbed the uncertain crags of masonry. But many in their weakened state were unable to. Scaling-ladders, which were normally used by the cadets for escalading practice, and rope-ladders of the gymnastic equipment, were fetched in haste from the basement, where during the first days of the siege they had been stored and catalogued. After much exertion the men reached their posts, but only just in time; for already great numbers of the enemy were swarming up the Zig-Zag and were pressing forward to the general assault.

The danger on the north side was nothing new. The breach had been open there for more than a fortnight. The risks created by it had been calculated and plans made. On the west, however, the men rushing to their posts found an appalling situation. For the rooms which they had till now defended and the loopholed windows at which they had stood, had ceased to exist. For more than forty yards the west side of the Alcazar had vanished; and through the thinning smoke the men saw the sunlight, the roofs of the town, and the empty hills beyond.

The situation can best be understood by looking at Plate No. 27. These show the breach, both from outside and from inside. In the outside view split-open rooms can be seen, one above the other. The lowest, now partly obscured by debris, had been known as the Arms Museum.

Till the explosion of the mines this room had been on an upper storey, over the Waggon Entrance, and some thirty feet above the ground. Within a single minute, not only the situation, but even the ground level itself had been completely changed. The wall had disappeared, as though it had been the door of a cupboard which had been torn off its hinges. And, instead of the room being thirty feet out of reach, it was now on ground level; and a long easy slope would lead the assaulting column straight into it. This is what the seven men who came scrambling through the smoke found.

The room had been as large and lofty as a ballroom in a country house. Now the whole south end of it was gone and, where it had been, there yawned the cellar choked with a tangle of ties and girders and rubble which had fallen into it from the floors above.[1]

There was no time to report or ask for orders. Nor did the men know who, except themselves, had been left alive. In wild haste they seized on anything to hand and began to build the

[1] Plate 9 shows the window of this room. It is the one just visible between the church tower and the white loft on the left of it. The level of the ground below the window can be estimated from the houses in the left corner of the picture. These faced the Arms Museum from across the road.

barricade which can be seen in Plate No. 27. Now, they were not building it only to protect themselves and some unimportant post, for behind them, on their left, was a doorway which led directly into the main courtyard—the heart of the Alcazar.

The men were weak from under-feeding. The work of throwing up the barricade was not quarter done, before the leading skirmishers of the enemy came clambering over the ruins below. Advancing slowly, they opened fire. But the men in the room had no time to reply. They went on fetching stones from the window barricade, and building them into this new one across the room. Bullets spattered on the wall behind them. But their end of the room was hidden from the enemy. Thus, as the seven carried the stones from the window towards the barricade, they remained unseen. However, as they drew near to it, they came into view. Then it was necessary, either to crawl, pushing the stones before them, or else to rush into view, place their stones and bolt back again. The barricade, to reach from one wall to another, had to be some thirty feet long. To finish it would have taken them an hour but within eleven minutes the enemy's assault began.[1]

In making plans to meet the explosion of the mines, the point which had been thought would be most dangerous had been the south-west corner of the building. It had been known that the tower and the whole corner had been mined, and would be demolished. This occurred. The tower which had formed, as it were, the dove-tailing of this great square box, had been blown out and, where it had been, there was now empty air. Yet this corner, in spite of all this destruction, had not been made easy to the enemy. The outer walls had van-

---

[1] The time between the explosion of the mines and the onslaught of the firot attacking columns is variously given. An Englishman who watched the assault from the Zocodover gave it as between ten and eleven minutes. The "official estimate" of the command of the Alcazar is, I believe, thirteen minutes. One of the officers who fought on the north breach gave it as fourteen minutes. But from whichever estimate we accept, there must be subtracted the time necessary for the men to reach their posts: and doing so had proved more difficult than had been expected.

ished, but the inner walls, those of the rooms behind, had only been felled to the level of the first storey. Now they looked down sheer into the hollows where the rooms had been. To mount them scaling-ladders would be needed. But to bring any to this point would have been almost impossible. For the whole space in front of these walls was encumbered by girders from the roof and from the floors above.

As no one had been able to tell what would be the effect of the mine explosions, no exact plan of defence had been possible. Now the men told off for it, swarming like ants in the ruins of a kicked-open ant-hill, scrambled about among the still crumbling ruins, trying to find some line which they could hold. With them they carried rifles, boxes of ammunition, cases of bombs, steel plates with which to build some sort of loopholes, a machine-gun. Crawling over the boulders and creeping under fallen girders, they finally established themselves in the outer crust of the ruins.

There remained the great breach upon the north. Plate No. 11 gives an easily understood picture of it. The terrace here was some thirty yards wide and the photograph was taken from the corner of it. Of this end of the Alcazar all that remained was the great bank of broken stones and rubble. In the foreground are two of those incongruous details, so commonplace in modern warfare; a lamp-post, still uninjured, and a burnt-out lorry.

To the right of the lamp-post, and above the breach, can be seen a plaster-covered wall. On it are arches, moulded in relief. These repeated the arches of the fallen upper arcades, and they enable the reader to understand where the floors of these galleries were; which is important, as much of the defence of the breach was conducted from them.

Just behind the summit of the breach itself the defenders had scooped out rifle-pits, and had built themselves head-cover with steel ammunition boxes, stones and the like. There may have been a dozen or more of these pits, large enough to hold two or three men. They were now manned. Into one or two, machine-guns had to be carried, into all a supply of ammunition and of hand-bombs.

The corners of both galleries were garrisoned, for from these cross-fire could be brought to bear over the forward slopes of the breach; and in the last extremity, should the enemy reach the courtyard, these galleries would form the last line of defence.

Within that dozen minutes, between the explosion of the mines and the delivery of the assault, those three breaches of the Alcazar were manned and their fortifications put into some sort of order. Meanwhile within the courtyard, on the stairs, in the basement, everywhere, parties were rebuilding those barricades which had been broken down by the explosion, and building new ones which breaches had made necessary. Those wild minutes in the Alcazar must have been something like those during scene-shifting in a great stage spectacle; but with the haste trebled, and with scene-shifters who had been starving for weeks and had had no sleep for three nights.

At the end of this period the assaulting columns closed in upon the Alcazar, to settle the issue with bomb and bayonet.

There were four distinct columns of assault; one directed against the great north breach; another against the breach of the Arms Museum; another upon that wide gap where the south-west corner of the Alcazar had been; the remaining one —unconnected with the breaches—across the waste land of the Corralillo. Many attacks were made on each one of these lines of approach. How many, it is difficult to say, for, when one wave of assault fell back, another rolled on.

The assault upon the great north breach began before the others; for no better reason than because this breach was nearest to the Zocodover, the most convenient massing-place for enemy troops. The first that the defenders saw of it was a crowd of Government militia-men swarming up over the ruins where the north-west tower had fallen across the Cuesta and blocked it. Seen from the breach this attack was somewhat on the left front. Fire was opened at once from all the rifle-pits, and from the end of the east gallery. But the militia-men came on in such numbers that it proved difficult to stay them with rifle-fire. The defenders in the west gallery, being unable on account of the walls to see this attack, began to throw bombs over the intervening ruins, and so down onto the heads of the unseen enemy. This brought the attack to a momentary standstill. But the enemy troops then crouched behind boulders and any cover they could find, and engaged the defenders with rifle-fire at point-blank range. And, hardly had this fire fight begun, than another wave of the attack came swarming up behind the first. It swept through it and reached the slopes of the breach itself. For some minutes there was hand-to-hand fighting, but apparently with rifles and bombs, and not with the bayonet. Eventually this wave, also, was checked. But as it rolled back, an entirely fresh assault was begun from another angle. For some minutes enemy troops had been pouring down from the Zocodover, through the arch of la Sangré, and through the ruins of the houses, where the Inn of Cervantes had stood. From there they had reached the Zig-Zag and been massing unseen just below the wall of the terrace, here some six feet high. The defenders were still engaged with the remnants of the attack upon their left front, when they saw these new enemy troops clambering up onto the terrace just in front of them. Fire was switched upon them but this did not bring them to a standstill. Crouching low they came forward; and, as they cleared the edge of the wall, others took their place. Soon the terrace was full of them. They drew close to the edge of the breach but, as they advanced, they fired. To fire, they checked. Those behind them checked also. Thus the power of this attack remained for some time that of a ragged line of indifferent shots, instead of the onward surge of several hundred men rushing but a score of yards to victory.

The militia-men had no experience of hand-to-hand fighting and no sense of it. Once on the slopes of the breach they halted and began throwing bombs. Most of those thrown at the crest went over it and burst far below in the courtyard. But those thrown up into the galleries proved most effective and drove back the marksmen of the Guardia Civil, who from there had been bringing cross-fire to bear. Still, to throw bombs the men of the leading line halted; and once halted they did not come on again. The attack had come to a standstill. Yet at each moment the danger increased. For more and more of the enemy were clambering over the wall of the terrace and, presently, their mere weight would drive their front lines up the slope, over the crest and down into the courtyard.

To meet this growing danger, reserves of the Guardia Civil were massed in the courtyard. It is said that bayonets were fixed. In almost solid formation they moved towards the breach, still unseen. They clambered up it and waited for the word. Then suddenly these lines of steady and responsible men came over the crest and swept down upon the militia-men. They were police advancing shoulder to shoulder upon a mob. The militia-men offered no resistance, they fired hardly a shot; they turned and fled before this phalanx. Falling over each other and over the dead and wounded they reached the farther side of the terrace and leaped over the edge onto the slopes below.

For a few moments the Guardia Civil scattered. They cleared the terrace of survivors. Then, still facing front, they backed towards the breach. They crossed it and reached the courtyard. With them they brought a big red flag which the enemy had carried, presumably to plant over the ruins of the Alcazar. After this there was for some time no sign of further attack upon this side. The enemy's dead and dying lay on the slopes of the breach, thickest at the edge of it, like seaweed along high water mark. Below the slopes the terrace was strewn with rifles, boxes of ammunition, ladders, tins of petrol, blankets and newspapers, all the odds and ends that the militia-men brought with them.

For a while the lull lasted on this side and it is now necessary to consider what was happening elsewhere; for, while this attack had been made upon the north breach, others had been thrust home against three separate weak spots.

On the side of the Corralillo the enemy launched a different type of attack. Here alone, the defenders had a clear field of fire; for the Corralillo was flat and bare, without a bush or blade of grass. However, from the enemy's point of view there was no obstacle to hold up an advance, and on the flanks was cover through which his men could work; on the left the houses, and on the right the slopes of the Tagus gorge. Yet, to manœuvre such irregular troops on any but the most direct course would have been impossible. The attack, therefore, was launched straight across the open waste land, and against the kitchens and the dining-hall, a hundred and twenty to a hundred and eighty yards away.[1] Ahead came the armoured cars, one mounting a light cannon in a turret, the other with machine-guns. They came forward at fine speed, rolling over the uneven ground and blazing away as they came. The number of these cars is variously given, as two, or three, or even four.

Behind them came the militia-men, it is said some five or six hundred strong. They came crowding out of the alleys and over the garden walls. They followed the cars as fast as they could, some of the better drilled companies being in lines, the rest straggling after their leaders.

The defenders from the Quarters-of-the-Soldiers, the Capuchinos, and the walls near the dining-hall, opened rapid fire.

[1] Plate 26 shows the line of attack.

The armoured cars, in no way disturbed by this, approached to within some forty yards. There they came to a standstill and brought their guns to play along the loopholes, only some of which were held. On this the defenders withdrew from behind the walls and, in places where it was possible, began lobbing bombs over them. This harried the cars. They began to move to and fro across the front; but once they were travelling laterally, their fire became ineffective. Yet once the defenders had been forced back from their loopholes, the advance of the militia-men was easy. They came on, not at all fast, but in a mass which stretched from one side of the Corralillo to the other. At that moment there seemed nothing to prevent them from reaching the dining-hall and the kitchens. Then from their left flank an intense enfilade fire was suddenly opened upon them. This came from the windows of a basement under the Capuchinos, from which till now no shot had ever been fired. The Capuchinos itself had long been nothing more than empty walls but, under the part of it which stood out into the Corralillo was a vaulted cellar used as a wash-house. The floor of this was sunk considerably below the surface of the Corralillo and the few small windows which lit it were thus almost at ground level. From the other side of the Corralillo these windows would hardly have been noticed; for the wall in which they were ran at an acute angle; and except in the morning was in deep shadow. Thus the enemy had probably never realized the existence of these windows.[1]

It was upon them, however, that the defence of this whole flank did in the end depend. The enemy, now almost a solid crowd, was close to the dining-hall and the kitchens. In another half-minute the leaders would have been clambering up the wall of the dining-hall and would have been entering it through

[1] The wash-house cellar is seen in Plate 26. It is in the shadow, behind the ruins of a low wall. But it had been so battered by subsequent bombardment that the windows which proved so effective on the morning in question had ceased to exist.

the wrecked and glassless windows.[1] But, just when they reached this point, a furious fire was suddenly and unexpectedly opened upon them from their left. They were taken completely in enfilade; one bullet might pass through five or six of them. The garrison in the wash-house was crowding to the windows and firing as rapidly as possible. The militia-men wilted under this. The leaders, almost within reach of the wall, wavered for a moment, not even realizing from where they were being mown down. Then, seeing man after man fall, the whole mob of them bolted back across the Corralillo, leaving little groups of dead and wounded along the front of the dining-hall.

But, while these attacks across the Corralillo and over the north terrace were being made, another two attacks were in progress. It is probable that it was upon them that the enemy had most counted for success. For they were against the breaches made but a quarter of an hour previously by the explosion of the mines; for which he had been waiting fully three weeks.

One of these two assaults was launched against the blown-out south-west corner, the other against the breach in the Arms Museum.

From a purely engineering point of view the mines had been well planned; from a tactical point of view they had not. A glance at the map will show that the approaches to the spots where the breaches had been made, were along narrow alleys. Two led into the south-west corner of the little Capuchinos plaza, the other led from the west, straight into the breach in the Arms Museum. But, however many men were directed through these alleys, they could only go slowly; and, once they emerged into the open, the ground upon which they would have to deploy for attack was now a wild confusion of mine craters and wreckage.

[1] The dining-room with its side consisting of wrecked windows is seen on the right of Plate 26.

The militia-men poured out of these alleys and even broke their way through the houses of the ruined streets. Soon the space to the west of the Alcazar was full of them. The ground here consisted only of craters, debris, boulders and dust; broken and uneven as the mountains of the moon.

Had any reconnaissance been made during those minutes between the explosion of the mines and the arrival of the assaulting columns, the militia-men might have been directed along certain lines of approach and against definite objectives. But there seems to have been no reconnaissance, no plan. The mines had been set off, before an admiring audience and with cinema cameras making their records, then the companies of militia-men came pouring out of the places where they had been sheltering. They reached the sites of the explosions and stood looking about them and waiting for their comrades. Presently they began making their way over the broken ground towards the Alcazar. All was confusion. Soon from the few remaining windows of the Alcazar, marksmen opened fire upon them. The militia-men continued moving forward over the craters but sometimes they stopped to shoot up at the windows.

The attack on the north side had been easy to launch. The men had been massed below a wall parallel to the breach. All they had to do was to clamber up onto the terrace and charge across it.

The assault upon the great breach at the south-west was a very different matter and the launching of attacks upon it would have been difficult, even with trained troops and a competent staff. The crazy slopes of the mine craters and the complexity of the debris on them might have been designed to hamper an assault. Beyond this, it is difficult in all cases to attack the angle of a fortress. Almost inevitably the attacking forces will divide and be deflected along the two sides. Added to this, here all recognizable points which might have acted as leading marks had disappeared.

The militia-men crossed the corner of the Capuchinos plaza

and descending into the mine crater, found themselves faced with exactly the view seen in Plate 25. Before them, where till a quarter of an hour previously the corner tower had stood intact, there rose a slope of ruins; and behind these a great gap, between the remnants of the west façade, on the left, and the still standing south façade, on the right. And across their front, blocking their way, stretched the wrecked framework of the cupola.[1] If the reader will imagine himself clambering over, or under, or through this tangle; if he will imagine, also, that he is being fired on from any window or corner of wall from which he is visible, he will have some idea of the difficulties which the militia-men found in their attack upon the south-west breach.

They floundered forward through the wreckage and up the slope beyond, sometimes throwing a bomb up into the empty rooms before them, sometimes stopping to gape at the enormity of the damage. The defenders recollect how curious it seemed to see these men within a few yards of them, yet gaping about as if they were sight-seeing.

But now from the rear others were pushing on and those in front were forced forward into the south-west breach till they found themselves confronted by walls, just too high and steep for them to scale. They halted. Their comrades pressed on and joined them. There, among the foothills of the ruins, they remained, effecting nothing, tossing bombs into empty rooms and firing up at any place where they suspected the defenders might be lurking. Thus on this corner the attack never developed into an assault.

From about a quarter to seven in the morning, for some four or five hours, the militia-men remained near the mine crater and the ruins of the fallen cupola. Sometimes they fell back and others took their place. Probably their losses were not great. In any case they achieved nothing.

---

[1] Seen on this Plate 25; the direction in which the camera is pointing being exactly the line of attack.

However, if the south-west breach offered no clear objective, and was blocked with obstacles, this was not true of the one fifty yards away, where the wall had been split open and the way lay straight into the Arms Museum.

Plate 27 shows this breach and how comparatively easy the approach to it was.

Within the lowest of the rooms seen in the photograph the seven men were still throwing up some barricade to protect themselves, when the first militia-men appeared from the alley, fifty or sixty yards away. These advanced slowly, clambering over the loose rubble which often turned under their feet. The men behind the barricade opened the rapidest fire they could. All that the militia-men had to do was to disregard this fire, charge on and capture the room. But undisciplined troops cannot endure to be fired at without replying. So, whenever they felt inclined to, the militia-men halted to return the defenders' fire. Thus was the first advantage lost.

When the enemy came to within some twenty yards of the breach, the men behind the barricade drew back into the corner of the room. From there, hidden in part by the barricade and in part by the floor which now jutted out like a terrace, they began hurling bombs out into the open air and so onto the slopes up which the militia-men must advance. This shower of bombs may have caused havoc. In any case it stopped the advance; while those bombs which failed to explode lay among the stones, dangerous for all who touched them.

It seems hardly credible that for a long period these seven men succeeded in driving back the attacks made upon the breach.

Once they gathered way, the militia-men came on with fine spirit. But on such rough ground their companies became mere crowds, each man working on some plan of his own, or on no plan at all. Forty resolute men, working under orders, would certainly have captured the room. But, as it was, never more than four or five followed the same idea, and even when a few, more daring than the rest, gained a footing on the floor of the room itself, they would remain unsupported and be shot down.

After a time the seven in the room were reinforced, and after a time, also, the dead and wounded on the slopes added to the difficulties of the assailants. By now there were, too, marksmen at the windows of the Alcazar, who picked off the militiamen while they were still forming up for an attack.

At intervals throughout the morning these gallant but futile men sacrificed themselves in attempts to gain this single room, held by a handful of Guardia Civil and Falangistas. But by noon it was clear that they would not succeed.

Meanwhile the attacks upon the north façade had weakened. Each had been feebler than the last. The enemy now prepared another, it is said with fresh troops. This attack was made with larger numbers than any of the previous ones, and it was led by a tank.

The tank, it seems, came up from the road beside the river, and turning up the calle del Carmen, came into view of the defenders of Stable No. 4. It passed their loopholes, blazing at them with its gun. The young soldiers of this stable being inexperienced and bombs being scarce, their ration of these had always been strictly limited. But this was a crisis and bombs were now rained down on the tank and on the road in front of it. These did no harm and the tank rounded the far end of the building and entered the Stable Approach. Here it was confronted by iron gates, of no special strength but carefully wired together by the defenders. The tank pressed against these and burst them open. Behind them, as a further obstacle, a large lorry laden with stones had been placed across the roadway, and the space beneath it filled with wire and obstacles. The tank nosed it out of the way. It then continued up the Zig-Zag,

PLATE 29

CARD HOUSES!

The second street away from the west side of the Alcazar, the intervening street having been blown to dust by the explosion of the mines.

VIVA RUSIA!

Scrawled in blood by Government troops upon a captured outwork of the Alcazar.

PLATE 30

THE HOUSE-OF-THE-MILITARY-GOVERNMENT

Seen from the Calle del Carmen which leads down towards the Tagus. The tunnel-like opening is the blown-out end of the famous Stable No. 4. The Santa Cruz, out of the picture, is on the reader's left.

THE INTERIOR OF STABLE NO. 4	VIEW FROM THE "BLOWN-IN WINDOW"
The blown-out end, the horse-troughs on the left, and the barricade in the foreground, can be seen. Across the stable is the light from the "blown-in window."	At the end of the street the Convent of la Concepcion is seen. Through a panel in the arched door, facing the reader, a field-gun engaged the window, through which the reader looks, at a range of 80 yards.

here joined by crowds of cheering militia-men who had come down from the Zocodover and out of the Santa Cruz.

Forcing its way past trees, felled by shell-fire, the tank breasted the slopes and reached the terrace. It then made straight for the breach, accompanied by the militia-men, cheering and waving red flags. Helped by its momentum the tank began to climb the side of the breach and, as it climbed, it fired point-blank at the loopholes only a few yards in front of it. But the men at the loopholes had fallen back and, out of sight, they commenced to toss bombs over the crest of the breach to where the tank was struggling on the other side. It looked for a moment as though the tank might reach the summit and come hurtling down the slope into the courtyard, but the surface was so loose that it could get no grip. Throwing back dust and stones, it slipped backwards to the terrace again. It made two or three attempts but failed at each.

Meanwhile from the galleries the Guardia Civil were lobbing bombs at it, and at the militia-men, who on this occasion had done no more than remain there, ready to follow up any success the tank might have.

Unable to mount the bank, the tank paraded backwards and forwards along the front of the breach, firing at the loopholes along the top of it, and blowing to pieces the ammunition boxes filled with stones, of which these loopholes had been made. Each time the tank approached, the defenders withdrew behind the slope, while their comrades in the ends of the galleries kept up enough fire to prevent the enemy from climbing the breach.

After a time the militia-men, discouraged, began to dribble back. Fresh companies were sent up, but the spirit had gone out of the attack and soon the tank was left alone. Still moving backwards and forwards in front of the breach, and sounding its klaxons to rally the militia-men, the tank fired from time to time into the roofs of the galleries. Eventually it became obvious that no further assault was forthcoming. The tank then waddled back towards the Zig-Zag and retired down it, amidst the shouts and jeers of the garrison.[1]

There seemed some doubt as to the hour at which the last of these various attacks collapsed. It is certain that they began almost exactly at a quarter to seven. Some say that the last was over soon after 10.30. Some say that they continued, at increasingly long intervals, until after 1 o'clock.

When it was clear that no chance remained of capturing the Alcazar that day, the "155" guns opened rapid fire; at first from the east and then from the north fronts. They continued this fire throughout the afternoon, the evening and the following night; so that the bombardment of one day overlapped the bombardment of the next.

Within the Alcazar, all was confusion. Enormous damage had been done by the explosion of the mines. Moreover the shell-fire on the east façade, which had preceded the explosion, had been by far the heaviest that had been experienced throughout the siege.

The spirits of the garrison, which had risen greatly when the last attack had been repulsed, sank when they thought of the night to come. Only when it did, was it possible to make some survey of the damage and the loss of life.

Infinite care had been taken to reduce the death-roll inevitable in the coming explosion. It is said that there had been at that moment only two moving sentries in the doomed corner of the building; one an officer, the other a civilian who some days before had volunteered for this duty. Chance had taken them for those two especial hours during which the mines were exploded, but others had gone on duty believing the risk to be

[1] There is a question as to whether the vehicle which made these attacks was actually a tank, or was only some very heavy armoured car. At least two officers, and several men who saw it, state that it was certainly a tank. But one officer and at least two men believe that it was some form of armoured car; perhaps one of those which had previously made the attack across the Corralillo. Civilians in the town, however, state that there were two tanks in Toledo on that day.

as great as they did that morning. These two men had vanished, together with this great mass of masonry and dust. No trace of them was ever found, nor in all likelihood ever will be.

The casualties for the day amounted to eighteen dead and sixty-two wounded.

THE NIGHT OF THE EIGHTEENTH-NINETEENTH SEPTEMBER

Night fell. The desultory artillery fire continued, and from all sides rifle and machine-gun fusillades remained heavy. The long-expected "day of the Mines" being over all felt entitled to a night of rest, but within ten hours the attacks would start again, and there was no time for it.

For the Command it was necessary to take stock of the position and rearrange the defences, to meet the greatly altered and worsened conditions. For the garrison there was arduous but essential work which must be done before the next day broke.

Within the Alcazar was havoc. Beyond the wrecking of the west side by the explosion of the mines, the shell-fire of the morning, unequalled throughout the siege, had done enormous damage to the east façade.

There was another matter, doubtless realized by the Command early in the day, but known to the garrison as a whole only after nightfall. It was that the outworks and their garrisons had, ever since the early morning, been completely cut off. The shell-fire which had preceded the explosion of the mines had blocked both the swimming-bath exit, and the exit from the Curved Passage. So, since the early morning there had been no communication between the Alcazar, and the Quarters-of-the-Soldiers, the Capuchinos, and the House-of-the-Military-Government. A fifth to a quarter of the total garrison had been thus completely cut off and it was uncertain how many survived. It could be seen that the Capuchinos and the Quarters-of-the-Soldiers were still holding out, but no one knew whether the House-of-the-Military-Government had not been captured and its garrison slaughtered. Many of the women in the Alcazar had sons in that building. There were many, also, whose husbands were in the Capuchinos or the Quarters-of-the-Soldiers. These did not know whether their sons and husbands were alive or dead.

Working-parties were sent to clear the two exits but found that the façade had been so hammered by shell-fire that they had ceased to exist. The blocks of stone which had fallen were so heavy, and the men themselves so weakened by under-feeding and exertion that they were unable to remove them. More help was sent. With crowbars and levers the work was begun. It proved dangerous, the wall having been so loosened by bombardments that, once a stone was touched, others above it often fell. The smell by the swimming-bath door was abominable. Several days before, a fall of wall had killed and buried some of the defenders at this spot. It had been impossible to unearth their bodies. The smell was so unbearable that the men at work, moving the stones, collapsed in fits of nausea, and in vomiting which brought up nothing, for they had had no proper meal that day. This work was done in complete darkness, under an intermittent shell-fire and under a wild but never-ceasing fusillade from across the river.

At length the exits were cleared. Reconnaissance parties were sent out to establish communication with all the outlying garrisons, and to take them food. These parties presently returned and reported that all was well; or, at any rate, as well as could be expected.

The Command seems to have felt that the chances of holding the outlying works had become slight. Orders were given, therefore, for the remaining horses and mules to be brought into the Alcazar itself and stabled in the swimming-bath. This meant much work for the men but came as a great relief to the women who had been housed in the swimming-bath for some days. For the smell of decomposing bodies had been so strong that some of them had not been able to keep down any food.

All this work done on the east side of the Alcazar was, of course, only a small fraction of that which was performed during that night. For instance, barricades and obstacles were built in the new breach at the south-west corner, and in the Arms Museum. Stairs and corridors were cleared. There were the dead to bury, and all the ordinary fatigues of sanitation and upkeep.

Beyond this another necessary work was taken in hand and completed before daybreak. The Curved Passage having been completely destroyed and there being no covered way of reaching the lower terrace, dining-hall, riding-school, Quarters-of-the-Soldiers, or the House-of-the-Military-Government, a barricade was built, giving cover from view between the Curved Passage exit and the doorway of the wrecked dining-hall. This, as long as it lasted, made the sending of messages and reinforcements possible.

The task of rebuilding the head cover of the rifle pits on the great north breach proved difficult, as this side of the building was floodlit by the enemy's searchlights.

Its outward slopes, and the terrace below, were strewn with dead. Some of the bodies had been crushed by the tank. During the night parties of the enemy crept up onto the terrace, to search for their comrades. No fire was opened on them.

Throughout the night there were bursts of artillery fire which hampered the working-parties. Many of the shells pitching in the courtyard made sleep impossible for those who had the chance of getting it.

It is said that on this night the women volunteered en masse to work on the barricades but the Command did not favour this.

Throughout the day Radio-Madrid had announced to the

world that the Alcazar had been completely destroyed by the
explosion of the mines, and the garrison exterminated. This,
for reasons which follow, was a cause of grave anxiety to the
Command. For several days the wireless reception had been
defective, and it had not been possible to know what point the
relieving force had reached. Now the road along which it was
moving led, not to Toledo, but straight to Madrid; and, were
General Varela to believe that the Alcazar had already fallen,
he would certainly press straight on towards the capital. During the morning some Nationalist planes had appeared, no
doubt sent to discover whether the reports of the capture of
the Alcazar were true. The fighting had been at its height.
Seen from above, the ant-like creatures creeping over the slopes
of the breaches might have been taken for friend or foe. And,
as there had been no artillery fire at that time, the planes might
well have reported that the Alcazar had fallen.

THE YOUNG SOLDIERS OF
STABLE NO. 4

The day of the mines had been the day of the Alcazar itself,
and its defence had been maintained chiefly by the steadiness
and discipline of the Guardia Civil. The night which followed
was the night of Stable No. 4 and the hand-to-hand fighting in
it was sustained by the boys who made up this garrison. Their
average age can have been barely eighteen and most of them
looked younger, but they had been fighting continuously for
seven weeks and had learned the self-reliance and resourceful-
ness of much older men.

During the whole of the 18th of September the House-of-
the-Military-Government had been completely cut off from
the Alcazar. Indeed the enemy occupying the Stable Approach
had, unknowingly but entirely, separated it from the rest of

the defences. Had he shown more initiative he could have overwhelmed the garrison in it.

As soon as it was dark on that night the fusillade from the Santa Cruz and from the roof of La Concepcion became unusually intensive. Suddenly a shell burst against the outer wall of the Stable, about half-way down its length. Almost before the garrison had taken cover another came, and another, and another. It was soon realized that the field-gun which, as far back as three weeks before, had fired through a panel in the door of La Concepcion, had once again begun firing at point-blank range. The shells bursting against the wall soon began to knock large pieces out of it. The gap around the window increased and practically cut the Stable in two; for it became impossible to run from one end of it to the other without being seen from outside.[1]

The boys of the garrison had now been in action for more than twelve hours and it is unlikely that they had slept for several nights. They were, of course, unable to man the loopholed windows at which the gun was firing, and two or three others on which a machine-gun was trained. Soon from the corner of the Santa Cruz, where a stone had been specially removed some time before, a spluttering and not very efficient flame projector began to blow its flame over all the loopholes of the Stable. Completely mastered by the field-gun, the machine-gun and these flames, the young men could no longer hold any of the loopholes. Their inability to do so enabled the enemy to creep out unseen from the cellars under the terrace of the Santa Cruz. Having stolen across the road they laid large explosive charges of T.N.T. along the wall of the House-of-the-Military-Government, and so under all the farther windows of the Stable itself. They then retired into the cellars and by some means succeeded in setting off this charge of T.N.T.

The explosion was violent and for some thirty yards the whole side of the house fell out across the roadway. The Stable

[1] See Plate 30.

was filled with smoke and dust and for some time no one in it was certain what had happened. Then, as the smoke cleared, they saw light where the other end of the Stable had been, and realized that some thirty yards of it had ceased to exist, and that the way lay open, by there, for an enemy assault. But hardly had they realized this than a jet of flame from the projector began to lick into the end of the Stable itself.

Two-thirds of the Stable were now untenable, almost a third had been blown away, while the gap caused by the shells of the field-gun had cut off the next third. The boys retreated into the lower part of the Stable. Here the concrete side of a loose box, some four feet high, stretched out from the wall, and gave them a little cover. Working with the greatest haste they began tearing down the barricades from the windows, and with this material continuing this little wall across the floor, so as to reach the other wall. But, before they had done, canisters of petrol had been hurled into the Stable through the windows from which they had removed the barricades. Everything was soused with it. They had only just time enough to withdraw into the east Stable, which with Stable No. 4 made a letter "L." A bomb was then thrown in by the enemy and the whole was in flames.

The fire was of course superficial. There was nothing in the Stable which would burn and presently the flames died down. The young soldiers then returned to complete their barricade. But, as soon as the enemy judged that the ruin was cool enough, a number of men came clambering over the rubble where the end of the Stable had been. All this took place in darkness, lit from time to time by the spluttering of the flame projector, which could not be made to work properly for long but which sometimes sent its flame through the window and licked the farther wall of the Stable. Plate No. 30 gives the scene exactly as the boys saw it. In the foreground is the barricade they built. On the left are the concrete horse troughs, and the walls and ceiling blackened with petrol flames. Above some of the troughs are the name-cards of the horses which had been stabled there. The light seen from the right is from the window which had been breached and widened by the field-gun in La Concepcion. The end of the Stable is seen to be open. Before the explosion it stretched on for another thirty yards. The debris, which rises in a steep slope beyond the open end of the Stable, consists of the remnants of the building which had just been blown up and which had fallen into it. Plate No. 30 shows also, from outside, what had happened.

At sight of the militia-men entering the end of the Stable, the boys took up their rifles and began firing. If the reader is still behind the barricade and facing the enemy, who in semi-darkness is crawling towards him; then there is behind him another ten or twelve yards of Stable; then through a doorway another and similar stable running at right angles and away to the left. From that, stable doors lead out onto the riding-school terrace. Whether this was already held by the enemy, or not, the boys had no means of knowing. Indeed, for all they knew, he might be in the ruined rooms above their heads, in the other stable behind them, in the Stable Approach on their left, and down in the calle del Carmen on their right.

As soon as the young soldiers opened fire, the militia-men halted and replied. Soon this cellar-like Stable became a veritable shooting-gallery, with firing going on from both ends. The light was indistinct; a little was given by the flame projector outside, but sometimes there was no light at all. The young soldiers soon discovered that by drawing back a little and keeping down, they would be protected from the enemy's fire; while they could aim at the wall at some point well in front on their right, and count on the bullet ricocheting off it and reaching the farther end of the Stable; much as a player at billiards aims off a cushion to hit a ball at the farther end of the table.

The enemy, not being able to get a glimpse of the defenders, gave up rifle-fire and began throwing bombs. But to throw a bomb in a long, low, narrow cellar is not easy. The bombs either hit the walls or the ceiling, or they fell short. In any case they burst far short of the barricade.

Presently the enemy retired.

After a long pause other militia-men clambered into the wrecked end of the Stable and the fight began again. All night, at short intervals, these attacks were made. Sometimes while they were in progress, petrol would be thrown through the windows and set on fire. But the flames which drove the defenders from the barricade made it impossible for the enemy at the end of the Stable to pass it. And, once the flames had died down, the garrison returned to their barricade.

All night the fight raged in this half-wrecked catacomb. Just before dawn a reconnaissance party arrived from the Alcazar, bringing with them the two meals which the defenders should have had during the previous day. They brought, also, a fresh supply of bombs.

They took stock of the situation and promised to report it to the Command. Then they retired, and the boys were alone again.

At dawn the militia-men abandoned their attempts to seize the Stable. They retired, pulling away with them their dead and wounded.

Thus ended the first night of the struggle for Stable No. 4.

THE NINETEENTH OF SEPTEMBER

Throughout the night the "155's" had kept up an intermittent bombardment of the courtyard and also of the east façade, and from time to time the "75" battery had shelled the Quarters-of-the-Soldiers.

At 7 a.m. all guns took up gun-fire and a general assault was expected.[1] The garrison stood to their posts. However, no attack was launched. For a long time the enemy kept up a furious rifle and machine-gun fire. To this no reply was made; for the men were too tired.

Strange as it may seem, all had suffered much from cold during the previous night; for Toledo stands very high and the summer was over. The women, therefore, were set to work, making capes out of horse blankets.

It soon became clear that the enemy had realized what had caused the failure of his attack against the Corralillo on the previous day. The houses overlooking it, and which till now had only been occupied by a few snipers, were therefore being put in a state of defence. Holes were being knocked through the walls, from one corner to another, and from one house to another; so as to make an advance through them possible. Beyond all else it had been rifle-fire from the wash-house under the Capuchinos which had stopped the enemy's advance. Now the "155's" began to shell this basement.

At noon there was a lull.

At 1.30 the artillery opened fire again and the fusillade grew severe. Once more a general assault was expected, but once more nothing happened.

At 4 p.m. this again occurred, and once again the garrison stood to their posts.

The bombardment had now been going on for some twenty-seven hours and the men were in a state of extreme exhaustion.

During the afternoon bombing was heard from the direction of the Santa Cruz and militia-men were seen moving or massing in that direction. By 5 p.m. anxiety began to be felt as to the safety of the House-of-the-Military-Government. All communication with it had failed and nothing had been heard of the garrison since the night before. There was no means of

---

[1] "Gun-fire" being the rapidest fire which the guns of a battery, each working separately, can deliver.

knowing whether this intense rifle-fire and bombing had not covered an attack upon this outlying post, and whether indeed it had not been captured. An officer and a number of men volunteered to go and ascertain what had happened. This reconnaissance in force made its way down to the lower terrace and into the Stable Approach. There some of the enemy were encountered and they were put to flight. A red flag and many boxes of bombs were captured. This fighting in the Stable Approach drew down artillery fire from across the river, and for some time it was feared that the reconnaissance party had fallen into a trap. However, it presently returned and reported that the garrison in the House-of-the-Military-Government was completely exhausted, after nearly thirty hours of continuous fighting.

In the late dusk lorries were seen approaching Toledo along a track on the farther side of the river. In them were guns, but of what size could not at first be decided. Later they were taken up to the Campimento de Alijares and brought into position. The observation posts then identified them as, one naval gun of 105 mm., one "75," and one anti-aircraft gun of a novel type.

The fusillade continued until late that night and the artillery, though their rate of fire was reduced, remained in action until the next morning.

The casualties of the day had been heavy; for, perforce, much work had been done under fire. Three men had been killed and thirty-five wounded.

THE BLESSED VIRGIN OF
THE ALCAZAR

This chapter must be written. For a long time I have put off doing so; partly as being unqualified to write it; partly because it is hard to explain what one divines rather than comprehends. Yet the story of the siege cannot be understood if this chapter is left out, for the religious fervour of those who defended the Alcazar was as much an element of the defence as was the water they drank or the cartridges they fired.

When studying the siege, and hearing of it from survivors, their religious faith comes to one almost at once as a sudden surprise. And, as the story is followed, the realization of the power their faith had, grows ever stronger. Defence of barricades, hunger and thirst, dead bodies, may all be things entirely of the material world. But what enables a man to endure these things is in essence, spiritual, whether it be linked with a religious belief, or not. For the defence of the Alcazar was a triumph, not of mind over matter, but of spirit over the fear of death.

In a town such as Toledo at least ninety out of every hundred are practising Catholics. They may not be any better citizens, but they have been brought up in that faith, they live in it, they die in it. They have their sacred pictures on their walls, on the doors of their tenements. Whether they are good, or evil livers, they are so accustomed to the outward symbols of their religion that they would greatly miss them were they not there. Almost all of those who stood the siege were men and women of the district, and this was the nature of their religion.

In Spain the army is consciously and strongly Catholic. The Alcazar is the cradle of the infantry officer and the Blessed Virgin of the Alcazar was the patron saint of Infantry. In the chapel was her image, in this realization of her. The ordinary soldier of infantry believes simply, even though it may not influence his thought or life, that he is under her special care. When in the 'eighties the terraces facing the river were rebuilt, a niche was made in the wall of the upper one and in it was placed a picture panel of the Blessed Virgin of the Alcazar, made in the glazed tiles for which Talavera, and to a lesser extent, Toledo, are famous.[1]

The Blessed Virgin was there, and from the early days of the siege the young soldiers, going and coming through the communication trench up the roadway just below, used to breathe a prayer to her as they passed. The terrace wall was often shelled. Rifle and machine-gun fire from across the river passed almost ceaselessly over it. The wall was struck by shells in many places. The little turrets which framed the niche, at a distance of four yards on either side of it, were struck many times. But the niche was never touched. It came to stand, as so often happens in such cases, for a miracle. One of the officers in command of the young soldiers of Stable No. 4 told me how he used to glance up, fearfully, in case the picture panel should have been harmed. For, if it had been, he knew how bad the effect would have been upon his men.

No doubt within the Alcazar there were many who in their normal lives were deeply religious, but for the majority this was how in the early days their faith most clearly showed itself. This was the first stage.

The weeks went by. Each day there were casualties; sometimes only a few wounded; sometimes many dead. At night there were burials in the darkness of the riding-school. The men were much alone. The organization of the defence depended upon moving sentries, working from loophole to loophole, ready to call at need on their comrades sheltering at some distance from their beat. Sometimes a man was at the loop-

[1] See Plates 20 and 39.

holes for hours on end; glancing through them, then drawing back and standing aside. The loopholes were the constant target of the enemy. Their bullets spattered against the walls outside. Sometimes one would come singing through the opening and smash itself against the wall behind. Every time the moving sentry glanced out he must chance meeting such a shot.

A man is unimaginative on whom this, continuing week after week, makes no effect. These men had taken prayer as natural, from their childhood. It is likely that many prayed each time before they faced a loophole. It is not hard to fancy that they often offered a prayer of thanks as they drew back again. That was the second stage.

The weeks went on. The ruin and the dirt and desolation about them grew ever greater. The present was often horrible to contemplate. There seemed no chance that they could ever be relieved. There was no future. So they drew aside into some space outside this world, just as they drew back from the shaft of dangerous light at a loophole, into the dark safety at its side.

For long spells at a time they drew back like this, from an earthly life which was near intolerable. And, as the hungry weeks went by, their failing strength made this ever easier for them.

They achieved an exaltation. They came to see themselves defenders of faith, under divine protection. There was no priest with them. There were no services, except those at the burials in the riding-school. Thus, and because they were so often solitary, the faith of each grew individual. Some came to feel themselves inspired. One recalled his feelings during those days.

"We are few, they are many. But numbers are not all. We believe, we have faith. They do not believe, they would destroy faith. They think; that is in the brain. We pray; that is in the heart. I myself, sometimes I cry. But I am not afraid. If I die, I die. But that is only myself. What I believe cannot die.

"As I take my aim I pray, as I throw a bomb I pray.

"We are filthy. We have not washed. Our clothes stench. We have insects. All that is around us is reeking and disgusting. We live half in filth. But we live half, away beyond it. We do not swear. We do not blaspheme. We do not allow ourselves carnal thoughts. Those who have wives within the Alcazar do not take them.

"The Reds think. Thinking is nothing. Presently they will give way. We believe. That endures for ever."

I have set this down, as he said it.

At night they heard the sound of mining. Few conceived that any could survive the explosion of the mines. Each night the chatter of the drills was nearer. If they allowed themselves to think, they could not put aside the thought that there was no future. But they went out beyond the future into that spiritual world which they had found.

In some spots on earth faith seems easier than in others. Toledo is one of these. Those who have known the true masterpieces of El Greco, few of which have ever left that city, must have felt that beyond all else in his work there was a sense of personal revelation.

At first, in some of his most characteristic paintings, the distortion of the figures is baffling. But as one grows to know them the thought of it, and later even the sense of it, is gone. And, beyond the skill and vision of the man, there stands that personal revelation and that exaltation which it brought to him. No other painter, perhaps, is bound up with any single city, as El Greco was. His models were Toledans, the landscape which he shows, often as though glimpsed by the light of doom, is Toledan, also. Perhaps those who know well these paintings may understand, through them, something of that exaltation, which it has been so hard for me to set down, but

PLATE 31

"THE LOST KEY OF THE ALCAZAR"

Mouth of a conduit which fell into the hands of the enemy, providing him with a ready-made mine shaft from which, on the last day of the siege, a mine was exploded.

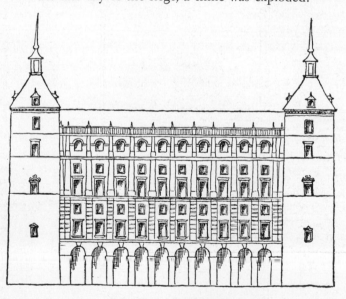

SOUTH FACADE -

Drawn by Miriam Pearce

The last to be built. Designed by Herrera, under the personal supervision of Philip II, husband of Mary Tudor.

PLATE 32

THE EAST FAÇADE FROM THE ESPLANADE

In the middle of it is seen a Moorish bastion and above it a
Moorish gallery. On the left, at the foot of the tower is the
vitally important "Carved Passage." Compare with Plate 22.

THE LEFT HALF OF THE SAME FAÇADE

On the right is what remains of the Moorish bastion, and above
it vestiges of the gallery. The slope of rubble on the left is the
"Cavalry Library Breach."

which, in the last days, alone, made the defence of the Alcazar possible.

THE TWENTIETH OF SEPTEMBER

DAY

Soon after midnight the rate of artillery fire increased and a bombardment of the east façade was begun by all the "155's" on the other side of the river; while those on the north intensified their shelling of the wrecked courtyard. Work on the barricades, however necessary, had to be abandoned; and for the third night in succession sleep became impossible.

The artillery fire continued till an hour after dawn. Then it ceased, except for the four "155's" in the Campimento de Alijares. These continued an intermittent fire upon the east façade, and especially upon the south-west tower, the only one still standing.

The damage done by the night's shelling had been heavy. The wash-house had now been bombarded for forty hours on end. At about 5 a.m., when this shelling ceased, it was reported that the little garrison in it was on the verge of collapse. An order was therefore issued that they should be relieved as quickly as possible by another garrison of the same strength. But before this was possible the bombardment began again, and remained so fierce that for another twelve hours nothing could be done for these men in the wash-house.

It seems that the enemy had now realized the difficulty which the garrison of the Alcazar had in keeping up communications with its outlying posts. So, to render all such communication impossible, two "155" guns were now kept ready, one trained upon the breach where the door of the swimming-bath had once been, and the other upon the similar breach where the Curved Passage had once begun. These exits now re-

sembled nothing more than the mouths of two large caverns.[1]
At the sign of the slightest movement at either of these exits
the gun trained upon it was fired. Sniping with guns of this
size proved terribly effective. The high-explosive shells were
fired so as to pitch and burst on the terrace, some fifteen yards
short of the wall. The splinters and the force of the explosions
made it practically impossible for anyone to leave the Alcazar
by either of these exits. Thus, for the second day running, the
Quarters-of-the-Soldiers, the Capuchinos, the dining-hall and
the House-of-the-Military-Government, were completely cut
off. The field telephone wires had long ago been destroyed and
signalling had become impossible.

Between 9 and 10 a.m. the artillery fire became so heavy that
a general assault seemed inevitable. And, since it was now uncertain whether the garrison of the wash-house were still capable of playing their part, a relief was always kept in readiness,
to rush to their help should a slackening in the bombardment
make this possible. A further attempt was made to relieve
them from the swimming-bath breach, but this was overwhelmed by a shell from the "155" gun trained upon it, by a
burst from the "75" battery, and by some bombs thrown by a
mortar in position somewhere behind the Convent of la Concepcion.

The hour was now approaching when a detachment from
the House-of-the-Military-Government might try to get
through, to fetch their meal and a fresh supply of bombs. It
was considered that this detachment must be stopped at all
costs; as an officer and two soldiers had already lost their lives
that day coming along this route. Knowing that the normal
line of communication was impossible, they had tried rushing
across the little iron bridge which spanned the Stable Approach, as a foot-bridge might a railway cutting. This bridge

[1] Plate No. 34 shows where the swimming-bath door had been. In the
enlargement a man in a white coat, seen standing inside the entrance, will give
an idea of the scale.

joined the upper storey of the House-of-the-Military-Government to a little garden at the corner of the Esplanade, and at other times had been a short cut for the officers going from their quarters up to the Academy. This officer and two soldiers, rushing across the bridge, had been blown to pieces by a shell.

It being considered so essential to stop the detachment coming up from the House-of-the-Military-Government, an officer volunteered for the errand, single-handed. Running out of the swimming-bath breach and bolting across the open terrace, he succeeded in accomplishing his mission, though shells had previously been falling over each yard of the ground he covered. He had taken with him instructions for some pre-arranged signal to be made hour by hour, so that the Command might in future know that the garrison in the House-of-the-Military-Government and in Stable No. 4 were still holding out.

The position of the House-of-the-Military-Government had become desperate. The west end had for weeks now been destroyed and was held only by posts which the garrison had made, half hidden, inside the ruins. But the enemy's complete occupation of the Stable Approach throughout the 18th and 19th of September had threatened to cut off the men holding these posts. They had therefore had to withdraw into the little wrecked courtyards in the centre of the building. Here in this wilderness of wreckage they were lost and unnoticed by the enemy, and the militia-men who had occupied the west end of the building had not shown any initiative. Thus the defence on the west had ceased to exist and all that remained, above ground, were a few men behind barricades in this honeycomb of broken walls and fallen roofs.

So much for the west and centre parts of the building. There remained only Stable No. 4, of which the whole west end had been blown out and in which the garrison had now been fighting for their lives for many hours. For a long time the enemy had been in occupation of the Stable Approach, and should any of his men be adventurous enough to penetrate onto the riding-school terrace, there would be practically nothing to prevent them from walking through the open doors of the House-of-the-Military-Government on that side. They would then be in the east stable. At the north end of that, a doorway led straight into Stable No. 4 and formed the only line of retreat from it.

It must be remembered that these militia-men came from Madrid and did not know the complicated geography of the Alcazar. It is probable, also, that they had no map or plans. For, had they understood the situation, they could have cut off the retreat of the young men in Stable No. 4 and could have attacked them in the rear.

True, the garrison of these posts had built a barricade across the Stable Approach to prevent the enemy doing this. But this barricade was in full view of the enemy's artillery, and men defending it would actually have had their backs to the gun-ners and rifle-men on the other side of the river. Thus this barricade was untenable.

Neither the boys defending the House-of-the-Military-Gov-ernment, nor the officers over them, had had sleep or rest for some sixty hours, and they had been fighting intermittently for forty of them. The officer who had volunteered to reach the garrison had had the following orders; that the garrison must hold out at all costs until nightfall; that they were then to abandon the building, set it on fire, and retire upon the Alcazar; that they were to bring with them anything of value which they could carry, and were to destroy the rest.

The signal which was to acknowledge the receipt of this order was, it seems, to have been made from a certain part of the roof of the building. But when attempts were made to do this, it was found that the garrison was so physically ex-hausted that no one could reach the spot. Thus the com-mander of the Alcazar remained in doubt all day as to whether the House-of-the-Military-Government had not already fallen into the hands of the enemy.

In the early afternoon observation posts reported the enemy to be massing in great numbers on the Zig-Zag. It was considered that these militia-men were unlikely to have anyone on the lookout, covering their concentration, and that therefore the boldest course was the wisest. A sortie was therefore made by strong forces of the garrison of the Alcazar. Crossing the north breach they made their way stealthily to the edge of the terrace. There, before the enemy a few yards below, had any idea what was happening, they poured heavy rifle-fire into them at the shortest range.

Taken utterly by surprise, the militia-men sprang to their feet and rushed helter-skelter down the precipitous slopes of the Zig-Zag into the road below. This put an end to any attempt at an assault that afternoon.

It seems that someone from the House-of-the-Military Government, perhaps the officer already mentioned, managed to make his way into the Alcazar while the men who had delivered this counter-attack were withdrawing. Whoever he was, the account he gave of the state of the garrison down there was so alarming that the plans for their relief were changed, and a large body of Guardia Civil were warned to stand by, to help in the retirement of the garrison and to carry up for them any stores that were left.

While this counter-attack across the terrace was being delivered, Nationalist planes had been seen approaching and attempts had been made to signal to them. Only a few moments later enemy planes appeared.

The shelling, though it had never ceased, had been at long intervals throughout the day, but soon after 5 p.m. it became intense, and continued so until dusk.

During the day it had become evident that the outworks could no longer be held. Structurally they were now untenable. The wash-house had been shelled so heavily that the whole of that side of the Capuchinos might fall at any moment. (Actually it remained standing for some two months and then the whole end of it, three storeys high, fell down during a windy November night.) The Quarter-of-the-Soldiers had no longer any floors and its walls were liable to collapse. The dining-hall would be untenable if the Quarters-of-the-Soldiers were abandoned; and in any case it was a roofless ruin offering no sort of cover. The House-of the-Military-Government had lost all its floors, the western third of it had been entirely demolished and the northern side had been split open by explosions. In truth all these wrecked outworks had come to be traps, rather than defences. Orders for the withdrawal of all garrisons as soon as night fell, were therefore given.

THE END OF STABLE NO. 4

The Twentieth of September

NIGHT

At 7.30 it was already dark. Soon the sortie party of the Guardia Civil made their way down to the House-of-the-Military-Government to rescue the young soldiers who had defended it.

They found them waiting in its broken and blackened ruins. The wheat which had been stored there, against the chance of the Alcazar being utterly destroyed by the mines and of this outwork alone surviving, the Guardia Civil now carried in. The bombs, rifles and equipment they brought in, also. Nothing was left, nothing which had been committed to the charge of the garrison and had not been destroyed. The young soldiers assembled for the last time in the Stable. Perhaps they felt as do a crew, forced to abandon the ship in which they have made many voyages and endured much. Yet that which they had held so long could be held no longer. They had been beaten. They had got to go. They took down, as souvenirs, name-plates of the horses they had groomed, and these they brought away with them. They shouldered what they could carry. They struggled out of the stuffy familiar darkness of the still-unburnt eastern stable, into the clean chilly darkness of the night. They filed into the communication trench, and up the long slope towards the Alcazar. This was the end of their separate effort.

A few of the Guardia Civil had remained behind, to fire the abandoned building. By 10.30 the garrisons of all the outlying posts had been withdrawn. The one which had held the redoubtable wash-house, below the Capuchinos, whose relief had been ordered for that morning but had been prevented by shell-fire, was found to be so collapsed that it was necessary to carry their rifles for them and to help them walk even so short a distance.

Presently they were all in. The relief had been accomplished without loss. The few Guardia Civil who had been left in the House-of-the-Military-Government and who had already sprinkled the ruins with petrol, now set fire to them. The flames caught. They lit the night. The men, their task performed, filed out, into the communication trench and through the flickering darkness, back to the Alcazar.

The House-of-the-Military-Government was blazing. It burnt all night. It called down a heavy rifle-fire. Yet for some reason the enemy did not realize that this conflagration indicated the withdrawal of the garrison.

Everything had been done according to plan and in perfect order. Not a rifle, not a box of bombs, nor a box of ammunition had been abandoned. All was brought in, checked and accounted for. Nothing had been lost to the enemy, except those outbuildings which from the first must have seemed hardly defensible. Yet to the garrisons withdrawn from Stable No. 4 and from the other outworks, this marked the end of a period in their lives, it signalled their failure and defeat.

The casualties of the day had been heavy; seven dead; fifty-seven wounded; one natural death.

THE LOST KEY OF THE ALCAZAR

The withdrawal from the outbuildings had been accomplished in good order and without loss. Both the Command and the garrison had reason to congratulate themselves. But one mistake had been made, a mistake for which no one could possibly have been blamed, but which almost led, even at the last moment, to the total destruction of the Alcazar.

The Command and officers of the garrison were not normally resident in the Alcazar, and even if they had been they could not have been expected to know every detail of the complicated drainage system of that immense building and of its precincts. So, when the troops were withdrawn from the House-of-the-Military-Government, and the Stable Approach was definitely abandoned, what was indeed the key of the Alcazar was left behind.

Inconspicuous in the brickwork of the south wall of the Stable Approach was a small arch, the size of a large dog kennel.[1] Yet no one who noticed it could fail to wonder where it led. It was a rain-water conduit: its course ran almost horizontally and presented no difficulties: it was large enough for a man to crawl up or down it with ease and to pull a load of explosives with him. It was in fact a ready-made mine-shaft and its farther end was beneath the Alcazar.

[1] See Plate No. 31.

THE TWENTY-FIRST OF SEPTEMBER

At midnight, only an hour-and-a-half after the outlying garrisons had been brought up into the Alcazar, all the "155's" opened fire; the two from the north dropping their shells into the courtyard; the rest hammering at the east façade.

At dawn the enemy's rifle-fire was heavy.

At 7.30 a.m. all the artillery ceased fire.

After an hour's interval all guns opened fire again upon the south-east tower, which alone remained standing. They fired also upon the part of the façade adjoining it. The shells were heavy, high explosive, and landed at frequent intervals. This bombardment was kept up all day. In the middle of the eastern façade was a half-round Moorish bastion, which can be seen on Plate No. 32. During the course of the day every part of the façade seen to the left of this bastion, was demolished. By the late afternoon this whole high cliff of wall had fallen and the rooms behind it were laid open, from the roof, right down to the level of the courtyard. The damage can be seen by comparing the two pictures on Plate No. 32. Two large shells entered the Cavalry Library and knocked the end out of it. Through the hole, so caused, there dribbled out over the wreckage, a stream of heavy atlases, great tomes on engineering, portfolios of maps, plans of forgotten battles, books of aerial photographs, old bound copies of "l'Illustration," of the "Illustrated London News," pamphlets, military records. The stream slid down slowly over the slopes of the wreckage and covered the Esplanade with sheets of torn paper and leather bindings.

Towards sundown the last remaining tower, that at this corner of the building, split from top to bottom. The eastern half of it toppled outwards and fell; and with it fell the last spire of the Alcazar. The militia-men as usual showed their joy. They cheered, they shouted, they set off rockets, they waved red flags. Men got up on flat roofs not a hundred yards away, and danced there.

At 6.30 the bombardment ceased. By then all the southern half of the east façade had been demolished; one eighth of what the Alcazar had once been; and one quarter of what had remained of it that morning.

All day long rifle and machine-gun fire had been particularly severe; but there had been no attack.

Here the advantage of a purely "passive defence" is seen to its full. For weeks the enemy had grown used to grey walls which often for days on end made no reply to their fire. Now all the outworks of the Alcazar had been abandoned, but the enemy had no idea of this. His troops might have occupied the whole riding-school and all the buildings near it. They might have closed in that afternoon upon the Alcazar. For three days they did nothing of the sort, for the simple reason that they did not discover that the garrisons of the outer posts had been withdrawn.

Within the Alcazar the day was a busy one. The withdrawal of the garrisons had increased the strength inside the main building and a general reorganization of services had been undertaken.

The casualties for the day had been twenty-six wounded.

THE TWENTY-SECOND OF SEPTEMBER

The early night was relatively calm and during that part of it, for the first time for five nights, it was possible to sleep.

At 3 a.m., however, the "155" guns across the river began to shell the east façade again.

At 5 a.m. this ceased abruptly and several enemy detachments, sallying from the doorway of the Santa Cruz, made an attack upon the Stable Approach. Machine-guns rattled down its empty roadway. Attacks were made with flame projectors against the undefended obstacles. Explosive charges were laid against the walls of evacuated rooms and they were blown up. Hand-bombs were hurled against the abandoned barricades. Eventually the enemy occupied all the north part of the building and bombed his way through it, room by room, apparently without discovering that there was no one there to stop him. The progress of this attack was clearly visible from the Alcazar and was watched with grim amusement.

Soon after 10 a.m. the artillery bombardment began again. However, the observation posts reported that under cover of this the "155's" in the Campimento de Alijares were being manhandled out of position and withdrawn. The news soon became known to the garrison and roused fresh hopes.

For some days the reception by the makeshift wireless set had been so bad that it had been impossible to tune in any station except Radio-Madrid. As a result there had been no means of knowing what progress the relieving force had made. But the withdrawal of these guns could only mean that they were urgently needed elsewhere, and presumably to stem the pressure of the advancing Nationalist forces.

Later it was noticed that the anti-aircraft gun was also gone from its accustomed position on the north, and there was movement among the heavy guns on that side, suggesting the possibility that they, too, might soon be removed.

However, shortly before noon these guns opened a very rapid fire upon the north breach and an angry fusillade broke out from all sides. Enemy troops were seen moving in the Zocodover and a general assault upon the north breach was expected. Defences were manned; fatigue work ceased within the Alcazar: the reserves stood to arms. But nothing came of it and presently all was normal again.

Later, militia-men were seen working their way cautiously out of the doorway of the Santa Cruz, and from there across the road, presumably for another attack upon the House-of-the-

Military-Government. Canisters of petrol were thrown into the ruins and some fires started. Then the enemy retired, still without having discovered that the whole building had been abandoned.

An hour later the enemy was again observed massing on the Zig-Zag. Once more an assault upon the north breach seemed imminent. But, as it is always wise to show an enemy something new rather than something to which he has grown accustomed, reserves were not sent out to chase him away. Instead, rifle-men and machine-guns were massed behind the highest accessible portions of the Alcazar which remained on that side. A burst of fire was then opened. At this the militiamen, as usual when surprised, fled.

The enemy's artillery on the north remained silent but the guns were not withdrawn, as it had been expected they would be.

Later in the afternoon the "75" battery fired several rounds but, when it ceased fire, it was seen that the guns were being manhandled out of position.

All this had been heartening to the garrison. But by now the men had become so weak that every exertion was a tax on them, and each day, on account of the increasing destruction, the difficulty of defending the Alcazar became greater. Another breach had been added. For the whole south half of the east façade had fallen and exposed the interior of the rooms, as completely as the pigeon-holes are exposed when the front of a desk is dropped. And where there had been a cliff-like wall facing blankly any attack, there remained a slope of debris which led up from the Esplanade straight into the basements of the building. All the outer wall of the upper storeys was gone, and even the vaulted classrooms of the basement, the windows of which had looked over the Esplanade, lay open. In Plate No. 33 these rooms gape like caverns above the debris. Now, were the enemy troops to mount the slope which led up to these rooms and were to capture even a single one, a doorway would lead them straight into the "catacomb-road" —upon which the whole defence of the Alcazar had for a long time in reality depended. If once enemy troops could gain a footing in it, the Alcazar would be lost.

It was certain that, as the enemy realized the outer defences were no longer held, he would occupy the whole of the riding-school terrace. This might happen at any moment. Then there would be no defence or obstacle between him and this newly made breach on the east, against which he would be certain to concentrate his efforts.

For the enemy troops the way would be easy. They could mass unseen in the roofless dining-hall. From there to the breach the distance was not more than forty yards, and there was ample cover from view amid the fallen masonry, burnt-out lorries and the general disorder. Once at the foot of the breach there would be but a short steep climb, before they would reach the mouth of these caverns, which had once been class-rooms and stairway windows.

Their defence, on the other hand, would be difficult. Almost as much of the rubble had fallen inside the building as it had outside and, to hold these breaches, rifle-men must establish themselves on the crests of these treacherous slopes of dust and debris. All the ladders were broken or in use elsewhere and the men were too weary to find material and make others. Most of the defenders were so feeble that they could not climb these slopes. All that could be done was this. Some of the fittest, helped from below, managed somehow to get up to the top and attach a rope and pulley to something strong enough to hold them. Then, when a rope had been passed through the pulley, all was ready. One end of it was tied under the arms of the man who was to be sent up for duty. Holding his rifle, and helping himself as he could, he was hauled up this crumbling slope.

The men hated these posts; for they disliked showing the state of weakness to which they had been reduced. Sometimes a man would vomit while being helped up the slope. Sometimes it was minutes before he could undo the knot and send the rope down again for the use of the next man. Yet, once there, he must be ever vigilant, ready to open and keep up the highest rate of fire possible.

The smell on these breaches and in the barricades had become terrible. Even weeks afterwards the reek of putrefaction in the swimming-bath was hardly to be borne. Passing the end of it, where the "showers" had been, one of the young soldiers apologized.

"We couldn't bury them deep, you see. They're only just under the ground. It wasn't our fault. It was so hard and we weren't very strong then. We did the best we could."

In the late afternoon two Government planes arrived and reconnoitred for a long time over the Alcazar. Later still, a flight of large Nationalist planes came from the west and bombed the enemy posts round the Alcazar and across the river.

The evening fusillade was weak, and there was no artillery fire. Soon after dark, red flares were lit at several points around the Alcazar and on the cliffs across the river. By the light of these the gorge of the Tagus appeared more unearthly and tragic than ever. Those who know El Greco's view of Toledo, revealed by a light so strange that it seems that of some other world, can realize the eeriness this ravine can have. The flares went on burning. Once again an assault was expected. All defences were manned. Nothing happened. The flares burnt out.

Towards midnight the alarm was sounded. A loud but undefined sound had been heard just outside the Arms Museum breach. Some described it as a subterranean explosion; others as a metallic sound, like the fall of a truck-full of girders. A bright light had flared up, just outside the breach. It illuminated all that side of the Alcazar for several minutes. Posts were manned but once again nothing happened.

After that the night was calm.

The casualties for the day had been two killed and twenty-seven wounded.

THE TWENTY-THIRD OF SEPTEMBER

The night was quiet and everyone off duty slept.

At dawn an intense fusillade began from all sides.

At 5 a.m. enemy troops suddenly appeared on the north terrace and charged forward upon the great north breach. This time they did not fire, but some threw bombs and others, presumably miners from the Asturias, threw sticks of dynamite. The defence was almost taken by surprise. The men who were in the rifle-pits opened fire at once. But, before supports could be sent up to them and reserves massed, they had been driven back into the courtyard. There they halted and by throwing bombs over the crest of the breach tried to keep back the enemy. Those on duty in the galleries ran to the ends of them, from where, having the advantage of a higher position, they were able to bomb the enemy with greater effect. For a few minutes the situation was extremely perilous, and had the enemy driven home his attack, the militia-men would have gained the courtyard. However, instead of that, they engaged in a bomb-throwing duel with the garrison in the galleries. So, just in time, supports began to arrive. Reinforcements were sent up into the galleries and the enemy was driven from the forward slopes of the breach by bombing and by rifle-fire.

Once it was clear that the surprise had failed the enemy made no great efforts and after a short time retired. But retiring into the Stable Approach the militia-men found it unheld and, progressing down it, passed the barricade at the bottom of it and suddenly found themselves upon the riding-school terrace. There, close under the wall of the upper terrace, they were hidden from all the observation-posts of the Alcazar, and what they did was not known. Presumably finding they were not fired at, they advanced cautiously southward, over the terrace they had never seen before, towards the riding-school. Well used to silent walls which suddenly blazed rifle-fire at them, they no doubt went dubiously. And drawing near to the riding-school they presumably found it empty. Doubtless they entered it uncertainly and looked about them at the strange and unsuspected cemetery inside it. To their left was the Quarters-of-the-Soldiers. This, too, was possibly still occupied and dangerous. But in the end they realized that the whole defences on the lower level had been abandoned and they spread over the terrace, calling to their comrades. Then for the first time they came into view of the observation posts in the Alcazar.

Meanwhile, as soon as the light made accurate observation possible, the look-out posts reported that all the "155's" had been withdrawn from the Campimento de Alijares. Where they had been taken no one could tell. The departure of these guns was not a matter of much relief to the defenders of the Alcazar. For the east façade, at which they had been firing, had suffered so much that in truth the artillery could now do it little more harm. And, instead of the artillery shelling from a distance of two miles, there was an unknown quantity of the enemy militia-men, out of sight and perhaps massing for an attack, occupying the lower terrace only a hundred yards away. Nor was this side of the Alcazar easily defensible. At one end there was the breach leading into the swimming-bath (seen in Plate 34); and at the other, the various breaches into the Cavalry Library and rooms near it; which the enemy could approach under cover till within forty yards of them. Indeed the new position was far more dangerous than it had been till that morning. Just before 8 a.m. the observation posts reported enemy troops massing once again below the north terrace. This time the numbers were much greater but on the other hand

PLATE 33

THE "CAVALRY
LIBRARY
BREACH"

The south-west tower has been brought down by shell-fire. In
the foreground is its cupola, upside down, having fallen a
hundred feet, but with most of its slates still in place.

VIEW FROM THE "CAVALRY LIBRARY BREACH"

Below is the Esplanade with its wrecked acacias. Beyond is the
gorge of the Tagus; across it the Castle of San Servando, and on
the right of that the hamlet which, till the last ten days, formed
the enemy firing line on this side.

PLATE 34

THE "SWIMMING-BATH BREACH"

This should be compared with Plate
No. 32, as the above photograph
shows the same portion of the façade
as is seen on the right in the upper
photograph on that Plate.

ENLARGEMENT OF THE SAME
BREACH

A man in a white rain-coat can be made out
inside it and to the right of the tilted water-tank
Compare with Plate No. 22.

they had not the advantage of a surprise. The garrison stood to arms and all was made ready to repel a serious attack. Presently a tank, mounting a light gun in an armoured turret, was seen swaying up the Zig-Zag and over the trunks of the fallen eucalyptus trees. As soon as it reached the terrace it opened fire upon the loopholes along the crest of the breach, and upon the barricaded ends of the galleries. No sooner had the tank opened fire than Government militia-men came swarming over the edge of the terrace and made for the breach, shouting, and throwing bombs and dynamite sticks.

Once again the men at the loopholes, unable to face the little shells of the tank's quick-firing gun, were forced to withdraw. But marksmen posted in new and unexpected crannies of the ruins, poured down their rapidest fire upon those of the enemy who were crowding at the foot of the breach.

For a time the decision hung in the balance. At several points a wave of the militia-men washed to the summit of the crest, only to fail and to recede. More and more men clambered onto the terrace and were brought forward to the attack. But the fire of the defence was too heavy for them and they were unable to mount the breach. Instead, they swung away to either side, where by keeping close to the wreckage of the towers they were to some extent under cover. There were now not two, but four other breaches on which an attack might at any moment be delivered.

Meanwhile the tank, unharmed by the bullets and bombs of the defence, kept passing along the foot of the breach, blowing away the loopholes and head cover, and anything or anyone that offered a target. The attack on the north was pressed with bravery and persistence. When some of the militia-men were already filtering away to the edges of the terrace and making their retreat, other companies clambered up. Yet, after some three-quarters-of-an-hour the heart was out of it and only a few of the militia-men remained upon the terrace. These, keeping well to the sides of the breach, continued to put up a fine fight, tossing bombs diagonally over the summit and so making the rear slopes untenable. For a long time the tank remained, trying to rally the militia-men by sounding its klaxon and by firing at random. But presently it became apparent that nothing more could be done and the tank, turning tail, made off down the Zig-Zag. By then the terrace and the forward slopes of the breach were strewn with new dead, lying over the crushed and decomposed dead of five days before.

Once the attacks had been abandoned a fusillade broke out from all four sides and now, on the east, the enemy was already firing up from the ruins of the dining-hall and other buildings, but a stone's throw from the breaches in the east side of the Alcazar.

At noon there was a long lull; no artillery fire, no rifle-fire.

At 4 o'clock the only "155's" left, opened fire from their position on the north, and began to shell the breach where the attack of the morning had failed. Presumably this was intended to prevent the loopholes and rifle-pits being repaired. The garrison of the posts remained under cover; thus not much harm was done; though the shelling of the dead lying on the forward slope made the breach more horrible than before. After a time the gunners lengthened their range a little and began dropping their shells into the courtyard. Much damage was then done to the new barricades which had been built to meet the changed conditions and the possibility of the enemy gaining a foothold even in the courtyard itself.

Towards sundown the guns ceased fire.

In the twilight a further attack was made from the Zig-Zag across the north terrace. However, this time there were long pauses between each wave of the attack and the numbers were less. Nevertheless the men taking part in it showed bravery, advancing up to the breach. The failing light favoured them; for while their objective was visible enough, growing darkness robbed the defenders of the advantage of their superior musketry. For nearly an hour-and-a-half the enemy struggled to gain the objective. Reinforcements coming up in the dusk approached the breach from both flanks. Once near enough, they threw canister after canister of petrol over the defences, soaking the rifle-pits on the inner slope. They then set fire to this with bombs. The flames lit up all the building and caused consternation in the basements where, through the chinks between the stones blocking the ventilation openings, the light could be seen. At length, when it was almost night, the enemy withdrew, leaving still more dead.

After the failure of this attack the enemy's rifle-fire was weak all night.

The casualties of the day amounted to one killed and thirty-one wounded.

The state of the north breach had become horrible. The forward slope was littered with corpses and it was hard to bear the smell of putrefaction and of charred bodies. The night was cold. There was a heavy dew.

Within the defences the confusion on every hand was beyond description. Once the young moon had set it was very dark and it was impossible for a man to move two yards away from his post, even when he wished to ease himself.

One of those who had endured the siege, speaking of these last days, said "Those were the bad times. Because there were corpses the rats came. Because there were rats the cats came. And soon at night the Alcazar seemed full of them."

THE TWENTY-FOURTH OF SEPTEMBER

By the first light of dawn it was seen that during the night the enemy had dug trenches all along the edge of the lower terrace of the Alcazar. These were close to the railings and, as the ground fell away steeply below them, the men occupying the trenches could enter or leave them at any time, unseen. The distance from these trenches to the Alcazar itself was not more than a hundred and forty yards. It can be seen in the photographs on Plates 32 and 34, that the battlemented Moorish gallery had been almost entirely knocked away by shell-fire, and that there remained so little of this side of the Alcazar that there were few windows which could be manned by rifle-men. As a result the enemy, being able to occupy the whole length of the terrace, could bring an overpowering number of rifles to bear upon the defence.

On the Zig-Zag, also, the enemy had thrown up some cover. There his snipers were within fifty yards of the north breach. But the nearest and greatest danger was that the Government militia-men now occupied the dining-hall and all the buildings on that corner of the Esplanade. Among these ruins there was ample space for them to mass unseen for an attack upon the breaches of the cavalry library. Loopholed barricades had been built by the enemy within forty yards of the breaches and of those cavernous openings where the basement classrooms had been. How difficult it was to hold some of these posts has already been stated, and how men on duty at the top of these breaches had to haul themselves up with ropes, or be hauled up by their comrades below.

Till now the Alcazar itself had been assailed by short-range rifle-fire only on the south and west. For on the north the enemy forces in the Santa Cruz had been able to engage only the outworks. While on the east their firing-line had been on the farther side of the river and a quarter-of-a-mile away. Now, however, the enemy's rifle-men were within forty yards on all sides; and it will be understood that after these weeks of practice their marksmanship had improved. Moreover, there were now five breaches, of which that by the cavalry library consisted of at least five separate openings. As soon as it was light enough to see, the militia-men opened rifle-fire from all sides and so disclosed these new positions.

As it grew lighter observation posts reported that all the

enemy guns were gone from the Campimento, on the other side of the river. But they had done their work and it would not have been possible for them to further reduce the defensive power of the Alcazar.

A little later the observation posts reported signs of activity, many coaches and lorries moving in both directions on the roads leading to Madrid and to Avila.

A little later, a Nationalist plane appeared from the west and drew a volume of ineffective enemy rifle-fire. It bombed the concentration of coaches near the bull-ring, which stands just outside the town and near the gate of Visagra. It dropped bombs, also, upon the Zocodover. It then flew back into the west.

At 10.45 a.m. the remaining "155's," those on the north, opened a slow fire. Their target was the courtyard of the Alcazar and such upper portions of the east façade as were still standing. This harassed the observation posts up there, and knocked out some of them.

At noon, instead of the normal lull, rifle and machine-gun fire increased and, with the enemy so close to all the breaches, there was within the Alcazar a state of constant tension.

In the afternoon the rifle-fire, after slackening for an hour or so, increased. It then remained violent till sundown.

During the late afternoon the observation posts reported various enemy troop movements. Some forces were apparently leaving the town by coach and lorry, while others were arriving.

With nightfall the rifle-fire diminished.

Despite the knowledge that the enemy were within forty yards of all breaches the evening proved a happy one. For several days the wireless reception had been so bad that it had been impossible to tune in any station except Radio Madrid. The news from this post, had it been believed, would have always greatly depressed the garrison. The matter of supreme importance was, of course, the position of the relieving force.

For there remained now but nine mules and horses; while the supply of wheat was running low and the enemy were in possession of the granary from which the supplies had been obtained. Various calculations, or rather guesses, had been made, as to the point which the relieving force must have reached. Some had feared that it had been held up at Marqueda, where it had to abandon the main road by which it had been advancing, and to bear off eastward to Toledo. Marqueda, with its medieval castle, stood on high ground, commanding the cross-roads. Radio-Madrid had spoken of the Government position there as being impregnable. Many of the optimists had placed the relieving column as being at Torrijos, another twelve miles nearer. Therefore, when the wireless set succeeded in picking up "Radio Club" of Portugal, and learned that the leading troops of General Yagüe's column had taken Barcience and Rielves, two villages yet another ten kilometres nearer to Toledo, this came as a most agreeable surprise.

Nevertheless, between the relieving column and Toledo, ran the Guadarrama river. This was likely to prove a considerable obstacle, as on the Toledo side it was commanded by a ridge which would offer the enemy an admirable position. Thus, when still later that night the Portuguese station announced, just before closing down, that the Nationalist forces were already across the river, the delight of the garrison can be imagined.

In this happy frame of mind, and free from artillery bombardment, those of the garrison who were off duty were able to go to sleep.

The casualties of the day had been fourteen wounded.

WRECKAGE

The successive stages of the destruction have been described so often; of the north façade, of the west façade, of the east façade. Indeed all that remained of the Alcazar was the great Herrera façade of the south, which still stood, pockmarked by bullets, its towers gone, unsupported; draughty, perilous, forlorn.[1] Yet, though inevitably so much of this destruction has been recorded here, it is perhaps worth while to give a description of a single upper room, as a sample of the rest.

It was a lofty chamber on the east side. Its windows had opened onto the Moorish gallery and had looked down upon the Tagus. It had been an artillery museum. To reach it it was necessary to climb to the gallery, much of which still remained to the end, along the east side of the courtyard. But reaching the gallery was not easy. The great stairs, one flight of which ascended to it, were lost under the avalanche of fallen architecture; and amongst the dust and girders were live bombs. The gallery was littered with cartridges and with fallen plaster. Amongst these were bones belonging to a wired-up, but now dismembered skeleton of a horse; for somewhere near here had been the classroom for veterinary studies. The ribs, the shanks, the jaw-bones of several horses, and teeth innumerable lay scattered about. And it was not at once grasped that these had no relation to the carnage of the siege. Glazed heraldic tiles of the wainscotting had fallen and lay smashed among the dust, glittering like mother-of-pearl. Farther down the gallery was a great hole, knocked through it by shell-fire. Bridging this there was a rickety plank. The hole extended right across the doorway of the artillery museum. To enter it, it was necessary to grip the mouldings of the doorway, and swing round it, over empty space.

[1] Plate 26 shows this façade standing almost intact, but quite alone.

The room itself was a foot deep in dust and destruction. The whole south end of it had fallen out; so that the room on that side lay open to the outside air. Framing the doorway, fixed to the walls and still in place, were two tall naval shells, cut open for inspection and with their various parts painted diagramatically. On the floor, across the debris, lay a tall wall-mirror of hammered silver, with panels of drums and banners and martial trophies. The glass was gone, the frame was riddled with bullets. Across it was the jacket of a Guardia Civil, with dark bloodstains. Scattered everywhere were specimen shells; those of pom-poms, old-time mortars; all neatly sectioned and with labelled and numbered parts. And mixed with these classroom specimens were other shells which had come hurtling in through the windows and the breached walls, and which had wrecked the room. Some had burst into fragments and had stained the surrounding confusion yellow with picric; some had been "duds" and, rusty and disgraced, lay nuzzling amidst the polished specimens of the museum.

The ceiling had largely fallen. Through the gap in the wall, where the next-door room had been and where there was now only giddy emptiness, there dangled a rope ladder by which the observers had mounted to some post on high.

Behind the barricade in one of the remaining windows was a mass of empty cartridge cases, almost knee-deep. The gallery outside the room had been chipped away, there were no window frames, no door.

On the day of the relief every part of the Alcazar was like this and everywhere there was the same wreckage and confusion: the same dirt: the same stink.

THE TWENTY-FIFTH OF SEPTEMBER

Soon after midnight the fusillade became intense. But no reply was made and it did no harm.

At dawn, from the north-west, a cannonade could be heard and it was realized with delight that at least some of the guns were those of the Nationalist columns.

As the sun rose two enemy batteries could be made out, far away in that direction, in action on a ridge commanding the valley of the Guadarrama.

Presently Radio Club of Portugal in its broadcast of news reported that the Government forces had suffered a heavy defeat on the previous day, on the line of the Guadarrama, and that they were in retreat. Now, probably for the first time, the garrison of the Alcazar believed that they would be able to hold out until the relieving column reached Toledo. It is said that the reception of this wireless news was noted down in the official log book of the Alcazar, and that after it was written: —"Thus passed the last hours of this siege, sustained by such sacrifice and with such spirit by all."

During the morning three large Nationalist bombing planes were seen approaching those enemy batteries just mentioned. They bombed these and evidently gave information as to their position, and so called down upon them fire from Nationalist guns, invisible behind the ridges.

Presently the first glimpse was caught of the actual battle. Detachments of militia-men on foot, columns of coaches, more detachments of militia-men, were seen passing the ridges and retiring towards Toledo, while shells from the Nationalist batteries burst high over their heads. At this the enemy's gunners also made ready to retire. They limbered up and made off as fast as they could, taking up new positions nearer Toledo, and on the western side of the road; so that, if needs be, they could make away across country and get to the Madrid road; which would be their line of retreat, should the Nationalist columns reach Toledo.

What the garrison of the Alcazar did not know, was that the Government troops, which had been sitting round the Alcazar for nearly ten weeks, had made no preparation to stop the advance of the relieving column.

Toledo lies in a loop of the Tagus. A line of defence across the neck of this loop need not have been more than two-and-a-half miles long, and would have run along a ridge, giving a good field of fire to the front and cover for manœuvre and communication in the rear. There were in Toledo at least four thousand Government troops, and half that number could in a single day have thrown up a serviceable trench line across this loop of the river. Had this been done, the besieging force could have held up the relief column and could have continued a passive investment of the Alcazar. And, even if the Nationalist column cut the main Toledo-Madrid road, there was an alternative one, by Mocejon and Aranjuez, more to the eastward and only twenty-five miles long; and, were that also to be cut, there remained another serviceable road, through Mora and Aranjuez, secure behind the Tagus and only thirty-five miles longer than the direct route.

Had such a line of entrenchments been dug, and held with but a quarter of that bravery which the militia-men had shown in assaults upon the breaches, the relieving force must have been delayed for a week, perhaps for two. Then the garrison of the Alcazar must have perished from starvation. With these facts clear to him, it seems hardly credible that the Government commander in Toledo had made no preparations at all.

The enemy which the garrison of the Alcazar had seen retreating did not enter Toledo. On reaching the open just outside the gates, where the Avila-Toledo road, along which they had been retiring, joins the main road to Madrid, they turned towards the capital. But after a time they branched off to the

left and took a second-class road which leads to a village called
Bargas, six miles due north of Toledo and a mile or so to the
west of the Madrid highway. The garrison of the Alcazar believed this to indicate that some Nationalist flying column had
already cut the Madrid road. But it seems that the Government forces moved to Bargas and took up a position there,
believing that they would thereby threaten the communications of the Nationalist column advancing upon Toledo; would
cover the retirement of the force besieging the Alcazar; and
would ultimately block a Nationalist advance from Toledo towards Madrid.

The "155" guns on the north still remained in their old
position but during the past twenty-four hours they had not
fired a shot.

In the mid-afternoon enemy planes were seen circling over
Bargas, no doubt keeping up observation for the commander
of the Government forces there. All through the afternoon
throngs of militia-men and numbers of motor-coaches were
seen just outside Toledo, between the gate of Visagra and the
bull-ring; that is, the point where the main road sets out for
Madrid. During the afternoon the enemy's battle front, still
out of sight behind the ridges on the Avila road, seems suddenly to have collapsed; for hundreds of militia-men were seen
breasting the crest, where the road first becomes visible from
Toledo. They were running as hard as they could towards the
town, were in no order at all, and were being shelled by Nationalist batteries, still out of sight behind the ridges. After a
time the new positions which the enemy's batteries had taken
up became known to the Nationalists and their guns began to
shell them. Whereupon the Government artillerymen limbered up again, made off eastwards across country, and were
not seen again.

At 5 p.m. three large Nationalist bombing planes, escorted
by pursuit planes, passed over the outskirts of Toledo and
bombed the concentration of men and coaches outside the

Visagra gate. They then turned north-westward and droned away towards Avila.

Despite the approach of the relief force the Government militia-men besieging the Alcazar showed no signs of considering their own safety and of abandoning their task. All through the afternoon their rifle-fire had been heavy and galling and the lookout men on the breaches had found their work difficult. Now that the enemy was everywhere within forty or fifty yards, his marksmen knew exactly where each man lay watching, and all day long bullets were rained at the loopholes through which at frequent intervals the men on duty must peer, so as to guard against a surprise attack.

The dusk brought these men relief, for the enemy's aim grew less accurate and presently his fire died down.

The casualties for the day had been:—one killed and thirteen wounded.

THE TWENTY-SIXTH OF SEPTEMBER

Till midnight the fusillade had been heavy but after that, for two hours, there was a rest. Then, at 2 a.m., the fusillade became so intense that it might have been the prelude to an attack. Later it slackened once more.

At dawn it was seen that the enemy had a battery of artillery and a considerable force of infantry in position on the slopes some four miles away to the north-west, near where the road to Avila mounted the ridges and swept out of sight. That was all that could be known of the dispositions and plans of either side. But somewhere behind those ridges to the north-west lay the relieving column, and that body of the Government forces which was endeavouring to prevent it reaching the Alcazar.

From dawn onwards a stream of coaches was seen coming and going along the road to Madrid. But what this signified was not clear. For, while the coaches which left Toledo were laden with men, others arrived from the direction of Madrid equally full. However, one thing was proved; that the main road to Madrid was still open to the Government.

At 7 a.m. an intense cannonade began in the north-west and it was realized that the Nationalist columns must be delivering an attack. But, as the operations were hidden by the high ground, the garrison of the Alcazar itself could not tell in what direction the attack was being made. It was considered probable that the relief forces, after crossing the Guadarrama, would not have moved directly towards Toledo, but would have aimed at the village of Bargas, some four miles due north of it. For, if they took the high ground there, they would command the Madrid road and, by threatening his line of retreat, would force the enemy to raise the siege of the Alcazar and to abandon Toledo.

Throughout the day the enemy's fusillade against the Alcazar alternated between moments of great intensity and periods of comparative calm. There was no sign that he was contemplating a withdrawal.

Of all the guns which had bombarded the Alcazar only the "155's" now remained. They were still in their old position on the north, but for many hours they had not fired a shot. However, presently they were swung round and began engaging some unseen target in the direction of Bargas. This, of course, went to confirm the guess that the relief column was moving towards that village.

In the afternoon there was considerable air activity, both over Bargas and over the district just north of Toledo itself. Many of the garrison stole to the loopholes and lookouts to watch this. They saw one big Nationalist bomber shot down by a Government pursuit plane, hardly a mile away from the Alcazar. The four occupants of the plane jumped clear and, making parachute descents, landed somewhere near the Arms Factory, but whether they fell into the hands of the enemy was not known by the garrison.[1]

During the afternoon a heavy cannonade heard from behind the ridges to the north and north-west, bore out the theory that the Nationalist columns were pressing forward towards Bargas. At dusk an enemy battery was seen to switch its fire in the direction of the village itself. This seemed to prove that it had now been captured by the Nationalists.

The evening fusillade was of no special intensity.

The casualties for the day were:—one killed, seven wounded.

THE CAP OF THE MAN FROM ALBI

The story of the siege is drawing to its close and I cannot end it without setting down something of my admiration for the bravery of the besiegers. Their line of retreat was threatened. By the next evening it would be cut. Then, whatever happened, there would be neither food nor ammunition. Should they escape and hold together, they would probably be taken prisoner; and, if they believed the broadcasts of their Government in Madrid, they would be lucky to be shot out of hand. While, if they escaped and scattered, they were likely to be killed by the peasants of the countryside.

The artillery on which they had depended had been withdrawn. Their battle was lost. They must have realized that they would be abandoned. Discipline in their companies was lax. They were often employed alone or in pairs on house-tops or at windows. It would have been so easy for them to have

[1] Toledans living outside the town in this quarter say that two of the airmen were literally torn to pieces by the girls whom the Government had sent from Madrid to work in the Arms Factory, and that the other two were tied by the hands behind a lorry and dragged over the rough slopes which led up to a gate of the town called del Cambron, until they were dead. Whether this was true I do not know, but I was told it by several persons, and an English friend told me that when the bodies were exhumed from the rubbish heap in which they had been buried, the state of them bore out this story.

slipped away, boarded a lorry, and made their way back home. They had come as volunteers, to capture the Alcazar. Now that the chance of doing so was gone, they, free workers of a Workers' Republic, might well have held themselves entitled to go.

They did not go. They stayed, they stayed and many of them met their death. They stayed and fought bravely to the very end. Even on the morning of that day on which the Alcazar was relieved, they delivered their last desperate assault upon it. They strewed the breaches and the terraces with yet more dead. Some continued firing at the Alcazar, when the soldiers of the relieving force had entered Toledo.

Even after that one man remained. He may have watched the legionaries, nimble but cautious, climbing the breaches and meeting those ragged creatures they had come from so far to save. He waited till night. Then, when the glow of the first bonfire lit within it, showed inside the courtyard of the Alcazar, he took careful aim at one of its loopholes, and fired the last shot of the siege.

Perhaps he got away. But hundreds did not. No one took the names of the dead or drew up a list of casualties. Their relatives heard no more of them, and with the resignation of the poor they reckoned them as dead.

It is probable that amongst those who died and whose death was not reported, was a man from Albi. For, weeks afterwards, I found his cap upon the Esplanade. It was a check cap, of the apache type which youth in the Midi affects, jaunty, deliberately a little sinister, worn over one eye.

The terrace was a scene of unimaginable confusion. The dead had been buried, except for the charred bodies of some of the militia-men which lay in a twisted black heap in the bottom of the last mine crater; but curiously gruesome were the skeletons of burnt-out motor-cars. The Esplanade looked as though there had been fought over it some mad, symbolic, Capek battle, between motor-cars and bedsteads—in which the bedsteads had won. There were scores and scores of iron bed frames—I fancy they had been placed there as a barricade but had been scattered by the explosion of shells. Some had mounted on the wrecked cars, as though to throttle them.

There amongst the battered but victorious bedsteads, and under the dwarf shell-splintered acacias, and amidst the ruins of the cadets' obstacle course, were petrol tins, buckets and cartridges; broken rifles, kettles and bandoleers; torn jackets, canvas shoes, newspapers; tattered books which had seeped out through the breaches from the library. There, amongst all this litter and this waste, which was Spanish, lay the cap of the man from Albi, which was French.

It had been trodden underfoot, it had been sodden with rain and dew; but the maker's name was visible, and the name of that Languedoc town in which he lived.

Why had he come, the owner of that cap, to this bitter foreign struggle? To win five pesetas a day? It is more likely that he came because, like all his race, he was a politician, and at home was a supporter of the Front Populaire; and that he came to fight for liberty and for democracy. But if he did, we others who stand also for democracy, must resent most bitterly how he was cheated. The Government of Madrid—though how should he have known it?—was no more democratic than that of General Franco. The Cortes had gone on holiday before the Civil War broke out. Since then the convening of it had been endlessly put off. Governments enough had been tried and finally, three weeks before the day of which we write, Largo Caballero had formed yet another. Now, by the law and by the constitution of Spain, a Government, before it acts, must face the Parliament and be approved by it. But Largo Caballero, who on one occasion had been sentenced to life imprisonment for treason, and on another had raised an Anarchist revolution, was not taking any such risk. True, had the Cortes been allowed to meet, no member of the parties of the Right could have sat. But this new Government, with its load

PLATE 35

A GOVERNMENT ATTACK ACROSS THE
LOWER TERRACE

On the right is the House-of-the-Military-Government which
has at last been captured. On the left is the Esplanade terrace.
Between the two, spanned by a footbridge, is the lane known
as the Stable Approach.

THE LAST MINE CRATER

This was exploded on the last day of the siege. The fragment
in it is part of the north-east tower and is as large as a two-decked
bus. The photograph is taken from the Swimming-Bath Breach.
The building is the wrecked laboratory at the corner of the
terrace.

PLATE 36

SURVIVORS

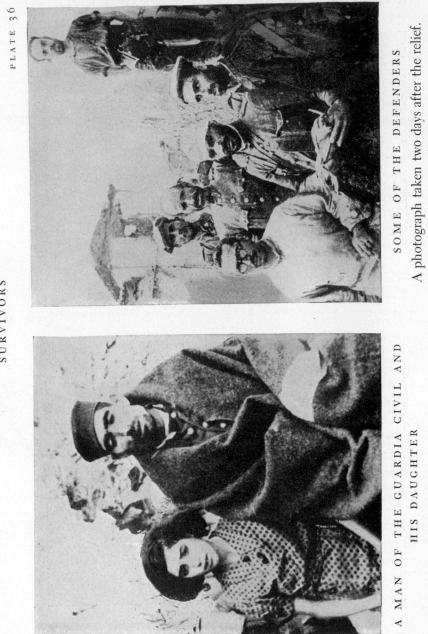

SOME OF THE DEFENDERS
A photograph taken two days after the relief.

A MAN OF THE GUARDIA CIVIL AND
HIS DAUGHTER

of Communist ministers, did not even dare to face the other deputies of the Left. It was ready enough to fight a war, to fly from the capital when it became dangerous, to send abroad loads of gold from the gold reserve of the Spanish people; but one thing it would not do, and that was to face the democracy to which it was responsible; and from before the date on which the Civil War broke out, until December, when this book was started, the Cortes was not allowed to meet.

So if this man from Albi came to fight for those things which he, and most of us believe in, then indeed he was cheated. Perhaps he escaped. Perhaps he lay with the other charred bodies, unburied in the crater of the final mine. His cap remained; the cap from Albi.

THE TWENTY-SEVENTH OF SEPTEMBER

Throughout the early hours the enemy from his barricades and trenches on the terrace kept up a fusillade.

At 5.30 a.m. the two remaining "155's" opened fire from the Pinedo. Their fire was as rapid as their gunners could make it. Suddenly, amongst the bursts of these high-explosive shells, there came an explosion a dozen times louder than the rest. The Alcazar shivered. Some thought this to be the shell of a new and enormous gun; but others believed a mine had been set off. Dense black smoke filled every room and passage, and for some time hung heavily above all the ruins of the Alcazar. Then, as this cleared, it was seen that a crater, some fifty yards across, and deep enough for a two-storey cottage to have been placed in it, had opened in the Esplanade, at the foot of where the north-east tower had been. The tower itself had fallen three weeks before, so that actually there was not much damage.

Almost immediately militia-men were seen swarming up from the Zig-Zag, from across the Esplanade, and over the terraces.

They swarmed out of the dining-hall and rushed at the slopes of rubble which led up into the several breaches which honeycombed the walls around the cavalry library. From the slopes below the ruined laboratory they scrambled up towards the breach where the exit to the swimming-bath had been.

They came forward with the valour of despair, for this was the last assault that could be delivered, and on it they set their final hopes. They came forward, cheering, shouting, throwing bombs; to be met by steady rifle-fire.

The assault against the breach of the north façade fared like others before it. The militia-men reached the slopes, mounted them, and hung there, unable to advance. They were shot at from the galleries, they were bombed by the defenders of the breach, who had been driven from the loopholes back into the courtyard. Then, as before, there were moments when the surge of the attack might have lapped over the rim of the breach and washed down into the Alcazar. For a while the militia-men held to the ground they had won. Then once again they realized that they had failed. They dribbled back from the breach, leaving fresh bodies among the corpses, rotting there.

The assault upon the breach of the swimming-bath is said to have been the most determined. For it was there that the new mine had been exploded and no doubt the enemy had massed his picked companies against this point.

But the mine had opened no new breach and had only slightly widened that where the door of the swimming-bath had been. Instead, the mine had made a crater so huge, so deep, and with such crumbling slopes, that on one side it acted as protection for the breach, against which attacks could now only be launched diagonally, and from the south-east. Here, too, the Alcazar walls still stood upright, and from the windows and from what remained of the Moorish gallery, fire was rained down upon the militia-men. They came forward in a dense crowd, but from the first they had no chance.

Presently they grasped this and withdrew to the corner of the Esplanade, where from amid the ruins of the laboratory they kept up an intense fire upon the cavern-like opening of the breach.

Of all the attacks, that upon the breached classrooms round the cavalry library was the most dangerous. Here the ground offered cover to the militia-men till they were on the actual slopes of the breaches, and these slopes gave foothold and were not too hard to scale. But here every opening into the Alcazar had been strengthened with loopholed barricades and the rifle-fire brought to bear upon the militia-men was more than they could endure. They were driven back into the wrecked dining-hall and, though for an hour or more they made further attempts, they were driven back each time.

Meanwhile, good news had been received from the observation posts. For, as the light grew stronger, the first skirmishers of the relief column were made out, far away and towards Bargas, trickling over the slopes towards the highroad to Madrid. They were meeting with some resistance but were not held up. And, as they advanced, solid formations of the Nationalist forces came into sight over the crest of the ridges. Once in sight they extended, and it was judged from the excellence of the line they kept, and from the speed of their advance, that they were Regulars or legionaries.

Soon afterwards, Nationalist shells began to fall about the bull-ring and around the Visagra gate of Toledo, which faced towards Madrid and near which concentrations of the enemy could be seen. To these unseen batteries the two "155" guns, still in the Pinedo, began to reply. But, when they themselves were shelled, the gunners limbered up and abandoned the position which they had held for so many weeks.

It was now realized that, were the speed of their advance maintained, the relief forces might enter Toledo that night. So, to show that the Alcazar was still holding out, an order was given that the old red-yellow-red flag of Spain should be set up on the highest part of the ruins which could be reached. The task proved difficult and the men were so weak that they could not climb as high as they would have wished. But presently they set the flag upon the ruins of the north-west tower; though not on the highest part of them.

The militia-men greeted the old monarchic colours with shouts and curses and with heavy rifle-fire. But a bullet passes through bunting without as much as stirring it and any harm they did to the flag was not apparent.

Soon after this the observation posts established contact with the relieving force by heliograph. Messages were exchanged. The Nationalist troops continued their advance smartly and in perfect order, as though on manœuvres. Presently they could be seen in the orchards and olive groves some miles north of the town. The Madrid road was cut.

Just before 11 a.m. subterranean explosions were heard in the streets and in the ruins around the Alcazar, and it was thought that land mines, placed there to prevent a sortie by the garrison, had now been set off.

Shortly after this many Nationalist planes came out of the west and began to bomb the enemy massing near the bull-ring. Then circling close to the Alcazar they dropped their bombs upon the Zocodover and behind the Santa Cruz.

By noon the skirmishers of the relief force, with formed troops behind them, had occupied the low hills north of the town from which, ten days before, the War Minister of the Government had watched the great explosion of the mines. Presently detachments of these troops were seen moving towards the Arms Factory, without drawing any enemy fire. In another hour, if they wished, they could be round the town.

The siege was over. The Command had some of the prisoners brought up and to them letters were entrusted, addressed to the commander of the Government forces in the town. With these in their hands they were sent out of the Alcazar. In the letters the Command stated that, if the lives of families

of those within the Alcazar were respected, the lives of the
enemy prisoners within the Alcazar would be respected in like
manner; that he begged that the Government troops might
be withdrawn, so as to avoid the horror of useless street fighting
and the destruction of monuments dear to all Spaniards; that
anyone who should surrender would be treated with perfect
humanity and not in the manner always alleged by the broadcasts from Madrid. This message was communicated, also, by
heliograph to the Nationalist forces outside the town.

Soon after noon the flight of Government forces from Toledo began and they were seen streaming away, some along
the highway to Mocejon, and many over the bridges, up into
the barren hills, and on the tracks leading to Sisla, and on the
old highroad to Ciudad Real. At this, there was brought up
from the basement the remaining one of the two light mountain guns which ever since the beginning of the siege had been
in the Alcazar. It was brought into position in the breach of
the cavalry library and with those shells, husbanded so carefully that not one had ever been fired, the Alcazar spat its final
defiance at the retreating enemy.

So now, with the dangers past and the besiegers in full retreat, it is time to take stock a little of the Alcazar and of its
garrison.

Of food there was enough for some days more. There remained five mules—mule flesh was hated and these had been
kept as a last resource, and one horse. The horse was called
Cajon, it was a racehorse, property of an officer of the Academy
who, when the Civil War broke out, was taking part in jumping
contests in Germany. The garrison did not know it, but he
was with the relief forces and was now within sight of Toledo.
It is reported that on the next day, when the officer entered the
Alcazar, his first question was as to the fate of Cajon; and
that, when he was brought down to the swimming-bath and
saw his horse, he threw his arms around his neck and wept.

There was wheat, also, enough perhaps for another six days. There was water for a slightly longer period. There were still half-a-million rounds of small arm ammunition. And that is all there was.

In the short report that the Command drew up, summarizing upon a sheet of foolscap the ten weeks of the siege, there was just one boast; it was at the end. The Command had tried to be exact. A record had been kept—inevitably inaccurate— of every shell that had been fired by the enemy upon the Alcazar; tabulated according to the calibre of the guns. There was a list of the various forms of attack which had been made and how many of each sort there had been.

Aerial bombardments 30
Attacks with flame projectors and petrol. . . 35
Mines exploded under the Alcazar 3

The number of dead and wounded were recorded also, according to their categories—but these proved incorrect, for many died of their wounds after the siege was over. The number of deserters was set down; the number of suicides; the number of births; the number of women dead from natural causes.

And after that there came the boast:—

"Number of women and children harmed by enemy
action . . . . None
Material destroyed by enemy action . . . . . All."

Yet that statement drawn up by the Command was, to an infinitesimal degree, an exaggeration; a libel on its own stewardship. For, down in some darkest basements, there remained the articles which had been stored and catalogued with such care; the great carved wooden doors, taken from off their hinges; the state carpet of the great stairs; some lamentable daubs, portraits of one-time commandants of the Academy.

Two memorials remained, almost unscarred. In the middle of the courtyard there had stood the bronze statue of Carlos Quinto, first and greatest of the Spanish Habsburgs, maker of all about him. This had been taken down from its pedestal and had been placed behind a barricade. One shell had struck the emperor on the stomach. But, when his armour—it was detachable—was removed, it was found that his naked body had not suffered from the blow.

Under the gallery on the west side of the courtyard a bronze panel still remained upon the wall. It had been spattered with bullets, but the figure of Fame with outstretched hands and laurel wreath, and the battle scene behind her, had not been much damaged; and the inscription was still legible. It was the monument to a cadet of former days; The Gentleman Cadet Don Juan Vasquez Afan de Ribera, who had died in the defence of the Parc de Montelon, and fighting against the French, at the age of 13 years, during Napoleon's occupation of the country.

The Alcazar was in ruins. The streets to the west of it had been wiped out by the explosion of the mines. For this the garrison had been in no way responsible. It seems that hardly one wanton shot had been fired by them. The pleasant little bourgeois houses, facing Herrera's façade, not having been held by the enemy, had hardly suffered; and the care with which the hard-pressed garrison had spared the façade of the Santa Cruz is something, perhaps, unique in war.

Higher up that same street great damage had been done, but not by the defenders of the Alcazar. The houses on the left had crumbled into ruins; amongst them the Inn of Cervantes which for centuries had been a pilgrimage for lovers of Don Quixote. This little house had never been exploited. It had remained an inn, and till the outbreak of the siege had carried on a humble trade. Now only some blackened walls of it re-

mained. Yet surely the shade of Cervantes will not grumble.
For he had believed the days of chivalry over; and in his story
of the poor gentleman of La Mancha he had laughed at those
fancies, and tales of wondrous feats of arms which had set his
hero out upon his travels. Yet, just above the inn where Cervantes had lived, there had been performed feats seeming as
crazily impossible as any that had filled the pate of that poor
gentleman, Don Quixote. The Inn is gone. The spirit of the
Alcazar remains. The joke is against Cervantes. But he, too,
was himself a Spanish soldier and he will make no complaint.

The siege had held those in the Alcazar under a spell and
the story of the siege should end before the spell is broken.
Yet something of what happened after it must be recorded.
Let us hear it. Then let us return and watch the last moments.

That night the Fifth bandera of the Legion entered the Alcazar, took over its defence and let the survivors of the siege
have rest.

On the next day the Army of Africa closed in and the Alcazar
had ceased to be an island. General Francisco Franco came,
and with the Command went round the ruins. He made a
speech. He awarded to every member of the garrison the cross
of St. Fernando. With him, for the first time in seventy days,
Colonel Moscardó walked in the Toledan streets. It is said that
he was greatly aged. He, who had held himself so well, stooped
and walked stiffly. He was distressed, it is said, that he had
failed to preserve the structure of the Alcazar better than he
had. His task was done. He asked for some employment
against the enemy. He took a grave farewell of the garrison
he had commanded. He slipped away, out of the news lines.

Two more days, and the great outside world swept in and
gaped among the ruins. The Press, the movie-men, came in
conducted parties; brought to Toledo by the High Command.
They wandered in among the survivors, they made their notes

and took their pictures. They got their stories.

"Jimmy, quick! See that dame . . . the one giving her kid nature's own breakfast food? She's one of them, O.K. See her arms? Like connecting rods. See her ribs, where her gown's gone open?"

"She isn't hard to look at, either."

"She sure isn't— She'd be a dream—if her hair weren't full of dust and her face like a skull. Boy, what a shot! What a shot!"

"Seems kind'er wild, don't she?"

"You've said it. Listen to her! What's she shouting about? . . . Where's that kid that does the talking for us?"

"Al . . . fonzo! . . . Al . . . fonzo!"

"I'm right here, gentlemen?"

"Listen here. What's this dame shouting? What's she wild for? What's bitten her? What? . . . Eh? Says they've killed her man? And they got him the last day? Isn't that just too bad; just too bad. My, I'm sorry. Jimmy, here! Here's a lead-story for you. They plugged her man the last day. Got it? You have Alfonzo tell you what the dame says, while I get a shot of her."

"Here, kid. Here, Al . . . fonzo—or whatever you call yourself. Quit making that cigarette, can't you? Just get the dame to cover up a bit; just to oblige my friend here. Steady. Not too much. She can hold the kid over one, and cover up the other."

"Jimmy, can you get her fixed for me first? Then you can get her story. . . . Señorita! . . . Señorita: Favor, Señorita. . . ."

"Señorita, my boot! She's married, ain't she? Señora! Aqui! Señora! Hi! Just a minute! Cover them up. Eh? No savvy? My friend here wants make a picture of you. Soo? Cover 'em up. Thi . . . s wa . . . y. See? This way . . . That's it! You've got it!"

"Gee . . . Jimmy, it's just swell. See? She's tearing out her hair. Boy, it's swell . . . but she'll have to keep them covered up."

"Señora. . . . See here! . . . Like this! . . . Eh?"

"Al . . . fonzo . . . Where's that God-damn bastard got to? . . . If this dame keeps on this way she's going to have me mad. She's going to spoil the swellest shot I ever had. She must cover 'em up. Can't you tell her, Jimmy? . . . Marvellous! Marvellous, shouting that way. And the kid and all. She'll get every mother in the country sobbing. Not a dry eye in the house!" . . .

"Señora . . . Eh? Cover 'em up . . . just for a minute."

"Oh Gaud! Cover 'em up! . . . No savvy? . . . Money. Give you money! Dinero. Eh? . . . Ten pesetas . . . Eh? . . . Jes——us! I'm missing the swellest shot I ever had. I'll just go crazy. . . . Cover 'em up! I tell you. . . . Don't you get me? . . . Over in the States they just . . . won't . . . stand . . . for . . . tits."

I would not have given this conversation, were it not almost word for word as it was spoken.

The survivors stood about. As yet they had nowhere to go. Indeed they did not know whether, if they had, they were free to depart.

The world swept round them and they found themselves objects of curiosity. There was no longer any danger, there was no longer any work that must be done. They blinked at the unaccustomed sunlight. They went in among the ruins and escaped. Sometimes they looked out at those people from the other world who gave them cigarettes.

They could smoke.

They were coming back. They were coming back, just as a patient after some long surgical operation comes back from under an anæsthetic; slowly, painfully, almost grudgingly.

PLATE 37

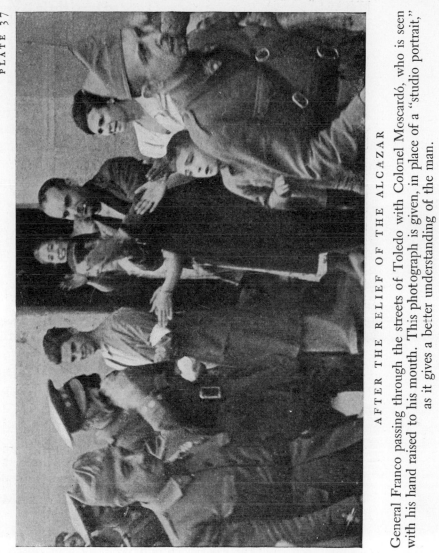

AFTER THE RELIEF OF THE ALCAZAR

General Franco passing through the streets of Toledo with Colonel Moscardó, who is seen with his hand raised to his mouth. This photograph is given, in place of a "studio portrait," as it gives a better understanding of the man.

PLATE 38

"The evening breeze stirs the flag . . . then the breeze fails
and the flag hangs limp again."

ADIOS!

Now let us leave them, let us go back again to the last moments of the siege. Let us take farewell of the defenders, before the world breaks in upon them, claims them, and swallows them up. They will hardly reach such heights again. Later, life may seem flat. Times may be hard. There may be moments when they will look back almost enviously to those tense and dreadful hours. Let us fade out now, upon the dusk of that last evening.

Into the emptiness of the Zocodover come the skirmishers of the Legion. Picquets double out automatically and block the exits from it. Scouts slip away and reconnoitre the fallen houses on the eastern side. All clear! Arrangements to meet a surprise attack are made as usual, while the men gaze up through the twilight at the ruins of the Alcazar.

Presently a lieutenant and platoon of men go stealing under the archway of La Sangré, towards the echoing ruins of the House-of-the-Military-Government. The platoon halts. A patrol from it stalks the entrance of the Santa Cruz. They pounce on it, find it deserted, take up position there, blocking the gateway. The rest come on; in through the mad disorder of the Stable Approach; up over the fallen tree-trunks of the Zig-Zag. They pick their way warily amongst the dead bodies, the abandoned arms. They reach the terrace. They pause.

The lookouts above the great north breach watch them silently.

The skirmishers of the Legion look to their dressing and extensions. Then with their rifles at the ready, cautiously, unbelievingly, they advance towards this vast bank of ruin. They reach the foot of it.

Suddenly from behind the summit of the bank a scarecrow of a man stands up. No one says a word. Other scarecrows come clambering up from behind and join him on the summit of the breach. They are ragged, incredible emaciated. Their unkempt hair and stubbly beards make their drawn cheeks appear even more hollow than they are. Their eyes are sunken. They seem half-wild creatures. They have an exaltation that is hardly of this earth. They stand there wordless, looking down at these men who have come six hundred miles to save them.

Let us leave them here, as they would wish it, with their task accomplished.

The night is closing in. No one has spoken yet. The evening breeze stirs the flag above the stump of broken tower. For a moment its folds lift, the ancient red-yellow-red of Spain just visible in the twilight. The spell is still around them. Then the breeze fails and the flag hangs limp again.

ADIOS!

Toledo, Oct: Nov: Dec.
Cushendun, Jan: Feb.

APPENDIX NO. 1

THE ALCAZAR

ITS ARCHITECTURE AND HISTORY

The original Alcazar of Toledo was a Moorish fortress—*al* representing the Moorish definite article, and *cazar* "castle."

After the reconquest of the city it became the home of the Christian kings of Castile. But these for generations employed Moorish masons and craftsmen when altering and improving its defensive character. And, in spite of the rebuilding of almost all the structure, traces of Moorish work remained clearly visible.

During the last years of the fifteenth century Ferdinand and Isabella made alterations, in order to adapt this, the royal residence of their capital, to the taste of the day and the demand for increased luxury.

Their grandson, the Emperor Charles V, greatest monarch of the Renaissance, determined to transform the fortress into a palace in the new taste. The designs for this were made out by Alonzo de Covarrubias.[1]

The ground plan of the building—a long rectangle—may to some extent have been determined by those four great corner towers which ever since then have given to the Alcazar its characteristic silhouette.

To the main east and main west wall Covarrubias made but few alterations. They were walls of a fortress; he left them so. But a few widely spaced windows were built into both of them, to serve the purpose of the new age.

The eastern façade, that which faced the river, consisted of a single and unbroken wall of great length and height. In the face of it were three half-round towers and a projecting battle-

[1] Whose portrait by El Greco many may know.

297

mented gallery. These belonged to the original building. Covarrubias appreciated this work of an earlier period. He kept his own subservient to it; with a lack of self-assertion unimaginable in an artist of any other country. The windows which he employed in the upper storeys of these two original fronts were similar—they will presently be described. But this façade was already so marked by the horizontal shadow cast by the gallery, and by the three half-cylinders of the Moorish towers, that the windows of this Renaissance adaption were hardly noticed. And to the end this façade remained stern and almost forbidding.

The other original front, that which faced the west, had not the grimness of the one just described, for it had neither bastion towers nor gallery, and here the architect was given his freedom on a vast bare expanse of ashlar wall. Here, too, he treated the past with respect. In the upper storeys he placed windows, large but delicate; he spaced them very widely and with sensitive decision. The carving which framed them, and the windows of the other two sides of the Alcazar for which he was responsible, was in the plateresque style—the Spanish low relief counterpart of the arabesques and candelabras of the Italian early Renaissance. The carved decoration around these windows had an innocent and eager happiness which contrasted with the gruff texture of the fortress wall. Except for their framing he used no single touch of ornament upon the whole wide surface. The result was calm and mature.

The lower storeys on both these façades he left almost blank. They were the lower storeys of a fortress and he left them as such. Actually there was need for light, so he put windows, treated as mere structural openings, low, framed in the simplest of mouldings and so unmarked that they disturbed the general scheme hardly more than the joins in brickwork do.

These two façades were only adaptations, but they exemplified perfectly the attitude of a Spanish architect towards his art; his desire to serve the present and the future, to respect the past, but not to express his own human individuality.

These two great fortress walls of the east and west being already in existence, only the fronts of the north and south were then needed to complete the exterior.

For the north Covarrubias designed an entrance façade. Others, since then, have destroyed its effect. The heightening of the towers which flanked it, and the setting of gigantic and foreign spires upon them, altered the balance, so that it became difficult to appreciate the original design; probably few have tried.[1]

As in all Spanish buildings the door, in this case a monumental gateway, was all-important. This stressing of the entrance may be the remnant of Moorish influence. For in Moorish work, where windows were small or non-existent, the door formed always the focal point and was the sole essential feature. In just this way the grandiose, and perhaps overladen gateway which Covarrubias gave to the Alcazar, was intended to dominate the whole north side of it.

Toledo is a city of gateways. Here as in all aristocratic countries the entrance of a house expresses the pretensions of its owner. Covarrubias was a Toledan, and the gateway of the Alcazar was Toledan. It should be compared with others in the city and not with those of Italy at that time. And, although there is an understanding of the Renaissance in this façade, it is transitional, and in the proportions of its gateway is still Castilian. When he designed this, Covarrubias was not a young man. He had grasped the Italian conceptions but he had stopped short of abandoning entirely his Toledan standards.

The windows of the north façade were similar to those upon the east and west. But here, the effect seemed always less happy. Yet this was due to no fault of design but to a disadvantage from which this façade always suffered. For the terrace which faced it was so narrow that there existed no spot

[1] See Plate 13.

from which it could be seen, squarely and as a whole. Viewed from a corner and at an oblique angle, all was fore-shortened and distorted. Indeed the too close spacing of the windows, apparent to the eye and to the camera, does not exist in prints showing the original design.

Though three of the façades, and the plan of the whole Alcazar, were the work of Covarrubias, he did not live to build the fourth side of it. This, and the great stairway that he had planned, were carried out by Juan de Herrera.

Herrera was the Wren of Spanish architecture. He was masterly, immensely proficient, but his work belongs to the August, and not to the Springtime of the Renaissance. Here, on the last remaining façade of the Alcazar, his task was indeed difficult. Owing to the lower level of the ground on this side, the building had to be at least one, perhaps two, storeys higher than he would probably have chosen.

He solved the problem of its overwhelming height in two ways. Firstly he used every artifice to reduce the apparent number of the storeys—there were indeed no less than six of them. Secondly he included the two flanking towers in the general treatment; thus decreasing the apparent height by increasing the apparent breadth.[1]

The three lower storeys, built of stone, he treated as a plinth, and to lighten them designed the lower one as an arcade—not unlike that beneath the Ritz Hotel in London. This arcaded plinth he mounted on a terrace, thereby to rid the building itself of yet a little more of its height. Upon this plinth of three storeys he set the next two, treated as one. Their windows, set in panels of red brick, were framed in an order of giant pilasters, and under a strongly stressed cornice. Above this cornice, and in appearance set back behind it, was an attic storey; treated almost as a frieze, with an order of smaller pilasters, to carry the crowning cornice of the building.

In the second, third and fifth storeys the windows were

[1] See Plate 31.

squat, small, and of approximately equal size. But the windows of the third floor, those which stood immediately upon the part treated as a plinth, were lean and lofty, reaching from the floor level of the rooms. Thus, to some extent, Herrera succeeded in forcing the impression that this, in reality the fourth and fifth floors treated as one, was actually the main storey of the building; with a plinth below, and a frieze above.

The other way in which the height of this façade was made less apparent was probably in accordance with the original plan of Covarrubias. At the other corners the towers stood out like ears, framing the façade between them. But here the façade had been built level with the face of the towers, thereby incorporating them.

The whole of this Herrera façade is very well done, a little donnish, rather chilly. Yet as one grows to know it, the varying heights of the storeys have a rhythm which becomes increasingly satisfying. It forestalled by two centuries those public buildings which made the cities of France models for the world. But this southern façade, even more than the north one, suffered from the difficulty of finding any place from which it could be viewed. Indeed the plaza beneath it was so small that from it no true conception of this side of the building could be formed. While from the housetops at a distance, from which the view of the façade is not foreshortened, the arcaded storey and the terrace below it, were invisible.

As already mentioned, at the corners of the Alcazar stood four great square towers. These were placed most unusually, for they stood almost outside the square which it formed; much like the ears at the corners of many early Georgian frames and mirrors. It may be that this curious plan was adopted for the following reason: Charles V had just built himself, at Granada, the most beautiful palace which the world has seen, but he had abandoned it, still unroofed, because of an earthquake which was believed to be an evil portent. On account of this, and because he was always short of money, he was obliged to leave two of the existing façades of the Toledan Alcazar more or less as they were, and to complete his plan with two new façades. Had these old and new sides been allowed to meet each other at the corners of the building, their incongruity would have been apparent. But by building the towers outside the rectangle, the differences of the façades are no more objectionable than the differences of the painted panels on the sides of an Italian chest.

The interior of the Alcazar consisted of a very large courtyard, surrounded by two storeys of arcades. These were carried on monolith columns with Tuscan capitals. In the spandrils between the lower arches were double-headed heraldic eagles, surmounted by the Imperial crown. The whole effect was magnificent; serene, yet curiously gay. Beyond these sculptured eagles and Tuscan capitals the courtyard was without decoration.

In the centre of it, upon a high pedestal, was a bronze statue of Charles V, bareheaded, in a Renaissance version of Roman battle-harness, and with his foot upon a conquered foe. This statue was only a copy, of the original by Pompeo Leoni; which had once stood there but which had been removed to Madrid. However, being a cast of the original, it was a perfectly faithful reproduction. It has one peculiarity: the armour, being slit vertically and made in two portions, can be removed, leaving Charles utterly naked. So splendid in his Roman armour, Charles, when naked, is seen as an ageing man; scraggy, disillusioned, sagging. Yet in his face there is all his tenacity, his imagination, his wisdom. Did Charles connive at the scheme of this nude portrait of himself? Or was it the artist's bitter jest? [1]

At the southern end of this courtyard was one of the largest stairways in the world. Steps, each a monolith, and fifty feet

[1] See Plate 19.

across, led to a low landing. From this, flights of steps ran right and left, to reach the arcaded galleries. This stairway was enclosed in a hall, of the whole height and the whole width of the Alcazar. It had immensity but yet brought a sense of frustration. For, having started with these giant steps, it broke into two flights, each of which ended, after the width of a passage, at a blank wall.

This stairway has strange links with history. It was the work of Herrera, who had built the south façade of the Alcazar, and who later built the Escorial. He was working under the orders, not of Charles V, but of his earnest, studious and almost morbid son, Philip II. There are letters existing, written by Philip when he was living in England as the husband of Mary Tudor, in which he gives Herrera minutest instructions about the building of these stairs. He left his stamp upon them; they were immense in conception, the work of culture and knowledge, but they were cold, and, like their master, they have about them the sense of frustration.

The subsequent history of the Alcazar is this: that, for some reason not easily explained, the four towers were heightened one storey each, and above them, in place of their tranquil roofs of pantiles, were set four enormous extinguisher spires. The form of these belongs to the North, not to Spain. This theory is offered: that they are modelled after the spire-like cupolas so common in Philip's Flemish possessions. It has been suggested that they are French, but they seem nearer to the spires of Dordrecht than those of Vendôme or of Chambord.

Who introduced these northern high-pitched spires into flat-roofed Toledo? They were erected within sixty years of the completion of the Alcazar. During that period the most influential architect of the city was El Greco's son. He built the Town Hall, and, either the spires of the Alcazar were modelled upon its, or its upon those of the Alcazar. The façade of the Town Hall is hardly conceivable without its spires. Thus it appears more likely that, these having been admired, somewhat similar ones were added to the Alcazar.

They crushed the original design; they were so vast, so full of effort. Yet, though spoiling its original design, they made the Alcazar one of the most inevitable buildings in the world. The Alcazar of Charles V and of Covarrubias was smiling and secular. The altered version, with its four stupendous spires, was distant and devout.

Rightly or wrongly the spires were added, and that was the Alcazar which stamped itself upon the memory of more than three centuries of men.

Until Philip II abandoned Toledo and made Madrid his capital, the Alcazar remained the centre of his great empire. Thereafter it was but one of the chief royal residences.

In 1710, during the war of the Spanish Succession, Toledo was occupied by the Austrian claimant, the Archduke Charles. England was backing his pretensions and his army was in part Germanic, with English detachments. After some months he was forced to abandon the town and the Alcazar was set on fire. Its walls were unhurt but it remained roofless for more than forty years; until the Archbishop set it in order, for use as a charitable institution.

During the Peninsular War it was occupied by French troops, who again burnt it and left it a roofless ruin, just as they did that other great rectangular palace, on the heights above Pressburg.

It was put in condition again in the mid-eighteenth century and became the Academy of Infantry for the Spanish army. In the 'eighties it was burnt once more, after which it was restored to the form in which it remained until 1936.

APPENDIX NO. 2

When first the Author saw the report of the Badajos "massacre" in the New York "Herald Tribune," under the signature of Mr. N. Reynolds Packard, he wrote to United Press Associations, asking for information. This they kindly gave him, in the following reply.

UNITED PRESS ASSOCIATION OF AMERICA.
30 Bouverie Street, E.C. 4.
February 16, 1937.

Geoffrey Moss Esq.,
Cushendun House,
Cushendun.

Dear Sir,

Replying to your letter of February 14, the account of the reported massacre after the storming of Badajos, which appeared in the New York "Herald Tribune" under the signature of H. Reynolds Packard, was not written by him.

Mr. Packard never was in Badajos and never wrote anything concerning the capture of Badajos. At that time he was in Burgos, and the details referred to by you were erroneously published under his name. He did not write anything at the time remotely resembling the material which appeared by error under his name in the New York "Herald Tribune."

You may have seen the letter from Mr. Andrew Rothstein in the "Manchester Guardian" of January 19, regarding the article in the "Herald Tribune." This was brought to the notice of United Press and on January 28 the "Manchester Guardian" published a letter from Mr. Webb Miller, European News Manager of the United Press, embodying the second paragraph of this letter.

Yours faithfully,
HARRY FLORY.
Assistant European News Manager.

305

The following is a copy of a telegram sent by Mr. Packard from Salamanca during the month of January. It came into the author's possession from another source. He had not asked for it; nor did he know of its existence. The telegram is worded in the manner usual among newspaper correspondents. It was addressed to Mr. Webb Miller, head of the London branch of "The United Press."

PRESS COLLECT AMUNIP LONDRES

25140 WEBB I HAVE BEEN SUMMONED TO SALAMANCA IN CONNEC-TION WITH A PARAGRAPH APPEARING IN A LETTER SIGNED BY ANDREW ROTHSTEIN PUBLISHED IN THE MANCHESTER GUARDIAN OF JANUARY THE NINETEENTH QUOTING ME AS DESCRIBING AN EYEWITNESS ACCOUNT OF MASS KILLINGS IN BADAJOZ. THE LETTER STATES THAT THE ARTICLE WAS PUBLISHED BY THE PARIS EDITION OF THE NEW YORK HERALD AUGUST SIXTEEN AND THE MESSAGE DATELINED BADAJOZ WAS DATED AUGUST FIFTEEN UNDER MY SIGNATURE. CAPTAIN BOLIN REPRESENTING THE NA-TIONALIST MILITARY PRESS AUTHORITIES DEMANDS THAT YOU IN-FORM THE MANCHESTER GUARDIAN THAT I NEVER WROTE SUCH ARTICLE ALSO THAT I HAVE NEVER BEEN IN BADAJOZ IF THIS IS TRUE. IF YOU RECALL I POINTED OUT TO YOU MONTHS AGO THAT THERE WERE A NUMBER OF MYSTERIOUS MESSAGES APPEARING UNDER MY NAME WHICH I NEVER WROTE AND DATELINED PLACES THAT I HAVE NEVER BEEN TO. I GIVE YOU MY WORD OF HONOUR THAT I KNOW NOTHING ABOUT THIS BADAJOZ MESSAGE WHICH OBVIOUSLY IS ONE OF THEM. I FRANKLY THINK THAT IN VIEW OF THE SERIOUSNESS OF THIS SITUATION YOU MIGHT INVESTIGATE THIS MESSAGE THOROUGHLY AND EXONERATE ME IN THE EYES OF THE NATIONALIST GOVERNMENT SINCE I WAS AT BURGOS DURING THE CAPTURE OF BADAJOZ WHERE I HAVE NEVER BEEN ONCE. I MUST EMPHASISE THAT THE NATIONALIST GOVERNMENT IS TAKING

A SERIOUS ATTITUDE WITH REGARD TO THIS MESSAGE. INCIDEN-
TALLY I HAVE POINTED OUT ONE REASON YOU GAVE WAS FOR NA-
TIONALIST SPAIN WAS TO TIGHTEN NEWS COVERAGE AND TO PRE-
VENT ANY SLIPS IN THE HANDLING OF SPANISH NEWS AND SINCE
THEN I AM SURE THAT ONLY THE STUFF THAT I HAVE WRITTEN
HAS APPEARED UNDER MY NAME AND NO UNITED PRESS OFFICE
OUTSIDE SPAIN HAS BEEN ALLOWED TO REWRITE STORIES AS
THOUGH THEY WERE COMING FROM WITHIN SPAIN.

REYNOLDS PACKARD.

That disposes of the only "eye-witness" account, for it proves that the journalist, under whose name it appeared, was four hundred miles away on the day in question.

Let us now deal with the French journalists who visited Badajos AFTER the taking of the town.

The official correspondents of the Havas Agency seem to have had somewhat the same sort of trouble as Mr. Packard. Here is a copy of a telegram which one of them sent to his Agency in Paris. It is given here to substantiate the view expressed in the chapter entitled "Asides." It came into the possession of the Author in the same way as the previous telegram. It ran:—

HAVAS PARIS

SALAMANQUE LUNDI SUITE CAMPAGNE AMORCEE ETRANGER SUR
EVENEMENTS AOUT DERNIER PARTICULIER SUR BADAJOZ OFICINA
PRENSA GENERALISSIME ME DEMANDE QUEL EST QUOTE CORRE-
SPONDANT SPECIAL HAVAS UNQUOTE DONT DEPECHE FUT PUBLIEE
SOUS CETTE MENTION DANS QUOTE POPULAIRE UNQUOTE LE SEIZE
AOUT ET QUI PRETEND AVOIR VISITE BADAJOS VEILLE PRISE CETTE
VILLE STOP DEMAND AUSSI QUEL EST QUOTE ENVOYE SPECIAL AVEC
LES INSURGES UNQUOTE DONT AUTRE DEPECHE MEME SUJET FUT

PUBLIEE LE DIXSEPT ENVOYEE DE ELVAS STOP INTERET POUR
AGENCE POUVOIR DONNER EXPLICATION RECLAMEE RAPIDEMENT
STOP NI GRAND NI MOI NALLAMES BADAJOZ STOP EST CE ABUSIVE-
MENT QUE POPULAIRE PARLE DENVOYE SPECIAL HAVAS ROG STOP
PRIERE REPONDRE MON OFICINA PRENSA GENERALISIMO SALA-
MANQUE AVEC MENTION QUOTE SERVICE CAPITAINE BOLIN UN-
QUOTE STOP SITUATION MALET DAUBANT TOUJOURS PENDANTE
D'HOSPITAL.

Here is a translation, supplied to me, and which is approximately correct—though *pretend* hardly translates into the
English "pretends."

HAVAS PARIS

SALAMANCA MONDAY. *As a result of the campaign started
abroad on the subject of the events of August last and particularly about Badajoz, the Press Bureau at G.H.Q. has asked me
who is the "Havas Special Correspondent" a telegram from
whom was published in "Le Populaire" of the 16th August
and who pretends to have visited Badajoz on the day before it
was taken. They have also asked me who is the "Special Representative with the Insurgents" from whom a further telegram was published on the 17th, despatched from Elvas. It
would be of interest to the Agency to be able to furnish the
explanation called for, rapidly. Neither Grand nor I went to
Badajoz. Is "Le Populaire", in speaking of a "Special Havas
Representative", making a misuse of the term? Please address
your reply to me c|o Press Bureau G.H.Q. Salamanca mention-
ing "Captain Bolin's Department". Position of Malet and
Daubant still unsettled.*

D'HOSPITAL

Reply from Havas to their correspondent ran:—

D'HOSPITAL ENVOYE ESPECIAL HAVAS PRENSA GENERALISIMO
SERVICE CAPITAN BOLIN SALAMANCA

26008 PARIS 97.–47.–26.–1732 EASTERNVIGO.

RECUMES QUATORZE QUINZE SEIZE DIXSEPT AOUT SUR BOMBARDE-
MENT PRISE BADAJOZ ET EVENEMENTS SUBSEQUENTS PLUSIEURS
TELEGRAMMES DE CORRESPONDANT DE GUERRE OCCASIONEL QUI
VISITA EFFECTIVAMENT BADAJOZ APRES ENTREE TROUPES NA-
TIONALISTES PUIS QUITTA ESPAGNE VIA PORTUGAL SANS Y REVENIR
—HAVAS

The following is a translation of the above:—

D'HOSPITAL, SPECIAL HAVAS REPRESENTATIVE, PRESS BUREAU,
G.H.Q. SALAMANCA. CAPTAIN BOLIN'S DEPARTMENT.

26008 PARIS 97–47–26–1732 via EASTERN, VIGO.

We received on the 14th, 15th, and 16th and 17th August on
the subject of the bombardment, and capture of Badajoz and
subsequent events several telegrams from an occasional war
correspondent who as a matter of fact visited Badajoz after the
National troops had entered that city and then left Spain via
Portugal and did not return to Spain.

The above telegram hardly clears up the matter, for the following reasons:—

1. M. d'Hospital had asked —— who could have been the
   "Havas Special Correspondent" who stated he had visited
   Badajos on the day BEFORE it was taken. The answer of the
   Havas Agency was —— that the correspondent in question

"as a matter of fact visited Badajos AFTER the 'National' troops had entered the city".

2. M. d'Hospital also asked —— who was the "Special Representative with the Insurgents" from whom a further telegram was published on August 17, despatched from Elvas (Portugal).

The answer of the Havas Agency states that this telegram had been from the same "occasional war correspondent". But this "occasional war correspondent" can hardly have been styled "Special Representative with the Insurgents", for in point of fact all he had to do with the "Insurgents" was that:—a Portuguese journalist (Señor Mario Neves) did obtain on August 15th permission for them to make a day's excursion into Spain and to visit Badajos.

3. Beyond this, the Havas Agency hardly made the position any clearer when they used the term "an occasional war correspondent". For their correspondent who visited Badajos (after its capture) and sent the cables in question was a M. Marcel Deny. The Portuguese who took him into Spain on this day's excursion wrote of him as "Monsieur Marcel Deny of the Havas Agency", and enquiries in Lisbon and Paris bear out that M. Marcel Deny was in fact the normal Havas Correspondent in Portugal at that time. My informants in Portugal also state that his "Red sympathies were well known".

Here is the account of their day's excursion, given by Señor Mario Neves, the Portuguese journalist who took M. Marcel Deny—and M. Jacques Berthet of "Le Temps"—into Spain. It explains how the excursion was undertaken and reports things which he saw during their "rapid tour of the city", and to which the two Frenchmen attached such very different implications. I am told that Señor Neves was not in sympathy with the Nationalists' cause in Spain and would not have been prejudiced in their favour. The report is a long one—some two thousand words—so only the relevant portions are given here. They read:—

FRONTEIRA DO CAIA. Aug. 15th. (By telephone.) I am the first Portuguese journalist to enter Badajoz after the taking of the city by the rebels. I have just been a spectator of a scene of desolation and terror which I shall never forget as long as I live.

To-day at 2 o'clock in the morning, in the company of two French journalists, Marcel Deny of the "Havas" Agency and Jacques Berthet of "Le Temps," I made another attempt to force my way into Badajoz. . . . .

. . . .

We got into contact with the military commandant's department, which, after repeated requests, finally gave us the required permit.

It was 3 o'clock in the morning. We had permission to go forward, but we had no car to take us. The night in spite of the starlight, was as dark as pitch. To attempt to make the trip on foot, would have been a useless and foolhardy procedure. For this reason we decided to wait until the morning.

It was 9 o'clock before we finally were able to secure places in the first car of the "Falangistas" which left for Badajoz. .

. . . .

We immediately reported to the Military Commandant's Office, in the front of which there is a great activity. Cowed by several days of continuous bombardment the inhabitants are now venturing to come out to the streets. White flags are to be seen in nearly all the windows. Women go past dressed in mourning. The streets present a grim and desolate aspect, with numerous visible signs of the recent bombardment. The lorries of the rebel columns block the traffic. They are coming in filled with war and engineering materials for trench-digging, bridge-building and road-repairing.

The walls near the Commandant's Office are spattered with blood.

We were able to talk with the local chief of the "Falangistas," Agustin Caranda, who accorded us full facilities for moving about the city.

We made a rapid tour of the city. The damage caused by the bombardment is very great. . . . .
. . . .

We went on to the bull-ring, where the lorries of the militiamen had been parked. Many of these lorries have been destroyed. On one side an armoured car is to be seen with the inscription "Frente Popular, D. Benito, No. 10."

This place has been bombarded several times. On the sand several dead bodies are still lying about, which lends a macabre aspect of anatomical theatre to the ring. Here there are still a number of unexploded shells lying on the ground, which makes a visit to this spot very nerve-racking and definitely dangerous. . . . .
. . . .

The Cathedral, in the tower of which machine-guns had been placed, has suffered very heavily. In the central nave two bodies are lying awaiting burial.

Three days ago, when the bombardment of the city commenced, a part of the population took shelter there.

The episcopal palace, where the Socialist Federation was installed, has also suffered considerable damage. . . . .
. . . .

Just a little before mid-day, when we were outside the gates of the city, near a stream, which was still blocked with dead bodies, we heard the humming of aeroplane motors at a great height over the city. The Legionnaires and the Regulars who were occupying several points outside the city, quickly sprang to arms at the clarion call of the bugle. . . . .
. . . .

It was at 4.30 when I managed to get back to Caia. It was the new mayor of the city, appointed by the Burgos Government, who facilitated transport for me. At the beginning, he wanted to requisition a car, but no cars were available. Providentially, just then a "Falangista" appeared, who offered to take me to the frontier, from where I am telephoning to you these hurriedly collated notes, which cannot even begin to give you a faint idea of the scene of desolation and horror from which I have just returned.

MARIO NEVES.

The various News Agencies have been most helpful to me. They—with one exception—have allowed me to purchase copies of the actual cables sent by their correspondents during this period. Having these I can assert that all stories I have come upon, dealing with alleged massacres at Badajos after its capture, have their origin in the three accounts which have been dealt with in this book.

This book is set in Electra, a linotype face designed by W. A. Dwiggins. This face cannot be classified readily as either "modern" or "old-style." It is not based on any historical model, nor does it echo any particular period or style. It avoids the extreme contrast between "thick" and "thin" elements that mark most "modern" faces, and attempts to give a feeling of fluidity, power, and speed.

This book was composed, printed, and bound by H. Wolff, New York. The paper was made by S. D. Warren Co., Boston. The binding is after designs by W. A. Dwiggins; the typography, by S. R. Jacobs.